THE ALMANAC OF WOMEN AND MINORITIES IN WORLD POLITICS

THE ALMANAC OF WOMEN AND MINORITIES IN WORLD POLITICS

Mart Martin

25 YEARS

Westview Press
A Member of the Perseus Books Group

Published in 2000 in the United States of America by Westview Press, 5500 Central Avenue, Boulder, Colorado 80301-2877, and in the United Kingdom by Westview Press, 12 Hid's Copse Road, Cumnor Hill, Oxford OX2 9JJ

Find us on the World Wide Web at www.westviewpress.com

Designed by Heather Hutchison

Library of Congress Cataloging-in-Publication Data
Martin, Mart, 1944-
The almanac of women and minorities in world politics
p. cm.
Includes index.
ISBN 0-8133-6805-7
1. Women in politics—Handbooks, manuals, etc. 2. Women politicians—Handbooks, manuals, etc. 3. Minorities—Political activity—Handbooks, manuals, etc. 4. Gays—Political activity—Handbooks, manuals, etc. I. Title.

HQ1236 .M347 2000
320'.082—dc21

99-057270

The paper used in this publication meets the requirements of the American National Standard for Permanence of Paper for Printed Library Materials Z39.48-1984.

10 9 8 7 6 5 4 3 2 1

To Bets,
for the time and effort spent on
me so long ago

Contents

Notes on the Text

It is a great pleasure to introduce this first edition of *The Almanac of Women and Minorities in World Politics.* To help better understand the scope of this reference work, some explanatory notes are in order.

Dates

Dates that appear immediately following a name in the politico-biographical entries indicate the period of time during which that person exercised a high degree of political influence. The usages of other dates in this book are self-evident.

Minority Entries

These entries, under various countries, are of several types. Some represent the largest ethnic or religious minority in a country; others represent significant or historical achievements by an individual; and still others are merely interesting notes to a country's politics. Many of the entries listed under "Minorities" are for males; when a minority entry is specifically for a female, it is so noted.

Missing Names and Entries

Various institutions—parliaments, national libraries, university libraries, women's groups, and so on—were contacted in every independent country in the world in order to make this reference volume as complete as possible. For one reason or another, many of these contacts chose not to reply. As a result, in some instances the specific names of individuals are missing, and only the dates and the number of people elected or appointed are provided. Efforts will continue to ensure that these individuals are properly identified so they can be included in future editions.

Names of Minority Groups

The names used in this book for minority groups are the ones most commonly used in the country being referenced. For example, in Guyana, the "native" peoples are referred to as *Amerindians,* not *Indians, Native Indians,* or *American Indians;* and in Uganda, East Indians are referred to as *Asians.*

Spelling

Determining the exact, correct spellings of names, especially in an international work such as this, is extremely difficult. Often two sources from the same country will submit different spellings—when transliterated into English—of the same name. Any perceived misspellings are most likely due to this circumstance.

Titles

Most titles, such as "Dr.," have been omitted, with the exception of royalty. In a few instances, the title "Mrs." precedes a woman's name. In these cases, the submission did not include the woman's personal given name, but instead that of her husband.

Readers' submissions for corrections and additions to appear in future editions are welcomed. A form for such submissions is included at the end of this book.

MART MARTIN

ACKNOWLEDGMENTS

One does not begin to assemble a work such as this without the support of many others. Leo Wiegman, senior editor at Westview Press, wins a deep bow of appreciation for believing that it could be done. Andrew Day, acquisitions editor, saw the promise of this book and encouraged me along the way. David McBride, acquisitions editor, made certain that I did not stray from the proper path.

Lisa Wigutoff, project editor, performed an excellent job of overseeing the entire project, attending to all the details and interfacing with all the people necessary to bring it to completion on schedule. Natasha Khomich Gorbach was kind enough to translate the communications written in the Cyrillic alphabet, which helped me over a formidable obstacle.

I am indebted to many truly helpful people from every corner of the globe who offered their assistance. They responded to my e-mails and letters with great accuracy and tremendous grace, showing patience with my additional queries for more and more details. Their assistance was truly wonderful, but I was more impressed with their expressions of genuine warmth and friendship. All of my contacts thought that this was a worthwhile project and were enthusiastic about making certain that the women (and minorities) in their countries were recognized. A complete list of these individuals appears at the end of this volume under "Special Research Contacts."

A special note of thanks must be extended to Martin Christensen of Copenhagen. He was unflagging in helping me to track people down and was relentless in seeking obscure bits of information. It was a pleasure swapping information with Martin on a daily basis and exchanging views on various political events around the world. Put simply: This almanac could not have been completed without his assistance. For that, I am truly grateful to Martin.

And, as always, my guardian angel continued to chide me to not neglect my daily chores and to not spend so much time working away on my computer.

M. M.

Chronology of International Female Heads of Government and State (Excluding Monarchs)

For a more detailed description of the political activities of the women listed below, see the section on each individual independent country.

1. **Sühbaataryn Nemendeyn Yanjmaa**
   Mongolia
   Chairman (Acting) of the Presidium of the State Great Hural: September 23, 1953–July 7, 1954
2. **Sirimavo Ratwatte Dias Bandaranaike**
   Sri Lanka
   Prime Minister: July 22, 1960–March 25, 1965; May 28, 1970–January 23, 1977; November 14, 1994–present
3. **Indira Nehru Gandhi**
   India
   Prime Minister: January 24, 1966–March 22, 1977; January 14, 1980–October 31, 1984
4. **Hilda Louisa Gibbs Bynoe**
   Grenada (Associated State)
   Governor: June 8, 1968–February 7, 1974
5. **Golda Mabovitch Meir**
   Israel
   Prime Minister: March 17, 1969–June 2, 1974
6. **María Estela (Isabel) Cartas Martínez de Perón**
   Argentina
   President: July 1, 1974–March 29, 1976
7. **Elizabeth Domitien**
   Central African Republic
   Prime Minister: January 2, 1975–April 7, 1976
8. **Lucinda E. da Costa Gomez-Matheeuws**
   Netherlands Antilles (see the Netherlands)
   Prime Minister: 1977

9. **Margaret Hilda Roberts Thatcher**
United Kingdom
Prime Minister: May 4, 1979–November 22, 1991
10. **Maria da Lourdes Pintasilgo**
Portugal
Prime Minister: August 1, 1979–January 3, 1980
11. **Lidia Gueiler Tejeda**
Bolivia
President: November 16, 1979–July 17, 1980
12. **Mary Eugenia Charles**
Dominica
Prime Minister: July 21, 1980–June 12, 1995
13. **Vigdis Finnbogadottir**
Iceland
President: August 1, 1980–August 1, 1996
14. **Maria Lea Pedini-Angelini**
San Marino
Captain-Regent: April 1–October 1, 1981
15. **Gro Harlem Brundtland**
Norway
Prime Minister: February 4–October 14, 1981; May 9, 1986–October 16, 1989; November 3, 1990–October 25, 1996
16. **Ching-ling Soong**
China
President (Honorary): May 16–May 29, 1981
17. **Elmira Minita Gordon**
Belize
Governor-General: September 21, 1981–November 17, 1993
18. **Agatha Barbara**
Malta
President: February 16, 1982–February 15, 1987
19. **Milka Malada Planinc**
Yugoslavia
Prime Minister: May 16, 1982–May 15, 1986
20. **Gloriana Ranocchini**
San Marino
Captain-Regent: April 1–October 1, 1984; October 1, 1989–April 1, 1990
21. **Jeanne Benôit Sauvé**
Canada
Governor-General: May 14, 1984–January 29, 1990
22. **Maria Philomena Liberia-Peters**
Netherlands Antilles (see the Netherlands)
Prime Minister: September 18, 1984–January 1, 1986; May 17, 1988–November 25, 1993

23. **Corazon Cojuangco Aquino**
Philippines
President: February 25, 1986–June 30, 1992
24. **Stella Sigcau**
Transkei (see South Africa)
Prime Minister: October 5–December 30, 1987
25. **Benazir Bhutto**
Pakistan
Prime Minister: December 2, 1988–August 6, 1990; October 19, 1993–November 5, 1996
26. **Ertha Pascal-Trouillot**
Haiti
President: March 13, 1990–February 7, 1991
27. **Kazimiera Danutë Prunskienë**
Lithuania
Prime Minister: March 17, 1990–January 10, 1991
28. **Violeta Barrios de Chamorro**
Nicaragua
President: April 25, 1990–January 10, 1997
29. **Sabine Bergman-Pohl**
German Democratic Republic (see Germany)
Head of State: May 5–October 3, 1990
30. **Ruth Nita Barrow**
Barbados
Governor-General: June 6, 1990–December 28, 1996
31. **Catherine Anne Maclean Tizard**
New Zealand
Governor-General: November 20, 1990–March 21, 1996
32. **Mary Bourke Robinson**
Ireland
President: December 3, 1990–September 12, 1997
33. **Begum Khaleda Zia**
Bangladesh
Prime Minister: March 20, 1991–March 30, 1996
34. **Edith Campión Cresson**
France
Prime Minister: May 15, 1991–April 2, 1992
35. **Edda Ceccoli**
San Marino
Captain-Regent: October 1, 1991–April 1, 1992
36. **Tansu Çiller**
Turkey
Prime Minister: June 13, 1992–March 12, 1996

37. **Hanna Suchocka**
Poland
Prime Minister: August 8, 1992–October 14, 1993
38. **Marita Petersen**
Faeroe Islands (see Denmark)
Prime Minister: January 18, 1993–September 15, 1994
39. **Patricia Busignani**
San Marino
Captain-Regent: April 1–October 1, 1993
40. **Kim Campbell**
Canada
Prime Minister: June 25–November 4, 1993
41. **Agathe Uwilingiyimana**
Rwanda
Prime Minister: July 17, 1993–April 7, 1994
42. **Sylvie Kinigi**
Burundi
Prime Minister: October 1, 1993–February 7, 1994
43. **Susanne Fransisca Coromoto Camelia-Römer**
Netherlands Antilles (see the Netherlands)
Prime Minister: November 25–December 28, 1993; May 14, 1998–present
44. **Chandrika Kumaratunga**
Sri Lanka
President: November 14, 1994–present
Prime Minister: August 19–November 14, 1994
45. **Reneta Indzhova**
Bulgaria
Prime Minister: October 17, 1994–January 24, 1995
46. **Claudette Werleigh**
Haiti
Prime Minister: October 23, 1995–February 7, 1996
47. **Sheik Hasina Wajid**
Bangladesh
Prime Minister: June 23, 1996–present
48. **Ruth Sando Perry**
Liberia
Chairperson of the Council of State: September 3, 1996–August 2, 1997
49. **Rosalia Arteaga Serrano**
Ecuador
President: February 9–11, 1997
50. **Janet Rosenberg Jagan**
Guyana
President: December 19, 1997–August 11, 1999
Prime Minister: March 17–December 19, 1997

51. **Pamela Felicity Gordon**
Bermuda (see United Kingdom)
Prime Minister: March 27, 1997–November 11, 1998
52. **Calliopa Perlette Louisy**
Saint Lucia
Governor-General: September 17, 1997–present
53. **Mary McAleese**
Ireland
President: November 11, 1997–present
54. **Jennifer (Jenny) Mary Shipley**
New Zealand
Prime Minister: December 8, 1997–December 10, 1999
55. **Jennifer Meredith Smith**
Bermuda (see United Kingdom)
Prime Minister: November 11, 1998–present
56. **Ruth Dreifuss**
Switzerland
President: January 1, 1999–January 1, 2000
57. **Rosa Zafferani**
San Marino
Captain-Regent: April 1–October 1, 1999
58. **Irena Degutienë**
Lithuania
Prime Minister: May 4–18, 1999; October 27–November 3, 1999
59. **Vaira Vike-Freiberga**
Latvia
President: July 1, 1999–present
60. **Mireya Elisa Moscoso Arias Rodriguez**
Panama
President: September 2, 1999–present
61. **Adrienne Poy Clarkson**
Canada
Governor-General: October 7, 1999–present
62. **Helen Clark**
New Zealand
Prime Minister: December 10, 1999–present

Afghanistan

Women

Right to vote: 1965
To stand for election: 1965

Royalty

Ex–influence behind the scene

Suraya Khanum, 1919–1928. Second wife of King Amânullâh (Aman Ullah). Regarded as the nation's most progressive king, Amânullâh was heavily influenced by his wife after their marriage in 1914. Beginning in 1921, two years after he had ascended the throne, Amânullâh promoted family-code legislation, which among other provisions limited child marriage. A woman's right to choose her own husband was declared in 1924. In what was perhaps the severest shock to the almost entirely Muslim nation, in 1928 Suraya, her daughters, and some of the leading women of Kabul appeared unveiled in public. By this time, Afghani legislation on women was the most progressive in the Muslim world. This modernization was not without strife, however. Afghani tribal leaders in the hinterlands revolted over the "ideas" of Amânullâh and Suraya, forcing the king to abdicate in January 1929. The royal couple drifted into exile, first to India and then on to Rome. Their progressive ideas didn't resurface in Afghanistan until the mid-1950s, only to be overwhelmed again by traditionalist forces. At the beginning of the twenty-first century, Afghani women once again find themselves living under the terrible conditions that existed when Suraya's husband first came to the throne, more than eighty years ago.

Executive

Ex–partner in power

Anahita Ratebzad, 1979–1986. Mistress of President Babrak Kamal. Anahita, a staunch feminist and fighter for women's equality in Afghanistan, ultimately did such immense damage to the women of her country, because of her leftist ideas and promiscuous lifestyle, that it will likely take decades before Afghani women recover. The daughter of an affluent and westward-looking family, Anahita was educated in Chicago, receiving a nursing degree in 1950. A degree from Kabul Medical College followed in 1963. After a marriage to the private physician of King Zahir Shah that produced two children, she left her husband to take up a career in politics, a step no other Afghan woman had ever taken. A participant in the founding of the Popular Democratic Party of Afghanistan (PDPA), the communist party, Anahita was soon romantically involved with its leader, Babrak Kamal. To strengthen their alliance, she even married her daughter to his brother. Babrak was a dedicated communist, and she shared his devotion willingly. After the Afghani monarchy was overthrown in 1964, Anahita became one of the first four women elected to the country's parliament. By the time the communists seized power in 1978, Anahita had become the preeminent woman in Afghani political life. She went on to serve in the cabinet of Kamal, who eventually became president; was named ambassador to Yugoslavia; and established the ultraleftist Democratic Organization of the Women of Afghanistan. Unfortunately, Anahita identified the battle for women's rights—carried out under her party organizations—too closely with both the communists and the Soviet Union, a fact that would soon come back to haunt all Afghani women. By 1986, the communists had splintered into violently opposed factions, and Kamal, who had faltered badly as president, was pushed out of office. He and Anahita sought refuge in Russia, where he died of liver cancer in 1996. She disappeared from view after his death, but unfortunately her style of communist-influenced feminism severely tainted the struggle for women's rights in Afghanistan. When the militantly conservative Islamic Taliban forces took control of the country shortly after the Russians and their Afghani allies had been driven from power, they turned with fury on what few rights Afghani women had won. All women in the country were driven back into almost total seclusion. The plight of women in Afghanistan today is probably worse than anywhere else in the world. They have almost no rights at all and exist in the most dire of circumstances.

First appointed to cabinet

Kobra Nourzai, Minister of Public Health, 1965

Notable service in cabinet

Anahita Ratebzad, Minister of Education; Minister of Social Affairs; Minister of Tourism; Minister of Culture

First appointed ambassador

Anahita Ratebzad, Ambassador to Yugoslavia, 1979

Legislative

First elected to national legislature (Wolosi Jirgah, Council of Representatives)

Rokia Habib
Anahita Ratebzad
Khadija Saljugi
Massouma Esmaty Wardak

All elected July 1965

ALBANIA

Women

Right to vote: January 21, 1920
To stand for election: January 21, 1920

Executive

Ex–Red Queen, partner in power

Nexhmjie Xhuglini Hoxha, 1945–1985. Spouse of longtime Stalinist dictator Enver Hoxha. A leader in the Union of Anti-Fascist Women and a component of the Albanian National Liberation Front during World War II, Nexhmjie soon partnered herself with the front's leader, Enver. When Hoxha came to power, she remade her group into the Albanian Women's Union. From that powerful perch, Nexhmjie, with Enver's blessing, became a deputy in the People's Assembly and eventually a member of the Central Committee of the ruling communist Albanian Worker's Party. Her power was only slightly less than that of her feared husband. His xenophobic, all-encompassing rule, which imprisoned or killed all who stood in his way, turned Albania into the world's first truly atheist state. Enver also boasted that he'd eradicated illiteracy and made Albania self-sufficient in food. His secret police, the Directorate of State Security or Sigurimi, was among the most feared in the communist world. After Enver's death in 1985, Nexhmjie devoted herself to keeping the flame of his memory burning, thus ensuring that their fiefdom remained on the narrow, isolationist path he had established. When the communists were swept from power across East Europe at the end of the 1980s, even secluded Albania couldn't withstand the tide of freedom. To prove its democratic credentials, the new government arrested the widow Hoxha, then in her seventies, putting her on trial in 1991. Charged with embezzlement and abuse of power, she drew a prison sentence of eleven years, most likely served in more humane conditions than she and Enver had meted out to their enemies in previous decades. Nexhmjie was released in January 1997 at age seventy-six, following a general amnesty for several classes of prisoners.

First appointed to cabinet

Naxhije Dume, Minister of Education, 1945

Notable service in cabinet

Tefta Cami, Minister of Education and Culture
Makebule Cecosi, Deputy Prime Minister
Arte Dode, Minister of Culture
Ermelinda Meksi, Minister of Economic Cooperation and Development
Roza Pati, Minister of Youth and Women
Marjeta Pronjari, Minister of Sports
Ingrid Shuli, Minister of Public Works and Transport
Themie Thomai, Minister of Agriculture
Arlinda Ymeraj, Minister of Labor and Social Affairs

First appointed ambassador

Syeda Laze, Ambassador to Vietnam, 1982

Legislative

First elected to national legislature (Kuvendi Popullor, People's Assembly)

Naxhije Dume
Liri Gega
Ollga Plumbi

All elected December 1945

Algeria

Women

Right to vote: July 5, 1962
To stand for election: July 5, 1962

Executive

Thwarted presidential candidate

Louiza Hanoune, 1999. Leader of the Worker's Party, a small leftist party, which won four seats in the 1997 parliamentary elections. Hanoune declared her candidacy for the 1999 presidential elections, but her plans were thwarted when she was unable to collect the required number of signatures to get on the ballot. Had she succeeded, Hanoune would have been the second woman to run for president in the Arab world, but the first in an independent country (see Palestinian Authority, under Israel).

First appointed to cabinet

Z'hor Ounissi, Secretary of State (Deputy Minister) for Social Affairs, 1982. She was promoted to full minister in 1984.

Notable service in cabinet

Leila Aslaoui, Minister for Youth and Sport
Zahia Benarous, Minister of Culture
Nafissa Lalliam, Minister for Health
Rabea Mechernene, Minister of National Solidarity and Family
Z'hor Ounissi, Minister of Education

First appointed ambassador

No woman yet appointed

Legislative

First appointed to national legislature
(al-Majlis al-Watani Ettaassissi, Constituent National Assembly)

Fatima Khemisti
And nine other women, all September 1962

First elected to national legislature (al-Majlis al-Watani, National Assembly)

Two women, September 1964

Andorra

Women

Right to vote: April 14, 1970
To stand for election: September 5, 1973

Executive

First appointed to cabinet

Mercé Sansa Renyer, Minister of Government Service, 1986

Notable service in cabinet

Susagna Arasanz, Minister of Finance
Olga Adellach Coma, Minister of Agriculture and the Environment
Carme Sala Sansa, Minister of Education and Sport
Monserrat Roncheras Santacreu, Minister of Tourism and Sport

First appointed ambassador

Meritxell Mateu Pi, Ambassador to France, Belgium, the Netherlands, and Luxembourg, 1993

Legislative

First elected to national legislature
(Consell General, General Council)

Mercé Bonell Bertran (Liberal Party), December 1994

Judicial

First appointed to supreme court

Assumpta Pujol Ribera, 1996

Angola

Women

Right to vote: November 11, 1975
To stand for election: November 11, 1975

Executive

Notable presidential candidate, 1992

Anália de Victoria Pereira. Leader and candidate of the Liberal Democratic Party. Pereira placed tenth out of eleven candidates, with less than 1 percent of the vote, in the presidential contest won by José Eduardo dos Santos.

First appointed to cabinet

Maria Mambo Café, Minister of Social Affairs, 1982. She had previously served as deputy minister of internal trade, beginning in 1977.

Notable service in cabinet

Albina Pereira Africano, Minister of Petroleum
Albina Faria de Avis, Minister of Petroleum
Joana Lina Ramos Baptista Cristiano, Minister of Women's Affairs
Maria Fatima Monteiro Jardim, Minister of Fisheries
Ana Dias Lourenco, Minister of Planning
Faustina Muteka, Minister for the Implementation of the Peace Process
Ana Maria de Oliveira, Minister of Culture
Candida Celeste da Silva, Minister of Family and Women's Affairs

First appointed ambassador

Maria de Jeses Haller, Ambassador to Sweden, 1978

Legislative

First elected to national legislature (Assembleia Nacional, National Assembly)

Nineteen women, November 1980

Antigua and Barbuda

Women

Right to vote: December 1, 1951
To stand for election: December 1, 1951

Executive

First appointed to an executive position

Yvonne Maginley, Deputy Governor-General, 1998

First appointed to cabinet

No woman yet appointed

First appointed ambassador

Deborah-Mae Lowell, Ambassador to Canada, 1992

Legislative

First appointed to national legislature (Senate)

Nathalie Payne
Millicent Percival

Both appointed April 1984

First elected to national legislature (House of Representatives)

Bridget Harris, March 1994

Head of national legislature

Bridget Harris, House of Representatives, 1994–1999
Millicent Percival, Senate, 1994–1999

Argentina

Women

Right to vote: September 29, 1947
To stand for election: September 29, 1947[1]

Executive

Power past

María Estela (Isabel) Cartas Martínez de Perón. Vice-President, October 12, 1973–July 1, 1974; President, July 1, 1974–March 29, 1976. Isabel, second wife of ex-dictator Juan Perón, met her future husband while dancing as a chorus girl in a pickup bar in Panama City. After a brief affair, they married and settled into exile in Spain. Despite having been ousted from power in a 1956 military coup, Perón's allure to Argentina remained strong, and he was finally permitted to return in 1973. He finagled himself into being elected president again, this time with Isabel as his vice-president, a feat he'd not been able to accomplish with his first wife, Evita (see below). Perón died unexpectedly within six months of taking office, leaving the hapless Isabel to succeed him. This turn of events was most unfortunate, both for her and for Argentina. Nearly illiterate with no intellectual abilities to speak of—she was addicted to reading comic books and watching cartoons—Isabel had a short but disastrous tenure. The Argentine economy spun out of control as inflation spiraled, while a vicious campaign of urban terrorism tore at the fabric of society. The military finally seized power in 1976, packing Isabel off to house arrest at a remote military base. Freed in 1981, she again left for Spanish exile. The only positive aspect of Isabel's term in power is that she was the first female head of government in South America.

Notable presidential candidate, 1998

Graciela Fernandez Meijide. A seventyish former French teacher, Graciela appeared at first sight to be an unlikely presidential candidate. Yet in early 1998, she topped the opinion polls as the people's choice for the position. Her involvement in politics began after the disappearance of her only son during Argentina's "dirty war" of the 1970s. First elected to the federal senate, she next ran for the more powerful Chamber of Deputies in 1997. Graciela

---

[1]In some provinces, women were given the right to vote and stand for election at an earlier date.

was a member of the center-left Frepaso group, which entered the 1999 presidential election in a coalition termed the "Alliance" with the Radical Party. In a first-ever party presidential "primary" in November 1998, Graciela lost the alliance's presidential nomination to Fernando de la Rua, mayor of Buenos Aires. As a consolation prize, she was named as her party's candidate for governor of Buenos Aires province, but lost that race also. In November 1999, she was appointed Minister of Social Affairs.

Ex–partner in power

María Eva (Evita) Duarte Perón, 1946–1952. Juan Perón's first wife was a charismatic schemer who rose from poverty, and reputed prostitution, to share power with her husband as an unelected "copresident." Many attribute Perón's whole career to Evita's energy. A one-time radio actress and aspiring film star, Evita dedicated her life to promoting her husband. She was a driving force behind his election as president in 1946, and once he was in office she built the Argentine working class into their bedrock of support. Working outside normal political channels, she established her first power base in the Confederation of Labor, an umbrella group for labor unions. Later, she established the Eva Perón Foundation, ostensibly a charity but in reality nothing more than a conduit for channeling money to her favorite causes, political and otherwise, with an ample share going into the couple's own coffers. After failing to be named as Perón's vice-presidential running mate in 1951 because of opposition from the military, Evita died of cancer the following year. Her husband tried to use her memory to inspire the country, but a series of political blunders damaged his credibility. He sought solace with teenage mistresses but couldn't replace Evita's political savvy. Four years after her death, Perón was overthrown in a military coup.

First appointed to cabinet

Aljandra Giovarini, Minister of Labor and Social Affairs, 1952

Notable service in cabinet

Maria Julia Asogaray, Minister of the Environment
Antonia Benitcz, Minister of Justice
Susana Ruiz Cerrutti, Minister of Foreign Affairs
Susana Decibe, Minister of Education and Culture

First appointed ambassador

Angela C. Romera Vara, Ambassador to Panama, 1962

Legislative

First elected to provincial legislature

Emar Acosta, San Juan provincial legislature, 1934

First elected to national legislature
(Cámara de Diputados, Chamber of Deputies)

Twenty-four women, November 1951. All twenty-four of these women were personally selected by Evita Perón for inclusion on the Perónista Party ticket.

Head of national legislature

María Estela Martínez de Perón, Senate President Pro Tempore, October 12, 1973–July 1, 1974

Minority: Arab-Argentinean

Executive

Carlos Saul Menem. President, July 1, 1989–December 10, 1999. Argentina's first president of Arab descent swept into office with a landslide victory, helped by the near collapse of the incumbent government of President Raul Alfonsin. The situation was so bad that Menem was sworn into office almost six months early. Born of Syrian immigrant parents and a Sunni Muslim by birth, Menem converted to Roman Catholicism to further his political career. He cultivated an image of machismo, which served him well as he struggled to bring a modicum of normality to Argentina's often chaotic economy and to level the country's political instability. He campaigned under the banner of the neo-Perónist Justicialist Party, yet never hesitated to abandon old tenets of "Perónisimo" if it suited him politically. By applying harsh economic policies, Menem worked such wonders with the country that he was able to overcome opposition and reinvent the constitution to give himself another term in 1995. Menem tried to maneuver himself into a third successive term but met far stronger resistance than the first time he redesigned the constitution to permit himself a second term. It is conceivable that he will return for at least one more presidential term.

Religious Minority: Jewish

Executive

First appointed to cabinet

David Blejer, Minister of Labor, 1958

Legislative

First elected to national legislature
(Cámara de Diputados, Chamber of Deputies)

Four persons, 1958

Armenia

Women

Right to vote: February 2, 1921
To stand for election: February 2, 1921

Executive

First appointed to cabinet

Karine Danielyan, Minister of Nature Protection, 1991

Notable service in cabinet

Nina Asmayan, Minister of Trade
Hranush Hagopyan, Minister of Social Security

First appointed ambassador

Sevda Sevan, Ambassador to Bulgaria, 1991

Legislative

First elected to national legislature[2]

Tamara Aloyan, Communist Party of Armenia
Jemma Ananyan, Communist Party of Armenia
Narine Balayan, Free Parliamentaries
Anahit Bayandour, Armenian National Development Party
Anahit Gevorgian, Free Parliamentaries
Hranoush Hakobyan, Communist Party of Armenia
Artzvik Hertvertsyan, Armenian National Development Party
Alina Hovhannisyan, Communist Party of Armenia
Karine Stepanyan, Armenian National Development Party

All elected May 1990

---

[2]Armenian women were previously elected to the Supreme Soviet of the Soviet Socialist Republic of Armenia and to the Parliament of the USSR.

Australia

Women

Right to vote: June 12, 1902
To stand for election: June 12, 1902

Notable First, 1897: **Catherine Helen Spence,** the world's first female candidate for an elective national political position, was unsuccessful in her bid for a seat at the Australian Constitutional Convention of 1897.

Executive

First appointed to cabinet

Enid Muriel (Dame) Lyons, Minister Without Portfolio and Vice-President of the Executive Council, 1949. **Annabelle Rankin** was appointed minister of housing on January 26, 1966. **Margaret Guilfoyle,** appointed minister of social security on December 22, 1975, was the first woman to be a member of the cabinet.

Notable service in cabinet

Bronwyn Bishop, Minister of Defense Industry, Science, and Personnel
Rosemary Crawley, Minister of Family Services
Margaret Guilfoyle, Minister of Social Security; Minister of Education
Ros Kelly, Minister of Arts, Sport, and the Environment; Minister of Tourism and Territories
Carmen Lawrence, Minister of Human Services and Health
Jeanette McHugh, Minister of Consumer Affairs
Judy Moylan, Minister for the Status of Women
Joyce Newman, Minister of Social Security
Susan Ryan, Minister of Education and Youth Affairs
Amanda Vanstone, Minister of Employment, Education, Training, and Youth Affairs

First appointed ambassador

Ruth Dobson, Ambassador to Denmark, 1974
Annabelle Rankin, High Commissioner (Ambassador) to New Zealand, 1971

First elected premier of a state

Carmen Lawrence, Australian Labor Party, Western Australia, 1990

First appointed to state cabinet

Florence Cardell-Oliver, Western Australia, 1936

First appointed governor of a state

Dame Roma Mitchell, South Australia, 1991

First elected mayor

Lilian Fowler, 1938

Legislative

First appointed to national legislature (Senate)

Enid Muriel (Dame) Lyons, United Australia Party, August 21, 1943

First elected to national legislature (House of Representatives)

Dorothy Margaret (Dame) Tangney, Australian Labor Party, elected August 21, 1943, and seated September 23, 1943

Head of national legislature

Margaret Elizabeth Reid, Liberal Party, Senate, 1996–present
Joan Child, Australian Labor Party, House of Representatives, 1987–1990

First elected to state legislature

Edith Dickersy Cowan, Nationalist Party, Western Australia, 1921

First to serve in other state or territorial legislatures

New South Wales: **Millicent Preston-Stanley,** 1925
Northern Territory: **Dawn Lewis,** 1978
Queensland: **Irene Maud Longman,** 1929
South Australia: **Jessie Cooper, Joyce Steele,** 1959
Tasmania: **Margaret E. McIntyre,** 1948
Victoria: **Lady Millie Peacock,** 1933

Youngest to serve in national legislature (Senate)

Natasha Stott-Despoja, Democratic Party, South Australia, appointed in November 1995 at age twenty-six years, two months

Past power, or potential power

Pauline Hanson, 1996–1998. Independent. A fish-and-chips shop owner from Queensland elected to the national House of Representatives, Hanson made quite a splash with her maiden speech decrying the "Asian invasion" of Australia. Denounced across the political spectrum as racist, she ignored her critics and launched the One Nation Party in April 1997. Within fourteen months her party had won 25 percent of the vote (and fourteen seats) in the Queensland state elections. Hanson immediately took her party to the national level, basing its platform on a rural, right-wing, anti-immigrant, anti-aboriginal stance. Heading into the October 1998 national elections, all other Australian parties had denounced One Nation but still feared that it might win enough seats to sway the balance of power in a closely fought election. Their fears proved unfounded. One Nation polled only 8 percent of the national vote, winning only one seat in the Senate and none in the lower house. Hanson herself lost the seat for which she was running, and even mulled leaving politics completely. The One Nation Party received almost $5 million in federal campaign funds, based on their showing in the national election, so the party itself could carry on even if Hanson doesn't. The party chairman, who seemed to be on the outs with Hanson after the election, claimed that the party would continue to fight on in future elections.

As for Hanson, it's hard to believe that she will be content to disappear from the political arena.

Judicial

First appointed to supreme court

Dame Roma Mitchell, 1965

Minority: Aborigine

Right to vote: June 18, 1962
To stand for election: June 18, 1962

Legislative

First appointed to national legislature (Senate)

Neville Bonner, Liberal Party, Queensland, 1971

First elected to national legislature (Senate)

Aden Ridgeway, Democratic Party, New South Wales, 1998

Judicial

First magistrate

Pat O'Shane, 1986

Minority: Asian-Australian

Legislative

First appointed to national legislature (Senate)

Thomas J. K. Bakhap, Liberal Party, Tasmania, Chinese descent, July 1, 1913

First elected to national legislature (Senate)

Bill O'Chee, National Party, Queensland, Chinese descent, 1993. O'Chee had been appointed to his seat in 1990, then sought reelection in 1993.

First woman appointed to national legislature (Senate)

Patricia Irene (Irina) Dunn, Independent, New South Wales, Macanese descent, July 21, 1988

First elected to a state legislature

Helen Sham-Ho, Liberal Party, New South Wales, Chinese descent, 1988

Minority: Gay/Lesbian

Executive

First appointed ambassador

Stephen Brady, Ambassador to Denmark, accredited to Finland, Iceland, Latvia, Lithuania, Norway, and Sweden, 1999

Legislative

First elected to local office

Bill Hunt

Craig Johnson
Brian McGahen

All elected to Sydney city council, 1984

First elected to national legislature (Senate)

Bob Brown, Green Party, Tasmania, 1996

First elected to state legislature

Paul O'Grady, Australian Labor Party, New South Wales, 1988

First woman elected to state legislature

Elizabeth (Giz) Watson, Green Party, Western Australia, 1997

Judicial

First appointed to supreme court

Michael Kirby, 1996

Minority: Vietnamese

Executive

First elected to public office

Phuong Canh Ngo, Fairfield city council, Victoria, 1987

First woman elected mayor

Mai Ho, Maribyrnong, Victoria

Political Entity: Christmas Island

Executive

First elected head of local administration (Shire of Christmas Island)

Lillian Oh, December 1992

Legislative

First elected to local legislature (Assembly)

Cheryl Wright, August 1989

Political Entity: Norfolk Island

Executive

First appointed to cabinet

Eleanore B. Read, Minister of Community Service, 1983

Austria

Women

Right to vote: December 19, 1918
To stand for election: December 19, 1918

Executive

Notable presidential candidates, 1998

Gertraud Knoll. Trained in theology, an ordained minister, and a Protestant bishop. Knoll ran as an Independent. She placed second, with 13.5 percent of the vote, behind President Thomas Klestil, who was running for reelection.

Heide Schmidt. Former Minister of Education and the Arts, member of Parliament, and a lawyer. Schmidt was the candidate of the Liberal Forum. She placed third in the 1998 balloting, with 11.1 percent of the vote. This was her second run for the presidency.

Notable presidential candidate, 1992

Heide Schmidt. Candidate of the right-wing Freedom Party, headed by Joerg Haider; placed third in the race. She broke with Haider shortly after the 1992 contest and founded her own party (see above), vowing to ensure that Haider never becomes head of Austria—as either president or chancellor.

Notable presidential candidate, 1986

Freda Meissner-Blau. Leader and candidate of the Green Party.

Notable presidential candidate, 1951

Ludovica Hainisch-Marcher. Independent, finished last of eight candidates with less than 1 percent of the vote.

First appointed to cabinet

Grete Rehor, Minister of Social Administration, 1966

Notable service in cabinet

Johanna Dohnal, Minister of Women's Affairs
Beatrix Eypeltauer, Minister of Construction
Maria Fekter, Minister of Construction and Tourism
Hertha Firnberg, Minister of Research
Marilies Flemming, Minister of the Environment, Youth, and Welfare
Gertrude Frölich-Sandner, Minister of Youth and Consumer Protection
Elisabeth Gehrer, Minister of Education and Culture
Hilde Hawlicek, Minister of Education, Arts, and Sport
Eleonora Hostasch, Minister of Labor, Health, and Social Affairs
Elfriede Karl, Minister of the Environment, Youth, and Family
Helga Konrad, Minister of Women's Affairs
Christe Krammer, Minister of Health
Ingrid Leodolter, Minister of Health
Sonja Moser, Minister of Youth and Family
Barbara Prammer, Minister of Women and Consumer Protection
Maria Rauch-Kallat, Minister of the Environment
Gertrude Wondrake, Minister of Social Affairs

First appointed ambassador

Johanna Mondschein, Ambassador to Norway, 1959

First head (Landeshauptmann) of a state (Bundesländ)

Waltraud Klasnic, Austrian People's Party, Steiermark, 1996

Legislative

First elected to national legislature (Nationalrat, National Council)

Anna Boschek, Social Democratic Party
Hildegard Burjan, Christian Socialist Party
Emmy Freundlich, Social Democratic Party
Adelheid Popp, Social Democratic Party
Gabriele Proft, Social Democratic Party
Therese Schlesinger, Social Democratic Party
Amalie Seidel, Social Democratic Party
Maria Tusch, Social Democratic Party

All elected February 2, 1919, and seated March 14, 1919

Head of national legislature

Heide Schmidt (Nationalrat, National Council), 1990–1994
Anna Elisabeth Haselbach (Bundesrat, Federal Council), January 1–June 30, 1991; 1995

Helga Hieden-Sommer (Bundesrat, Federal Council), July 1–December 31, 1987

Helene Tschitschko (Bundesrat, Federal Council), January 1–June 30, 1965; July 1–December 31, 1969; January 1–June 30, 1974

Johanna Bayer (Bundesrat, Federal Council), July 1–December 31, 1953

Olga Rudel-Zeynek, Christian Socialist Party (Bundesrat, Federal Council), December 1, 1927–May 31, 1928; June 1–November 30, 1932

Notable first, 1927: When **Olga Rudel-Zeynek** assumed office as head of Austria's Federal Council on December 1, 1927, she became the first woman in the world to head a national legislature.

AZERBAIJAN

Women

Right to vote: May 19, 1921
To stand for election: May 19, 1921

Executive

Notable presidential candidate, 1998

Lala Shovkhet-Hajiyeva. Candidate of the Liberal Party. The campaign against President Haydar Aliyev, former Azerbaijani Communist Party boss, who was running for reelection, was mired in charges and countercharges. Lala's name appeared on the ballot, but she protested more than she campaigned. All of Aliyev's opponents claimed that the election was rigged and limited their involvement to protesting the election. Naturally, Aliyev won, claiming in excess of 75 percent of the vote; Lala, along with the rest of his rivals, split the remaining 25 percent.

First appointed to cabinet (Azerbaijan SSR)

Tira Aza-kyzy Tairova, Minister of Foreign Affairs, 1959

First appointed to cabinet (after independence)

Lidiya Rasulova, Minister of Labor and Social Security, 1991

Notable service in cabinet

Sudaba Hasanova, Minister of Justice

First appointed ambassador

Eleonora Husseynova, Ambassador to France, 1993

Legislative

First elected to national legislature (Milli Majlis, National Council)[3]

Maryam Hassanova, Popular Front of Azerbaijan, November 1991

Head of national legislature (Azerbaijan SSR)

Elmira Mikail-kyzy Gafarova, Chairwoman, Presidium

[3]Azerbaijani women were previously elected to the Supreme Soviet of the Soviet Socialist Republic of Azerbaijan and to the Parliament of the USSR.

The Bahamas

Women

Right to vote: February 18, 1961
To stand for election: February 18, 1961

Executive

First appointed to cabinet

Doris Johnson, Minister Without Portfolio, 1968

Notable service in cabinet

Janet G. Bostwick, Minister of Foreign Affairs; Minister of Housing and National Insurance
Ivy L. Dumont, Minister of Education; Minister of Agriculture, Trade, and Industry
Doris Johnson, Minister of Transport
Theresa Moxey-Ingraham, Minister of Labor, Immigration, and Training

First appointed ambassador

Margaret McDonald, Ambassador to the United States, 1986

Legislative

First appointed to national legislature (Senate)

Three women, July 1977

First elected to national legislature (House of Assembly)

Janet Gwennett Bostwick, Free National Movement, June 1982

Head of national legislature

Rome Italia Johnson, House of Assembly, 1997–present
Doris Johnson, Senate, 1973–1983

Judicial

Notable service on supreme court

Joan Sawyer, Chief Justice

Bahrain

The right to vote does not exist in Bahrain. There is no parliament, and political parties are forbidden. There is a council, the Majlis as-Shura, which has forty appointed members—none have ever been female—and which functions only on a consultative basis. No woman has ever been appointed to the cabinet.

First appointed ambassador

Sheika Hayya bin Rashid al-Khalifa, Ambassador to France, 1999

Bangladesh

Women

Right to vote: November 4, 1972
To stand for election: November 4, 1972

Executive

Sheik Hasina Wajid, Prime Minister, June 23, 1996–present. Wajid became Muslim Bangladesh's second female prime minister in a row after she and her Awami League finally defeated her bitter political rival, Begum Khaleda Zia (see below). Wajid is the daughter of Bangladesh's first president, Shaikh Mujibur Rahman. He was assassinated by army officers in 1975, and almost all of his family were killed; Wajid escaped the slaughter because she was in India when it occurred. Given that she drove Khaleda Zia from power, it is only natural to assume that her rival will attempt to return the favor as soon as an opportune moment arrives.

Power past

Begum Khaleda Zia, Prime Minister, March 20, 1991–March 30, 1996. Zia came to power under circumstances highly unusual for women in any country, much less a Muslim one. She is the widow of former president Zia-ur Rahman, murdered in 1981 by rebel military officers. She fought a long-running battle against the autocratic and corrupt rule of Hussain Ershad, who had eventually succeeded her slain husband. After finally driving Ershad from office, Zia then led her Bangladeshi Nationalist Party to victory in a general election in which her main opponent was another woman, Sheik Hasina Wajid (see above). Zia was finally driven from power by her female rival, after several years of political infighting, in a hotly contested election.

First appointed to cabinet

Badrunnessa Ahmad, Minister of Education, 1973

Notable service in cabinet

Matia Choudhry, Minister of Agriculture, Food, and Disaster Management

Syeda Sajeda Chowdhry, Minister of Forestry and the Environment
Begum Nurjahan Murshed, Minister of Social Affairs and Planning
Sarwari Rahman, Minister of Women and Children's Affairs
Zinnatunnesa Talukder, Minister of Primary and Mass Education

First appointed ambassador

Tahmina Khan Dolly, Ambassador to Sri Lanka, 1980

Legislative

First elected to national legislature (Jatiya Sangsad, Parliament)

Fifteen women, March 1973

Barbados

Women

Right to vote: October 23, 1950
To stand for election: October 23, 1950

Executive

Power past

Ruth Nita Barrow, Governor-General, June 6, 1990–December 28, 1996. Barrow, the sister of independent Barbados's first prime minister, Sir Errol Barrow, had a long career in public service before being chosen as governor-general, the representative of the British monarch. She was a trained nurse and had served in many positions with national and international health and service agencies, including the presidency of the World Body of the YWCA. A relentless campaigner for women's rights, Barrow proved that she could compete in a predominantly male political world when she headed the Barbadian delegation to the United Nations. A very popular leader in Barbados, she died unexpectedly during the 1995 Christmas season.

First appointed to cabinet

Billie Miller, Minister of Health and National Insurance, 1976

Notable service in cabinet

Billie Miller, Deputy Prime Minister; Minister of Foreign Affairs; Minister of Tourism
Mia Mottley, Minister of Education, Youth Affairs, and Culture
Elizabeth Thompson, Minister of the Environment; Minister of Health
Maizie Barker Welch, Minister of Labour

First appointed ambassador

Cyralene Gale, High Commissioner (Ambassador) to Canada, 1975

Legislative

First appointed to colonial legislature (Legislative Council)

Muriel Hanschell, 1949

First elected to colonial legislature (Parliament)

Edna E. Bourne, Barbados Labor Party, December 18, 1951

First elected to national legislature (Parliament)

Gertrude Eastmond, Democratic Labor Party, September 1971

Historical Notes

Barbados has the second-oldest Parliament in the Western Hemisphere—it was established in 1639 as the House of Assembly. The first black to be elected as a member was **Samuel Jackson Prescod** in 1843; his election made him the first black male to sit in a parliamentary assembly in the "Western" world. In 1886, **Sir Conrad Reeves** was named as the first black chief justice of the Barbados supreme court. He was also the first black male granted a knighthood in the British Empire.

Belarus

Women

Right to vote: February 4, 1919
To stand for election: February 4, 1919

Executive

Power in exile

Ivonka J. Survilla, 1997–present. President of the Rada (Council) of the Belarusan Democratic Republic in exile. Proclaimed independent on March 25, 1918, the Belarusan Democratic Republic refuses to acknowledge any of the governmental changes that have taken place in Belarus since it was forced into exile in November 1920. Survilla, born in Belarus but now residing in Canada, is the latest in a line of exiled leaders who have fought for the true independence of their country ever since. The Rada's activities are now directed at the removal of President Aleksandr Lukashenka of Belarus from his post and the holding of truly free elections in the country.

First appointed to cabinet (Belorussian SSR)

Evdokiya Ilinichna Uralova, Public Commissar of Education, 1938

First appointed to cabinet (after independence)

Olga Bronislavovna Dargel, Minister of Social Security, 1993

Notable service in cabinet

Inessa Drobyshevskaya, Minister of Health
Tamara Krutivtsova, Minister of Social Welfare

First appointed ambassador

Nina Nicolaevna Mazy, Ambassador to France, 1993

Legislative

First elected to national legislature[4]

Tatyana Michaylovna Anisenko
Anna Ivanovna Boborukina
Inessa Drobyshevskaya
Olga Nicholaevna Golubovich
Nadezhda Yakovlevna Izvalova
Ylyana Feoktistovna Krishtalevich
Zoya Vladimirovna Krupnik
Zinaida Vasilevna Penkova
Raisa Nicolaevna Samusevich
Galina Georgievna Semdynova
Nina Ilinichna Soldatova
Elena Nicolaevna Uctinovich
Valentina Arcadevna Yastreb

All elected March 1990

[4]Before independence, Belorussian women had been elected to the Supreme Soviet of Belorussia and to the Parliament of the USSR.

Belgium

Women

Right to vote: May 9, 1919;[5] March 27, 1948[6]
To stand for election: February 7, 1921;[7] March 27, 1948

Royalty

Ex–power behind the scenes

Marie Liliane Baels, Princess de Rethy, 1941–1983. Second wife of King Leopold III. The second spouse often suffers from comparison to the first. Such was the case with Leopold's beautiful and ambitious second wife. His first, Princess Astrid of Sweden, was quite popular in Belgium, but died in 1935 in a car accident. Leopold's grief at his loss was magnified by the fact that he had been driving the car. When World War II broke out, Leopold—unlike many other European monarchs who fled abroad and directed governments-in-exile for their countries—made no attempt to flee, surrendering abruptly to the Germans. In 1941, he made a morganatic marriage to Marie Liliane Baels, a commoner who was accused, perhaps falsely, of being pro-Nazi. As the war dragged on, the Nazis installed a regent for Belgium and sent Leopold and Marie Liliane off for "safekeeping" to Salzburg, Austria, where they began to raise a family. When the war ended, the royal couple returned home, but Leopold met fierce resistance from the Belgians when he tried to reclaim his throne. The issue was finally decided by a plebiscite in March 1950, which Leopold narrowly won. His victory seemed to spark even more protests—which were directed at both him and his wife—and he finally decided to formally abdicate the following year in favor of Baudouin, his son by his first wife. Even though Baudouin formally ascended the throne, Leopold and Marie Liliane continued to live with him in the royal palace at Laeken. Many Belgians felt that their young king was under the profound—even pernicious—influence of his father and stepmother. It took years for the Belgians to gradually warm to Baudouin, with his own marriage to a Spanish princess, Doña Fabiola, helping immensely. By the time of Leopold's death in 1983,

---

[5]The law of 1919 gave the right to vote in national elections to the widows and mothers of servicemen killed in World War I, to the widows and mothers of citizens shot or killed by the enemy, and to female political prisoners who had been held by the enemy.

[6]The law of 1948 gave all women the right to vote with the same conditions that applied to men.

[7]The law of 1921 gave women the right to stand for election in communal, provincial, and parliamentary elections.

both he and Marie Liliane had become practically irrelevant to the scope of Belgian political life, a far cry from the furor the couple had evoked during the 1940s and early 1950s.

Executive

First appointed to cabinet

Marguerite de Reimacher-Legot, 1965

Notable service in cabinet

Magda Aelvoet, Minister of Health
Rita de Backer-Van Ocken, Minister of Flemish Cultural Affairs
Magda De Galan, Minister of Social Affairs
Isabelle Durant, Minister of Transport and Mobility
Laurette Onnckelinx, Minister of Social Solidarity, Health, and the Environment
Miet Smet, Minister of Employment and Labor
Paula D'Hondt Van Opdenbosch, Minister of the Interior

First appointed ambassador

Edmonde Dever, Ambassador to Sweden, 1973

Legislative

First elected to national legislature (Chambre des représentants/ Kamer van Volksvertegenwoordigers, House of Representatives)

Lucie DeJardin, Socialist Party, May 26, 1929

Minority: Algerian-Belgian

Legislative

First elected to national legislature (Chambre des représentants/ Kamer van Volksvertegenwoordigers, House of Representatives)

Dalila Douifi, Socialist Party, 1999

Minority: Gay

Executive

Notable service in cabinet

Elio di Rupo, Deputy Prime Minister; Minister of Energy and Telecommunications

Minority: Moroccan-Belgian

Legislative

First seated in national legislature (Chambre des représentants/ Kamer van Volksvertegenwoordigers, House of Representatives)

Chokri Mahassine, Flemish Socialist Party, January 1999. Mahassine replaced a member who resigned.

First elected to national legislature (Senad, Senate)

Mohamed Daif
Chokri Mahassine

Both elected June 1999

First woman elected to national legislature (Chambre des représentants/ Kamer van Volksvertegenwoordigers, House of Representatives)

Fauzaya (Fouzia) Tahlaoui, AGALEV (Ecolo-Flanders), June 1999

Minority: Turkish-Belgian

Legislative

First woman elected to national legislature (Senad, Senate)

Meryem Kaçar, AGALEV (Ecolo-Flanders), June 1999

Belize

Women

Right to vote: March 25, 1954
To stand for election: March 25, 1954

Executive

Power past

Elmira Minita Gordon, Governor-General, September 21, 1981–November 17, 1993. Gordon, a longtime supporter of former prime minister George Price's People's United Party, was rewarded for her years of service with an appointment as governor-general, the Queen's representative in Belize. She was the first woman in the British Commonwealth honored with that position in an independent country (see also Dame Hilda Louisa Bynoe of Grenada).

First appointed to the cabinet

Gwendolyn Margurite Lizarraga, Minister of Education, 1965

Notable service in cabinet

Faith Babb, Minister of Human Resources, Women's Affairs, and Youth Development
Dolores Balderamos Garcia, Minister of Human Development, Women, and Sports
Guadalupe Pech, Minister of Trade and Industry

First appointed ambassador

Ursula Barrow, High Commissioner (Ambassador) to the United Kingdom, 1993

Legislative

First elected to colonial legislature (House of Representatives)

Gwendolyn Margurite Lizarraga, 1965

First appointed to national legislature (Senate)

Kathlyn Hope, People's United Party, December 1984

Head of national legislature

Sylvia Flores, House of Representatives, 1998–present
Elizabeth Zabaneh, Senate, 1997
Jane Usher, Senate, 1989–1993
Carla Castillo, House of Representatives, 1985–1989
Doris June Garcia, Senate, 1984–1989

BENIN

Women

Right to vote: 1956
To stand for election: 1956

Executive

First appointed to cabinet

Rafiatou Karimou, Minister of Health, 1989

Notable service in cabinet

Grace Abamon, Minister of Justice and Law
Véronique Ahoyo, Minister of Labor and Social Welfare
Ramatou Baba-Moussa, Minister of Social Welfare and Women's Condition
Marina d'Almeida-Massougbodji, Minister of Public Health, Social Welfare, and Women's Affairs
Marie-Elise Gbedo, Minister of Commerce, Handicrafts, and Tourism
Véronique Lawson, Minister of Public Health
Conceptia Ouinsou, Minister of Education and Scientific Research

First appointed ambassador

Bernardine do Rego, Ambassador to Nigeria, 1980

Legislative

First elected to national legislature (Assemblée nationale, National Assembly)

Twenty-eight women, November 1979

BHUTAN

Women

Right to vote: 1953
To stand for election: 1953

Executive

First appointed to cabinet

Princess Dechen Wangchuk Dorji, Minister of Agriculture, 1985

Notable service in cabinet

Princess Dechen Wangchuk Dorji, Minister of Communications; Minister of Finance
Princess Sonam Chhoden Wangchuk Dorji, Minister of Finance; Minister of Agriculture

First appointed ambassador

No woman yet appointed

Legislative

First elected to national legislature (Tshogdu, National Assembly)

Three women, 1975

Bolivia

Women

Right to vote: 1938; July 21, 1952
To stand for election: 1938; July 21, 1952[8]

Executive

Power past

Lidia Gueiler Tejeda, President, November 16, 1979–July 17, 1980. During a period of intense political instability—Bolivia has suffered more than 180 abrupt changes of government since winning its independence in the 1820s—the country turned to Gueiler for help. As head of the Parliament's Chamber of Deputies, she was elected by her fellow members to serve as interim president until new elections could be held. Gueiler's colleagues knew that she was well equipped to handle the position. A longtime supporter of the National Revolutionary Movement, which had led a revolution in 1952, Gueiler was a former commander of the party's armed militias. In fact, she was the only woman to head a battalion during the 1952 revolution. After only a few months in office, she, too, like many of her presidential predecessors, was ousted in a military coup.

Notable presidential candidate, 1997

Remedios Loza, candidate of the Conscience of the Fatherland Party. Loza tied for fourth, with 16 percent of the vote, in a contest that saw ex-dictator Hugo Banzer Suarez return as a freely elected president.

First appointed to cabinet

Alcira Espinoza de Villegas, Minister of Labor and Social Security, 1969

Notable service in cabinet

Maria Amparo Ballivan, Minister of Housing and Basic Services

---

[8]Literate women and those with a certain level of income were given the right to vote and stand for election in 1938. These rights were extended to all women in 1952.

Ana Maria Cortes de Soriano, Minister of Justice and Human Rights
Elena Velasco de Urresti, Minister of Housing and Urban Affairs

First appointed ambassador

Teresa Alexander Dupleich, Ambassador to the Organization of American States, 1969

First elected mayor

Monica Medina, Patriotic Conscience Party, La Paz, 1993

Legislative

First elected to national legislature
(Cámara de Diputados, Chamber of Deputies)

Lidia Gueiler Tejeda, National Revolutionary Movement
Erna Gutierrez de Bedregal, National Revolutionary Movement

Both elected 1956

First elected to national legislature
(Cámara de Senadores, Chamber of Senators)

Leticia Antezana de Alverdi, 1966

Head of national legislature

Lidia Gueiler Tejeda, Chamber of Deputies, 1978–1979
Lidia Gueiler Tejeda, Senate, 1979

Judicial

First appointed to supreme court

Maria Josefa Saavedra, 1974

Minority: German-Bolivian

Executive

First to serve as head of state

Gérman Busch, May 1936

Minority: Indian

Executive

First elected vice-president

Victor Hugo Cardenas, Aymara Indian, 1993. Cardenas was the first full-blooded Indian elected to such a high office in South America.

Religious Minority: Jewish

Executive

First appointed to cabinet

Moisés Jarmusz Levy, Minister of Development and the Environment, 1992

Bosnia and Herzegovina

Women

Right to vote: January 31, 1949
To stand for election: January 31, 1949

Executive

First appointed to cabinet

Martina Raguz, Minister of Social Affairs, Health, and Labor, 1992

Notable service in cabinet

Svetlana Silkegovic, Minister of Information, 1996

First appointed ambassador

Sadzida Silaidzic, Ambassador to Pakistan, 1992
Bisera Turkovic, Ambassador to Croatia, 1992

Legislative

First elected to national legislature
(Skupstina Republike, Assembly of the Republic)[9]

Seven women, December 1990

Political Entity: Bosnian Serb Republic

Executive

Power past

Biljana Plavsic, President, June 30, 1996–November 14, 1998. A former dean of the Biology Department at the University of Sarajevo, Plavsic has moved from being a Serb hard-liner to

[9]Women from Bosnia and Herzegovina were previously elected to the Parliament of Yugoslavia.

taking a more moderate position. From 1990 through 1992, she was a member of Bosnia and Herzegovina's collective presidency. In April 1992, when the country declared itself independent of Yugoslavia, Plavsic left that position to become one of the two vice-presidents of the Republika Srpska, the Serbian entity that proclaimed its own independence from the government in Sarajevo. President Radovan Karadzic of the rump state was forced—under pressure from NATO—to relinquish his post, and Plavsic succeeded him in June 1996. Most indications were that Karadzic continued to exercise actual power, while hers was only a nominal authority. She was finally confirmed as president in elections held in September 1996. Relations soon soured, however, between the former Serb allies. Plavsic adopted a more amenable attitude toward the Dayton peace accords that had ended the fighting in Bosnia and Herzegovina, while Karadzic maintained his hard-line position. By September 1997, she had been expelled from the Serb Democratic Party and accused of corruption and having dismissed the Bosnian Serb Parliament without the authority to do so. A new round of elections in November 1997 saw her recently formed National Alliance Party take 20 percent of the parliamentary vote. Political control, however, continued to be split: Plavsic held sway from the city of Banja Luka, while Karadzic ruled the rest of the roost from Pale, near Sarajevo, effectively splitting the Bosnian Serb Republic between them. The schism in the Bosnian Serb ranks seemed to end with the elections of September 1998. Plavsic was beaten when she stood for reelection by a hard-line Serb nationalist candidate allied with Karadzic and his faction.

Botswana

Women

Right to vote: March 1, 1965
To stand for election: March 1, 1965

Executive

Ex–partner in power

Ruth Williams Khama, 1948–1980. Wife of Prime Minister and President Sir Seretse Khama (1965–1980). At the age of four, Seretse Khama became the hereditary paramount chief of the Bamangwato, the most important tribe of what was then Bechuanaland, a British protectorate bordering South Africa. The regent, his farsighted uncle, ultimately sent Seretse to England to complete his education, where he attended Oxford and studied law. At the end of his studies, Seretse met and married Ruth Williams, a white British woman, and took her home with him, setting off a furor that rocked southern Africa. Although the Bamangwato Kgotla (tribal assembly) finally approved Khama's marriage, the racist South African government, which hoped to absorb Bechuanaland, was infuriated by it. The British government finally intervened, forcing the interracial couple to leave the country and not permitting them to return until 1957. When they did, Ruth set about winning over the hearts of her husband's people, eventually becoming so popular that she was commonly called "Mama Ruth." Seretse, meanwhile, worked on gaining independence for his country, first as prime minister and then as president in 1966, when free Botswana was born. He brought to the country—with Lady Ruth beside him—a stability and prosperity, grounded in firm democratic rule, such as has rarely been found on the African continent. His death, after fourteen years in office, was cause for great national mourning. Lady Ruth has continued to live in her adopted country, universally respected and loved. She still plays a role in Botswana's daily life, currently serving as president of the nation's Red Cross organization. In 1998, her son, Lieutenant General Seretse Khama Ian Khama, resigned his position as head of Botswana's armed forces to become vice-president. He is likely to follow his father into the president's office. Former Tanzanian president Julius Nyerere once said of the Khamas, "The romance of Seretse Khama and Ruth Williams was one of the great love stories of the world. It brought home to people the realities of colonial life and racial discrimination."

First appointed to cabinet

Gaositwe Keagakwa Tibe Chiepe, Minister of Commerce and Industry, 1974

Notable service in cabinet

Gaositwe Keagakwa Tibe Chiepe, Minister of Foreign Affairs; Minister of Natural Resources and Water Affairs; Minister of Education
Margaret Nasha, Minister of Local Government, Lands, and Housing

First appointed ambassador

Gaositwe Keagakwa Tibe Chiepe, High Commissioner (Ambassador) to the United Kingdom, also accredited to Belgium, Denmark, France, Nigeria, Norway, Sweden, and the European Economic Community, 1970

Legislative

First elected to national legislature (National Assembly)

Gaositwe Keagakwa Tibe Chiepe
Emelda Mathe

Both elected October 1979

Judicial

First appointed to high court

Unity Dow, 1998

Brazil

Women

Right to vote: July 16, 1934
To stand for election: July 16, 1934

Executive

Notable presidential candidate, 1998

Thereza Ruiz. Ruiz placed ninth, with less than 1 percent of the vote, in the election that saw President Fernando Henrique Cardoso returned for a second term.

First appointed to cabinet

Esther de Figueirado Ferraz, Minister of Culture and Education, 1982

Notable service in cabinet

Claudia Costin, Minister of Administration and Reform of the State
Zelia Cardoso de Mello, Minister of Economics
Iris Rezende Machado, Minister of Justice; Minister of Agriculture
Margarida Procopio, Minister of Social Welfare
Dorothea Woerneck, Minister of Trade and Tourism

First appointed ambassador

Ivete Vargas, Ambassador on a special mission to Lebanon, 1951
Dora Vasconcelos, Ambassador to Canada and Trinidad and Tobago, 1965

First elected governor

Iolanda Lima Fleming, Acre, 1983

Legislative

First elected to national legislature
(Cámara dos Deputados, Chamber of Deputies)

Carlota Pereira de Queiroz e Berta Lutz, May 3, 1933

Minority: African-Brazilian

Executive

First elected governor

Three men, 1992

Legislative

First woman elected to national legislature
(Cámara dos Deputados, Chamber of Deputies)

Benedita da Silva, Rio de Janeiro, Worker's Party, 1986

First woman elected to national legislature (Senado, Senate)

Benedita da Silva, Rio de Janeiro, Worker's Party, 1994

Minority: Japanese-Brazilian

Executive

First appointed to cabinet

Shigeaki Ueki, Minister of Mines and Energy, 1974

Notable service in cabinet

Seigo Tsuzuki, Minister of Health

First elected mayor of a state capital

Cassio Tanuiguchi, Curitiba, Parana, 1996

Legislative

First elected to national legislature
(Cámara dos Deputados, Chamber of Deputies)

Yukishige Tamura, 1958

Minority: Native Indian

Legislative

First elected to national legislature
(Cámara dos Deputados, Chamber of Deputies)

Mário Juruna, Democratic Labor Party, Xavante tribe, 1982

Religious Minority: Jewish

Executive

First appointed to cabinet

Horácio Lafer, Minister of Finance, circa 1940

Brunei

The right to vote does not exist in Brunei. There is no parliament, and political parties are forbidden. A twenty-member Legislative Council exists, but its tasks are purely consultative; no female has ever been appointed as a member. No woman has ever been appointed to the cabinet.

First appointed ambassador

Princess Hajah Masna Haji Ahmed, Ambassador-at-large, 1996 or 1997. In 1998, Pengiran Hajah Masrainah Haji Ahmed served as non-resident ambassador to four Nordic countries. She was appointed, in 1999, as Brunei's first female resident ambassador, accredited to France.

Bulgaria

Women

Right to vote: October 16, 1944
To stand for election: October 16, 1944

Executive

Power past

Reneta Indzhova, Prime Minister, October 17, 1994–January 24, 1995. Indzhova, a former cabinet minister, served as head of a caretaker cabinet, after new elections were scheduled when the previous government was defeated on a no-confidence motion.

Blaga Dimitrova, Vice-President, January 1992–July 6, 1993. A poet and dissident under the former communist regime, Dimitrova was elected vice-president in January 1992 to serve under president Zhelyu Zhelev after the communists were ousted from power. She resigned abruptly in 1993, explaining that she felt deliberately shut out of decision-making processes and that she believed preparations were under way for the imposition of a new dictatorship in Bulgaria.

Notable presidential candidate, 1996

Vera Ileva, candidate of the Bulgarian Communist Party (BCP). It was an indication of how badly the fortunes of the formerly all-powerful BCP had fallen when Ileva drew such a small percentage of the vote—less than 5 percent—that statistics lump her with "Others." Interestingly, Ileva's running mate, Iskra Janeva, was also a woman.

Ex–power behind the scenes

Ludmilla Zhivkova, 1971–1981. Daughter of longtime communist dictator Todor Zhivkov, Ludmilla studied at Oxford University after receiving her primary education in Bulgaria. In 1971, she was made deputy chair of the Committee for Art and Culture, with added responsibility for radio, television, and the press in 1976. She began to show an interest in religion and emphasized Bulgaria's historical heritage, particularly during the 1981 celebrations of the 1,300th anniversary of the nation's statehood. Rumors swirled that "Papa Todor" was grooming Ludmilla as his successor—especially after she was appointed to the politburo in 1979. That promotion, as well as her increasing emphasis on "Bulgarianness," made Bulgaria's Soviet overlords nervous. Whatever Zhivkov's plans, they were all for naught, as Ludmilla died in 1981 under mysterious circumstances. Rumors swirled that the Russians had somehow contributed to her death, viewing Ludmilla as a threat to their hegemony over Bulgaria.

First appointed to cabinet

Tzola Nincheva Dragoicheva, Minister of the Post, Telegraphs, and Telephones, 1948

Notable service in the cabinet

Irina Boskova, Minister of Foreign Affairs
Svetla Daskalova, Minister of Justice
Reneta Indzhova
Evdokia Maneva, Minister of the Environment and Water
Emiliya Maslarova, Minister of Social Welfare
Nadezhda Mihailova, Minister of Foreign Affairs
Ema Moskova, Minister of Culture
Mimi Vitkova, Minister of Health
Christina Vutcheva, First Deputy Prime Minister

First appointed ambassador

Stela Dimitrova Blagoeva, Ambassador to the Soviet Union, 1949

Legislative

First elected to national legislature (Narodno Sobranie, National Assembly)

Stoyanka Ivanova Ancheva
Ekaterina Stafanova Avramova
Tzola Nincheva Dragoicheva
Stanka Hrisova Ivanova
Tzvetana Prokopieva Keranova
Elena Vladimirova Ketzkarova
Mara Ivanova Kinkel
Venera Stoyanova Klincharova
Viara Kostova Makedonska
Stefana Vladimirova Markova
Ekaterina Hristova Nikolova
Rada Iordanova Noeva
Rada Ivanova Pophlebarova
Mata Nikolova Tjurkedlieva
Maria Naidenova Toteva

Viara Dimitrova Zlatareva

All elected November 16, 1945

Head of national legislature

Sneahana Botyshorova, 1992

Minority: Roma (Gypsy)

Legislative

First to serve in national legislature

Manush Romanov, Independent
And three other persons, 1990

First appointed to national legislature (Narodno Sobranie, National Assembly)

Assen Hristov, Union of Democratic Forces, 1998

Burkina Faso

Women

Right to vote: September 28, 1958
To stand for election: September 28, 1958

Executive

Notable presidential candidate, 1998

Deborah Nazi Boni

Ex–partner in power

Nathalie Felicite Monoco Adama Yaméogo, 1965–1966. Ex–beauty queen, second wife of president Maurice Yaméogo (1960–1966). When the twenty-two-year-old ex–Miss Ivory Coast married the president of Upper Volta (Burkina Faso's previous name) in October 1965, she probably didn't expect the reception she would receive: outraged reactions and rioting in her new country. The excessive cost of the couple's wedding and honeymoon provided a focus for President Yaméogo's enemies. They channeled their energy into organized protest and refused to participate in the country's November 1965 parliamentary elections, finally forcing the president to resign in January 1966. But the couple, having tasted power, refused to go quietly. After being implicated in a plot to overthrow the government of his successor, Lieutenant Colonel Sangoulé Lamizana, later in 1966, Yaméogo unsuccessfully attempted suicide. In 1969, he was tried and convicted for embezzlement, but was released in 1970 on the tenth anniversary of the country's independence. As for Mrs. Yaméogo, she was implicated in yet another plot to restore her husband to power in September 1967. That led to a trial in May 1968 and a conviction for treason, but her sentence was suspended. Both Yaméogos have since then dropped from sight.

First appointed to cabinet

Macoucou Célestine Ouëzzin Coulibaly, Minister of Social Welfare and Labor, September 1958. Célestine was the first woman in Africa to attain cabinet rank. Her appointment came while the country was still part of the French Community, two years before gaining independence. Her husband, Daniel, was the premier of the colonial entity when he died suddenly in October 1958. Due to Célestine's lifelong involvement in politics, many hoped that she would assume his office. Instead, Maurice Yaméogo did, becoming prime minister of what was then called the Voltaic Republic. Yaméogo promptly appointed Célestine to his cabinet. When the country gained independence in 1960, with Yaméogo as its first president, she continued to serve in the cabinet, but gradually passed into obscurity in the years following independence.

Notable service in cabinet

Juliette Bonkoungou, Minister of Civil Service and Institutional Development
Viviane Yolande Compaore, Minister of Regional Integration
Beatrice Damiba, Minister of the Environment and Tourism
Konaté Domba, Minister of National Education and Culture
Gisele Guigma, Minister of Women's Affairs
Neda Rose Marie, Minister of Action and the Family
Bana Ouandaogo, Minister of Social and Family Affairs
Josephine Ouedraogo, Minister of Family Welfare and National Solidarity
Adele Ouegraogo, Minister of Budget
Bernadette Sanou, Minister of Regional Integration
Rita Sawadogo, Minister of Sport and Leisure
Alice Tiendrebeogo, Minister for the Promotion of Women

First appointed ambassador

Maimouna Ouattara, Ambassador to Ghana, 1985

Legislative

First elected to national legislature (Assemblée de députés du peuple, Assembly of the Deputies of the People)

Nignan Lamoussa, National Union for the Defense of Democracy, April 1978

Burundi

Women

Right to vote: August 17, 1961
To stand for election: August 17, 1961

Executive

Power past

Sylvie Kinigi, Prime Minister, October 1, 1993–February 7, 1994. Kinigi served temporarily while a truce was being concluded between the various ethnic factions in Burundi over the composition of future governments. An ethnic Tutsi and member of the Unity for National Progress Party, she was appointed by President Melchior Ndadaye, Burundi's first popularly elected Hutu chief executive. Shortly after her appointment, Ndadaye was assassinated during an army coup and his government collapsed. Kinigi was replaced, early in 1994, by another Tutsi.

First appointed to cabinet

Euphrasie Kandecke, Minister of Women's Affairs, 1974

Notable service in cabinet

Claudine Matuturu, Minister of Reintegration and Resettlement of Displaced Persons
Marcienne Mujawaha, Minister of Human Rights and Women's Development
Monique Ndakoze, Minister of Civil Service
Romaine Ndorimana, Minister of Women, Welfare, and Social Affairs
Julie Ngiriye, Minister of Labor; Minister of Social Affairs
Christine Ruhaza, Minister of Social Action and Promotion of Women

First appointed ambassador

Julie Ngiriye, Ambassador to Denmark, Finland, Iceland, Norway, and Sweden, 1994

Legislative

First elected to national legislature (Assemblée nationale, National Assembly)

Six women, October 1982

Cambodia

Women

Right to vote: September 25, 1955
To stand for election: September 25, 1955

Royalty

Power past

Sisovath Kossamak Nearirat Serey Vathana, Queen, March 2, 1955–April 3, 1960. Joint ruler with her husband, King Norodom Suramarit, and mother of present ruler Norodom Sihanouk. Kossamak was the daughter of King Sisowath (1904–1927) and sister of King Monivong (1927–1941). When her brother died, the French, who controlled Cambodia as a protectorate at that time, placed her son Norodom Sihanouk on the throne. In 1955, when the king finally achieved total independence for Cambodia, he held a referendum on whether he should step down from the throne, to serve instead as prime minister, and elevate his parents as coregents. Once the accession was agreed to by Cambodia's people, Kossamak ruled quietly with her husband until his death in 1960.

Executive

First appointed to cabinet

Pung Peng Cheng, Minister of Labor and Social Action. In 1958, she had served as secretary of state (deputy minister) for the same portfolio.

Notable service in cabinet

Princess Bopa Devi, Minister of Culture
Ho Hon, Minister of Industry
Sochua Mu, Minister of Women's Affairs and War Veterans
Keat Sakun, Minister of Women's Affairs
Ieng Thirth, Minister of Education

First appointed ambassador

No woman yet appointed

Legislative

First elected to national legislature (National Assembly)

Pung Peng Cheng, March 1958

Cameroon

Women

Right to vote: October 1946
To stand for election: October 1946

Executive

First appointed to cabinet

Delphine Zanga Tsogo, Minister of Social Affairs, 1975. Beginning in 1970, she had served as deputy minister of health and public welfare.

Notable service in cabinet

Madaleine Fouda, Minister of Social Affairs
Lucy Gwanmesia, Minister of State Control
Elizabeth Tankeu, Minister of Planning and Regional Development
Aissatou Yaou, Minister of Social Affairs and Women's Affairs

First appointed ambassador

Simone Mairie, Ambassador to the United Nations, 1982

Legislative

First elected to national legislature (Assemblée nationale, National Assembly)

One woman, April 1960

Canada

Women

Right to vote: September 1917; May 1918[10]
To stand for election: July 1920

Executive

Adrienne Poy Clarkson, Governor-General, October 7, 1999–present. Clarkson, Canada's second female governor-general (see below), came to the country as a war refugee from her native Hong Kong in 1942. She has been a leading figure in Canada's cultural life during her entire career. Clarkson has authored three books; served abroad promoting the province of Ontario's business and cultural interests; produced, written, and hosted television programs; directed films; and served on the executive boards of international cultural organizations. In 1992, she was appointed an officer of the Order of Canada, one of the country's highest civilian awards. Significantly, Clarkson is of Chinese descent. Her appointment to the post by Prime Minister Jean Chrétien (which was approved by Queen Elizabeth II) is an obvious nod to the growing influence of Canadian Asians in all walks of life in the country.

Power past

Kim Campbell, Prime Minister, June 25–November 4, 1993. After the resignation of Prime Minister Brian Mulroney, Campbell, Canada's defense minister, was chosen by her Conservative Party to succeed him as both party leader and prime minister. A member of the House of Commons (1988–1993) and previous holder of two additional cabinet portfolios (Justice and Attorney General; and Indian Affairs and Northern Development), Campbell's political career did not come to full fruition. She served only four months, then called a new general election. The voting was a disastrous rout for her personally—she lost her own seat—and for the Conservative Party generally, which lost all but two of its parliamentary seats. In 1996, she was appointed consul-general in Los Angeles, far from the seat of her nation's political power.

Jeanne Benôit Sauvé, Governor-General, May 14, 1984–January 29, 1990. Sauvé was a journalist, legislator (House of Commons, 1972–1984), cabinet minister (Science and

[10]Women who had close male relatives serving in the military were granted the right to vote at the federal level in 1917. All women won the right to vote federally in 1918.

Technology; Environment; and Commerce), and longtime Liberal Party member; she served a stint (see below) as the first female speaker of the Canadian House of Commons. She was chosen in 1984 to represent the British monarch in Canada. Sauvé died in 1993, without holding any additional political offices after her tenure as Canada's de facto head of state.

First named deputy prime minister

Sheila Maureen Copps, November 1993

First appointed to cabinet

Ellen Louks Fairclough, Secretary of State, June 21, 1957; Minister of Citizenship and Immigration, 1958

Notable service in cabinet

Monique Begin, Minister of National Revenue; Minister of National Health and Welfare
Suzanne Blais-Grenier, Minister of the Environment
Iona Campagnolo, Minister of Fitness and Amateur Sports
Kim Campbell, Minister of Defense; Minister of Justice and Attorney General
Elinor Caplan, Minister of Citizenship and Immigration
Mary Collins, Minister of Health
Sheila Maureen Copps, Minister of Canadian Heritage
Julie LaMarsh, Minister of National Health and Welfare
Monique Landry, Minister of Indian Affairs and Northern Development
Flora MacDonald, Minister of External Affairs; Minister of Finance
Diane Marleau, Minister of International Cooperation and the Francophonie
Barbara McDougall, Minister of External Affairs; Minister of Employment and Immigration
Anne McLellan, Minister of Justice and Attorney General
Maria Minna, Minister of International Cooperation and the Francophonie
Lucienne Robillard, Minister of Citizenship and Immigration
Jeanne Benôit Sauvé, Minister of Science and Technology; Minister of the Environment; Minister of Commerce
Bobbie Sparrow, Minister of Natural Resources
Christine Stewart, Minister of the Environment
Jane Stewart, Minister of Indian Affairs and Northern Development
Monique Vézina, Minister of External Relations

First provincial head

Pauline McGibbon, appointed Lt.-Governor (head of a Canadian province representing the federal government), Ontario, 1974

First other provincial heads

Lise Thibault, Quebec, 1997
Margaret Norrie McCain, New Brunswick, 1994
Marion Reed, Prince Edward Island, 1990

First provincial premier

Rita Johnson, Social Credit Party, British Columbia, 1991. Johnson headed the government for only a short time during a transition period. In 1993, Liberal **Catherine Callbeck** was elected premier of the provincial government of Prince Edward Island, after leading her party to an election victory in which the Liberals swept all but one seat in the legislature.

First appointed to provincial cabinet

Mary Ellen Smith, Minister Without Portfolio, British Columbia, 1921. Smith was also the first woman in the British Empire to hold a ministerial-rank post.

First appointed ambassador

Margaret B. Meagher, Ambassador to Israel, 1958. In 1930, Prime Minister R. B. Bennett appointed **Irene Parlby,** minister without portfolio in the United Farmers of Alberta government of Alberta, as a delegate (ambassador) to the League of Nations.

First elected mayor of a major city

Charlotte Whitton, Ottawa, 1951

Legislative

First elected to national legislature (Chambres des communes, House of Commons)

Agnes Campbell McPhail, United Farmers of Ontario Party, December 6, 1921

First appointed to national legislature (Sénat, Senate)

Cairine Reay MacKay Wilson, February 15, 1930

Head of national legislature

Jeanne Benôit Sauvé, Liberal Party, House of Commons, 1980–1984
Renaude La Pointe, Senate, 1974–1979
Muriel Fergusson, Liberal Party, Senate, 1972–1974

First nun to serve in Parliament

Sister Mary Alice Butts, Senate, 1977

First elected to provincial legislature

Louise McKinney, Non-Partisan League, Alberta, 1917. McKinney was also the first woman in the British Empire to serve in a legislative body. **Roberta MacAdams** was elected the same day, but McKinney was sworn in first.

First elected to other provincial or territorial legislatures

British Columbia: **Mary Ellen Smith,** Independent Liberal, 1918
Manitoba: **Edith Rogers,** Liberal Party, 1920
New Brunswick: **Brenda May Robertson,** Progressive Conservative Party, 1967
Newfoundland: **Helena Strong Squires,** Liberal Party, 1930
Northwest Territories: **Lena Pedersen,** 1970
Nova Scotia: **Gladys M. Porter,** Progressive Conservative Party, 1960
Nunavut: **Manitok Thompson,** 1999
Ontario: **Agnes Campbell MacPhail,** Independent, and **Margarette Rae Morrison Luckock,** Cooperative Commonwealth Federation Party, 1943. MacPhail was sworn in first.
Prince Edward Island: **Ella Jean Canfield,** Liberal Party, 1970
Quebec: **Marie-Claire Kirkland-Casgrain,** Liberal Party, 1961
Saskatchewan: **Sarah K. Ramsland,** Liberal Party, 1919
Yukon Territory: **Jean Gordon,** 1967

First elected head of provincial legislature

Nancy Hodges, British Columbia, 1950

Judicial

First appointed chief justice of supreme court

Beverly McLachlin, 1999

First appointed to supreme court

Bertha Wilson, 1982

First appointed judge

Alice Jamieson, Calgary juvenile court, 1914. Jamieson was the first woman in the British Empire appointed to a court.

First female Asian judge

Maryka Omatsu, Ontario, 1992

First female Native Indian judge

Terry Vyse, 1991

Minority: African-Canadian

Executive

First appointed to cabinet

Lincoln MacCauley Alexander, Minister of Labor, 1979

First provincial head

Lincoln MacCauley Alexander, appointed Lt.-Governor (head of a Canadian province representing the federal government), Ontario, 1985

First elected mayor

Montesime St. Vincent, Mattawa, Ontario, 1974

First woman elected mayor

Daurene Lewis, Annapolis Royal, Nova Scotia, 1984

First elected to office

Abraham Shadd, town council, Raleigh, Ontario, 1853

Legislative

First elected to national legislature
(Chambres des communes, House of Commons)

Lincoln MacCauley Alexander, Progressive Conservative Party, Ontario, 1968. He had previously been a candidate for the same seat in the 1964 elections, which he lost by slightly more than 2,000 votes.

First woman elected to national legislature
(Chambres des communes, House of Commons)

Jean Augustine, Liberal Party, Ontario, 1993

First woman appointed to national legislature (Sénat, Senate)

Anne Clare Cools, Liberal Party, Ontario, 1984

First appointed to provincial legislature

Donald Fairfax, Nova Scotia, 1959

First elected to provincial legislature

Leonard A. Braithwaite, Liberal Party, Ontario, 1963

First woman elected to provincial legislature

Rosemary Brown, British Columbia, 1972

Judicial

First woman appointed judge

Corrine Sparks, Cherrybrook, Nova Scotia, 1987

First appointed to supreme court

Julius Alexander Isaac, Chief Justice, 1991

Minority: Chinese-Canadian

Executive

First governor-general

Adrienne Poy Clarkson, October 1999

First provincial head

David Lam See-chai, appointed Lt.-Governor (head of a Canadian province representing the federal government), British Columbia, 1987

Legislative

First elected to national legislature
(Chambres des communes, House of Commons)

Douglas Jung, British Columbia, 1957. The second was **Raymond Chan,** Liberal Party, British Columbia, 1993.

First woman appointed to national legislature (Sénat, Senate)

Vivienne Py, Liberal Party, 1998

First woman elected to national legislature (Chambres des communes, House of Commons)

M. Sophia Leung, Liberal Party, British Columbia, 1997

Minority: East Indian–Canadian

Executive

First appointed to provincial cabinet

Ujjal Dosanjh, Attorney General, British Columbia, 1995

First appointed to national cabinet

Herb Dhaliwal, Minister of National Revenue, 1997

Legislative

First elected to local office

Narjan Grewall, city council, Mission, British Columbia, 1950

First elected to provincial legislature

Manmohan (Moe) Sihota, New Democratic Party, British Columbia, 1986

First elected to national legislature (Chambres des communes, House of Commons)

Jag Bhaduria, Independent Liberal, Ontario, 1993
Herb Dhaliwal, Liberal Party, British Columbia, 1993
Gurbax Singh Malhi, Liberal Party, Ontario, 1993

Judicial

First appointed to provincial supreme court

Wally Oppal, British Columbia, 1982

Minority: Filipino-Canadian

Legislative

First elected to national legislature
(Chambres des communes, House of Commons)

Rey Pagtakhan, Liberal Party, Manitoba, 1988

First elected to provincial legislature

Conrad Santos, Liberal Party, Manitoba, 1980

Minority: Gay/Lesbian

Executive

First elected mayor of a major city

Glen Murray, Winnipeg, 1998

First lesbian (closeted) elected mayor of a major city

Charlotte Whitton, Ottawa, 1951

Legislative

First elected to national legislature
(Chambres des communes, House of Commons)

Sven Robinson, National Democratic Party, British Columbia, 1979. Although first elected in 1979, Robinson didn't wage an election campaign as an openly gay legislator until 1988.

Minority: Greek-Canadian

Legislative

First woman elected to national legislature
(Chambres des communes, House of Commons)

Eleni Bakopanas, Liberal Party, Quebec, 1993

Minority: Hispanic-Canadian

Legislative

First elected to national legislature
(Chambres des communes, House of Commons)

Ricardo Lopez, Conservative Party, Quebec, 1984

Minority: Inuit

Executive

First appointed ambassador

Mary May Simon, Ambassador for Circumpolar Affairs, 1994

Legislative

First elected to national legislature
(Chambres des communes, House of Commons)

Peter Ittinuar, Liberal Party, Northwest Territories, 1979

First appointed to national legislature (Sénat, Senate)

Willie Adams, Liberal Party, Northwest Territories, 1977

Minority: Métis

Legislative

First elected to national legislature
(Chambres des communes, House of Commons)

Louis Riel, Independent, 1873

First woman appointed to national legislature (Sénat, Senate)

Thelma J. Chalifoux, Liberal Party, Alberta, 1997

Minority: Native Indian

Right to vote: 1950
To stand for election: August 1960[11]

[11]In 1950, the federal franchise was extended to Native Indians (regardless of gender) only if they waived their tax exemption under the Indian Act. In August 1960, the unqualified extension of federal voting rights to all Native Indians was made under the Act to Amend the Canada Elections Act. Quebec, in 1969, became the last province to extend franchise rights to all Native Indians at the provincial level.

Executive

First provincial head

Ralph Steinhauer, Alberta, 1974. Steinhauer, of Ojibway-Cree descent, was appointed Lt.-Governor (head of a Canadian province representing the federal government).

First appointed to cabinet

Leonard Marchand, Minister of State for Small Business, 1976

Legislative

First elected to national legislature
(Chambres des communes, House of Commons)

Leonard Marchand, Liberal Party, British Columbia, Okanagan tribe (Interior Samish), 1968

First woman elected to national legislature
(Chambres des communes, House of Commons)

Ethel Blondin-Andrew, Liberal Party, Northwest Territories, Dene tribe, 1988

First appointed to national legislature (Sénat, Senate)

James Goldstone, Independent Conservative, 1958

Minority: Ukrainian-Canadian

Executive

First governor-general

Ray Hnatyshyn, 1990

First provincial head

Stephen Worobetz, Saskatchewan, appointed Lt.-Governor, 1969

First appointed to cabinet

Ray Hnatyshyn, 1979

Legislative

First appointed to legislature (Sénat, Senate)

Ray Hnatyshyn, Progressive Conservative Party, Saskatchewan, 1959

First woman elected to provincial legislature

Mary Fodchuk Batten, Saskatchewan, 1956

Minority: Vietnamese-Canadian

Legislative

First nominated for national legislature (Chambres des communes, House of Commons)

Quoi Nguyen, Liberal Party, Alberta, 1993

Religious Minority: Jewish

Executive

First to serve as premier of a province

David Barrett, Social Credit Party, British Columbia, 1972

First appointed to federal cabinet

Herb Gray, Liberal Party

First appointed to provincial cabinet

Allan Grossman

Legislative

First elected to legislature

Ezekial Hart, legislature of Lower Canada, 1808. Hart was not seated, however, because the law prohibited non-Christians from taking their oath of office on the Bible. He was the first person of the Jewish faith to be elected to any parliament in the British Empire.

First appointed to national legislature (Sénat, Senate)

David Croll

First elected to national legislature
(Chambres des communes, House of Commons)

George Benjamin, 1857

First woman elected to national legislature
(Chambres des communes, House of Commons)

Simma Holt, British Columbia, 1974

Religious Minority: Muslim

Legislative

First woman elected to legislature

Fatima Houda-Pepin, Liberal Party, National Assembly of Quebec, 1994

Religious Minority: Sikh

Legislative

First elected to national legislature
(Chambres des communes, House of Commons)

Herb Dhaliwal, Liberal Party, British Columbia, 1993
Gurbax Singh Malhi, Liberal Party, Ontario, 1993

Cape Verde

Women

Right to vote: July 5, 1975
To stand for election: July 5, 1975

Executive

First appointed to cabinet

Maria Helena Semedo, Minister of Fisheries, Agriculture, and Rural Development, 1993. She had been appointed secretary of state (deputy minister) for fisheries in 1992.

Notable service in cabinet

Anna Paula Almeida, Minister of Public Administration
Odina Maria Fonesca Rodrigues Ferreira, Minister of Education and Sports; Minister of Culture and Communication
Manuela Teresa Silva Gomes, Minister of the Fight Against Poverty
Orlanda Maria Duarte Santos, Minister of Employment, Training, and Social Integration
Maria Helena Semedo, Minister of Tourism and Transport

First appointed ambassador

Marly de Menezes Barbosa-Vincente, Ambassador to Denmark, Estonia, Finland, Iceland, the Netherlands, Norway, and Sweden, 1997

Legislative

First elected to national legislature (Assembleia Nacional, National Assembly)

Carmen Pereira, July 1975

Head of national legislature

Carmen Pereira, 1975–1980

CENTRAL AFRICAN REPUBLIC

Women

Right to vote: 1986
To stand for election: 1986

Executive

Power past

Elizabeth Domitien, Prime Minister, January 2, 1975–April 7, 1976. Domitien was appointed to her position by then-president Jean-Paul Bokassa and was rumored to have had a hand in raising Bokassa when he was a child. She had political credentials for the appointment, since she had previously served as vice-president of the political party Movement for the Social Evolution of Black Africa. After a despotic tenure as president, Bokassa declared himself emperor of the now renamed Central African Empire. Domitien opposed this move and spoke out against it, prompting Bokassa to dismiss her as prime minister. He went ahead with his plans, being crowned in a lavishly ridiculous coronation that mocked the country's impoverished condition; the ceremony was paid for mostly by France. When Bokassa was finally overthrown in 1979, Domitien was briefly imprisoned, then put on trial, but was acquitted. She was modern Africa's first female head of government.

First appointed to cabinet

Marie-Christine Mbokou, Minister of Finance, 1975

Notable service in cabinet

Genevieve Goyemido, Minister of Public Health and Social Affairs
Marie-Noelle Koyara, Minister for the Promotion of Women and National Solidarity
Betty Marasse, Minister of Justice and Law Reform and Keeper of the Seals
Albertine Mbissa, Minister of National Solidarity
Eliane Mokodopo, Minister of Family and Social Affairs
Anne-Marie Ngouyombo, Minister of Social Welfare for the Promotion of the Family and Handicapped
Juliette Nzekou, Minister of Parliamentary Affairs
Marie Joseph Songomali Toungovala, Minister of Culture

First appointed ambassador

Not yet identified

Legislative

First elected to national legislature (Assemblée nationale, National Assembly)

Two women, July 1987

Chad

Women

Right to vote: Unknown
To stand for election: Unknown

Executive

First appointed to cabinet

Fatimé Kimto, Minister of Social Affairs and Women, 1982

Notable service in cabinet

Selguet A. Aguidi, Minister of Social Affairs and Women
Agnes Allafi, Minister of Social Welfare and Family Support
Achta Tone Gossingar, Minister of Social Affairs and the Promotion of Women
Monique Ngarlbaye, Minister of Social Welfare and Family Support

First appointed ambassador

Martine Djoumbi, Ambassador to Zaire (Democratic Republic of Congo), 1989. The current government of Chad recognizes **Malloum Bintou,** Ambassador to Germany, 1995, as the first female ambassador.

Legislative

First elected to national legislature
(Assemblée nationale, National Assembly)

Louise Boukou
Oumar Hadje Halime
Brahim Haowei
Guembang Kaltouma

All elected 1962

Chile

Women

Right to vote: May 30, 1931; May 15, 1949
To stand for election: May 30, 1931; May 15, 1949[12]

Executive

Notable presidential candidate, 1999

Gladys Marin, candidate of the Chilean Communist Party. A longtime party worker and general secretary of the Communist Party, Marin narrowly escaped being caught up in the thousands of arrests following the 1973 army coup against President Salvador Allende. Her domestic partner, Jorge Muñoz, was not so lucky. He was arrested and became one of the "disappeared" people, never to be heard from again. Gladys sought refuge in the Dutch embassy, then left Chile altogether in 1974. After her return years later under the democratic regime that replaced the administration of right-wing dictator Augusto Pinochet, Marin resumed her work for the communist cause. Her presidential run was not very successful: She won third place with 3 percent of the vote.

First appointed to cabinet

Adriana Olguín de Baltra, Minister of Justice, 1952

Notable service in cabinet

Soledad Alvear, Minister of Justice
Josefina Bilbao, Minister of Women's Affairs
María Teresa del Canto Molina, Minister of Education
Haydée Castillo, Minister of Development
Carmen Grez, Minister of Family
Monica Madariaga Gutierrez, Minister of Justice; Minister of Education
Adriana Del Piano Puelma, Minister of National Resources
Marcia Scantlebury, Minister of Culture

---

[12]Women were granted the right to vote and stand in municipal elections in 1931, and in legislative and provincial elections in 1949.

First appointed ambassador

Ana Figuero, Special Ambassador to the United Nations, 1951. Mention should also be made of **Carmen Vidal de Sencret,** who was married to the Chilean ambassador to the United Kingdom. She was accredited in her own right as the envoy (with rank of minister) to the Netherlands in 1947. **Gabriela Mistral,** winner of the Nobel Prize for Literature in 1945, was appointed in 1933 as a kind of ambassador-at-large for Latin American culture by the government. During this time, she also served as a Chilean representative at the League of Nations in Switzerland, where her official title might have been ambassador.

First elected mayor

Graciela Contreras de Schnake, Socialist Party, Santiago, 1938

Legislative

First elected to national legislature
(Cámara de Diputados, Chamber of Deputies)

Inés Enriquez Frödden, April 24, 1951

Minority: Mapuche

Legislative

First elected to national legislature
(Cámara de Diputados, Chamber of Deputies)

Francisco Milivilu Herniquez, 1924

CHINA

Women

Right to vote: October 1, 1949
To stand for election: October 1, 1949

October 1, 1949, was the date of the proclamation of the People's Republic of China. Shortly after the 1911 revolution, led by Sun Yat-sen, many women began agitating for the right to vote. That same year the Kwangtung Provincial Assembly granted them that right. Ten women were elected to that body in 1912, the first women ever elected to public office anywhere in Asia.

Royalty

Power Past

Cixi (Tz'u-hsi), Empress Regent, August 22, 1861–November 14, 1908. Cixi was authoritarian, reactionary, cruel, temperamental, uncompromising, and quick tempered. In her defense, one might add that she was ruthless and power hungry. Born in 1835, she came to the imperial court as a minor concubine of Emperor Kian Feng and immediately distinguished herself by bearing his only son. The emperor died when Cixi was only sixteen, and she had herself named as coregent, along with a senior wife, for her infant son. Soon, absolute power was in her hands, where it remained until her death forty-seven years later. All obstacles—including her coregent and her son—were quickly eliminated. Needing a new emperor after disposing of her son when he proved troublesome, she adopted a four-year-old nephew and seated him on the throne.

Ruthless to an extreme, Cixi managed to sabotage every government reform that might have limited her hold on power. Her greed and wanton disregard for all but herself at the nation's expense is legendary. She once diverted funds that had been earmarked to modernize China's navy to build a marble boat in a palace lake. The 1900 Boxer Rebellion and its aftermath left the country prostrate before invading foreign armies, signaling that imperial China's end was drawing near. Cixi managed to cling to power for a few more years, after poisoning her nephew to ensure that she remained in control. Her final gesture of absurdity was played out in 1908, a few days before her death. She installed as emperor the three-year-old Pu Yi, China's last emperor. When he was deposed a few years later, Cixi's tomb was looted and her embalmed body abused by crowds celebrating their democratic freedom.

Executive

Honorary power past

Ching-ling Soong, President (Honorary), May 16–29, 1981. Ching-ling, the American-educated older sister of Mei-ling Soong (see below), married President Sun Yat-sen (1911–1925), China's first democratic leader, in October 1915. After Sun's death, she drifted away from her democratic affiliations and closer to the communists, although she never formally joined the party. When her sister (and brother-in-law, Nationalist president Chiang Kai-shek) fled to Taiwan in 1949 after the communist takeover of the mainland, Ching-ling stayed behind. In 1954, she was made a vice-chairman of the People's Republic, ranking behind only Chairman Mao Zedong. The position was mostly window dressing, an attempt to link the new communist regime to the memory of Sun's democratic aspirations for China. Other honors followed, but Ching-ling's career was relatively quiet, punctuated only by an occasional public appearance to add a "democratic" veneer to the communist administration. In May 1981, as Ching-ling drew close to death from leukemia, China named her its "honorary" president and granted her membership in the Communist Party. She died two weeks later while in a coma, unaware of the final honors bestowed upon her by her country.

Ex–Red Queen, partner in power

Jiang Qing, 1965–1976. The third wife of Chairman Mao Zedong was one of the most nefarious characters ever to blot the Chinese landscape. An actress with a questionable background, she met and married Mao shortly after his historic Long March. Scandalized by their relationship and by her past, Mao's communist cohorts demanded that Jiang Qing be kept thoroughly behind the scenes. She emerged with a fury in the mid-1960s, when Mao unleashed his Great Cultural Revolution. If Mao's words inspired the turmoil, then Jiang Qing was the sword that set it off, and she garnered formidable political power as a result. In April 1969, Jiang Qing was elevated to the politburo, becoming the first woman to sit on China's ruling panel. From there, she wielded considerable power, striking at enemies, real and perceived, at whim. For her, the Cultural Revolution became an opportunity to settle old scores with all who had ever opposed her. The death toll of the Cultural Revolution, including Jiang Qing's whimsical contributions to the slaughter, is estimated to be in the millions.

Mao died in 1976. Within a month, Jiang Qing was placed under house arrest. On trial in 1980 for her excesses, she dumped all the blame back on her husband: "I was Mao's dog; what he told me to bite, I bit." Her conviction bore a death sentence, soon commuted to life imprisonment. After almost a decade in prison, where she was forced to make handicrafts, Jiang Qing committed suicide in May 1991. One measure of when China truly becomes free will be when a made-in-China film honestly depicts the life of Jiang Qing and the terror she wrought on the country.

First appointed to cabinet

Shi Liang, Minister of Justice, 1949

Notable service in cabinet

Chen Muhua, Vice–Prime Minister; Minister of Economic Relations with Foreign Countries
Chen Zhili, Minister of Education
Gu Xiulian, Minister for the Chemical Industry
He Xiangnin, Minister for Overseas Chinese
Lie Te'Chu'an, Minister of Health
Peng Peiyun, Minister of Family Planning
Wu Wenying, Minister for the Textile Industry
Yi Wu, Vice-Premier; Minister of Foreign Trade
Zhu Lilan, Minister of Science and Technology

First appointed ambassador

Deng Xuesong, Ambassador to the Netherlands, 1979

Legislative

First elected to national legislature
(Quanguo Renmin Daibao Dahui, National People's Congress)

One hundred forty-seven women, April 1954

Head of national legislature

Chen Muhua, 1988
Shi Liang, 1985
Deng Yingchao, 1980
Ching-ling Soong, 1976–1978

Minority: Tibetan

Executive

Notable service in cabinet

Doje Cering, Minister of Civil Affairs

Hong Kong

Executive

First woman appointed to executive body (Executive Council)

Joyce Symmons, 1976

First Chinese woman appointed to executive body (Executive Council)

Lydia Dunn, 1982

Legislative

First woman appointed to legislature (Legislative Council)

One woman, 1966

First woman popularly elected to legislature (Legislative Council)

Emily Lau, 1991

Tibet

Executive

First woman appointed to cabinet

Jetsun Pema, Minister of Education and Health, 1990[13]

Notable service in cabinet

Rinchen Khando Choegyal, Minister of Education[14]
Yangkyi Samkhar Dashee, Minister of Health and Home Affairs

First woman appointed diplomatic representative overseas

Mrs. Kesang Y. Takla, Head, Dalai Lama's office in London, 1987

---

[13]Pema is the younger sister of the Dalai Lama.

[14]Choegyal is the wife of the youngest brother of the Dalai Lama.

Republic of China: Taiwan

Executive

Ex–partner in power

Mei-ling Soong (Madame Chiang Kai-shek), 1927–1975. The American-educated younger sister of Ching-ling Soong (see above), Mei-ling married Generalissimo Chiang Kai-shek in 1927. She and her family exerted enormous influence on Chiang throughout his life, first as a warlord, then as China's dictator, and finally as the country's president. In 1937, the powerful couple shared the cover of *Time* magazine as "Man of the Year and Wife." Madame Chiang was the official head of the Chinese air force when the Japanese invaded in the 1930s. During World War II, she traveled widely, drumming up support for the Chinese people—and for her husband. She fled to Taiwan with him after the communist victory on the mainland in 1949. From that perch, the Chiangs maintained power until 1975, when the generalissimo died. After her stepson, Chiang Ching-kuo, with whom she was reputed to have less than cordial relations, succeeded her husband, Madame Chiang moved to the United States.

First appointed to cabinet

Kuo Wan-jung (Shirley), Minister of Finance, 1988

Notable service in cabinet

Huang Chu-wen, Minister of the Interior
Yeh Chin-fong, Minister of the Interior
Yeh Ching-seng, Minister of the Interior; Minister of Justice

First appointed ambassador

Katharine S. Y. Chang, Ambassador to St. Kitts and Nevis and Dominica, 1997

Legislative

Head of national legislature (Kuo-Min Ta-Hui, National Assembly)

Yeh Ching-seng, 1980–1992

Colombia

Women

Right to vote: August 25, 1954
To stand for election: August 25, 1954

Executive

Notable presidential candidates, 1998

Beatriz Cuéllar de Rios, candidate of the Christian Union Movement. Cuéllar drew less than 1 percent of the vote but led the pack of all the minor-party candidates in the race.

Noemi Sanin de Rubio, Independent (running under the party label of Life Choice). Former ambassador to Venezuela and then minister of foreign affairs under Conservative president Cesar Gaviria, Sanin ran a strong race, carrying the capital, Bogotá, and the cities of Cali and Medellín. Sanin hoped to break the longtime domination of the Liberal and Conservative Parties over the presidency, and she came dazzlingly close to making it into the runoff. She placed third with 27 percent of the vote, behind front-runners Liberal Horacio Serpa and Conservative Andres Pastrana, both of whom had 35 percent. She seems unlikely to fade away and will probably be a contender in a future presidential race.

Notable presidential candidate, 1994

Regina Betancur de Liska, leader and candidate of the United Metropolitical Movement. Betancur placed fourth with slightly more than 1 percent of the vote; she had also been a candidate in 1986 and 1990.

Notable presidential candidates, 1974

María Eugenia Rojas de Moreno Diaz. Daughter of ex-dictator Gustavo Rojas Pinilla (1953–1957) and a federal senator, María Eugenia sought to remove some of the tarnish from her father's name by running for president herself. As the candidate of the National Popular Alliance, the party founded by her father in 1966, she placed third in the balloting. After Gustavo's death in 1975, María Eugenia and her party vanished as an electoral force in Colombian politics.

Maria Socorro Ramirez. Candidate of the Socialist Workers Party, Ramirez attracted only a very small number of votes.

First appointed to cabinet

Josephine Valencia de Hubach, Minister of Education, 1956

Notable service in cabinet

Elena Bravo, Minister of Culture
María Sol Calderón, Minister of Labor and Social Security
Priscila Ceballos, Minister of Public Works and Transport
Maria Cuéllar de Martinez, Minister of Finance and Credit
Olga Duque de Ospina, Minister of Education
Doris Eder de Zambranco, Minister of Education
María Farero de Saade, Minister of Public Health; Minister of Labor and Social Security
Claudia de Francisco, Minister of Communication
Monica de Graff, Minister of Justice
María Elena Jiménez de Crovo, Minister of Labor
Cecilia López Montaño, Minister of the Environment
María Emma Mejia, Minister of Foreign Affairs
Lillian Suarez Mello, Minister of Education
Margarita Mena de Quevado, Minister of Mines and Energy
Esmeralda Arboleda Morales de Cuevas Cancino de Urribe, Minister of Transport
Marta Lucia Ramirez, Minister of Foreign Trade
Almabeatriz Rengifo Lopez, Minister of Justice
María del Rosario Sintes Ulloa, Minister of Agriculture
Gina Magnolia Riano, Minister of Labor
Noemi Sanin de Rubio, Minister of Foreign Affairs

First appointed ambassador

Esmeralda Arboleda Morales de Cuevas Cancino de Urribe, Ambassador to Austria and Yugoslavia, 1966

Legislative

First appointed to national legislature
(Cámara de Representantes, House of Representatives)

Two women, August 25, 1954

First elected to national legislature
(Cámara de Representantes, House of Representatives)

Eight women, March 16, 1958

First elected to national legislature (Senado de la República, Senate)

Esmeralda Arboleda Morales de Cuevas Cancino de Urribe, March 16, 1958

Minority: Gay

Executive

First elected governor of a department

Gustavo Alvarez Gardeazabal, Coalition Group, Valle del Cauca Department, 1997

Minority: Native Indian

Legislative

First elected to national legislature (Senado de la República, Senate)

Gabriel Muyuy Jacanamejoy, National Organization of Indians of Colombia, Putumayo Department

Two other persons, one each from the Indigenous Social Alliance and the Indigenous Authorities of Colombia

All elected 1992

First elected to national legislature (Cámara de Representantes, House of Representatives)

Five representatives, 1992

Comoros

Women

Right to vote: 1956
To stand for election: 1956

Executive

First appointed to cabinet

Mahamed Sittou Radhadat, Minister of Social Affairs, Labor, and Employment, 1993. In 1991, she had been appointed secretary of state (deputy minister) for population and women's affairs.

First appointed ambassador

No woman yet appointed

Legislative

First elected to national legislature (Assemblée fedérale, Federal Assembly)

One woman, December 1993

Democratic Republic of the Congo (Kinshasa)

Women

Right to vote: May 3, 1967
To stand for election: April 17, 1970

Executive

Ex–power behind the scenes

Marie-Madeline Yemo Mobutu, 1963–1971. Mother of dictator Mobutu Sese Seko, and the most powerful female influence on him. Mama Yemo—as she was known in the country—was widowed in 1940, with several children to raise. Extremely poor, she always emphasized education and made certain that her favorite son obtained the best she could secure for him. Mobutu rarely referred to his father during his rule but lavished attention on his mother: The country's foremost medical center, in the capital, Kinshasa, was named the Mama Yemo Hospital. Although Mama Yemo stayed in the background during his rule, Mobutu always paid close attention to her, apparently still trying to be the "good" son she had tried to raise. His more extravagant and avaricious tendencies—his home village had an airport capable of landing the Concorde—didn't fully emerge until after her death in 1971. One thing is certain: Mobutu treated his mother better than he did his wives, one of whom he reportedly beat to death. Ordinary citizens risked the terrible wrath of Mobutu when he felt that they had not paid Mama Yemo proper respect. In a notable example, Mobutu's troops shot student demonstrators protesting his rule in 1971, mainly because they had passed out leaflets implying that Mama Yemo had once been a prostitute.

First appointed to cabinet

Lusibu Zala (Sophie) N'kanza, Minister of State for Social Affairs, 1966

Notable service in cabinet

Odette Babandoa Etoa, Minister of Transport and Communications
Florentine S. F. Eyenga, Minister of Health and the Family
Justine Mpoyo Kasavubu, Minister of Civil Service

Sophie Lihau-Kaza, Minister of Social Affairs
Ekila Liyona, Minister of Foreign Affairs; Minister of Women and Social Affairs
Juliana Lumumba, Minister of Culture and Arts
Kinkela Vikansi, Minister of Post and Telecommunications

First appointed ambassador

Bintou A-Tshabola, Ambassador to Austria, 1983

Legislative

First elected to national legislature (National Assembly)

Twelve women, November 1970

Congo Republic (Brazzaville)

Women

Right to vote: December 8, 1963
To stand for election: December 8, 1963

Executive

First appointed to cabinet

Emilie Manima, Minister of Social Affairs, 1975

Notable service in cabinet

Marie Therese Avemeka, Minister for the Development of Women
Jeanne Dambenzet, Minister of Labor and Social Security
Charlotte Kisimba, Minister of Public Service
Cecile Matingou, Minister of Family Affairs
Maréme Ndebeki, Minister of Culture and the Arts

First appointed ambassador

C. Eckomband, Ambassador to Guinea, 1985

Legislative

First elected to national legislature
(Assemblée nationale, National Assembly)

Three women, December 1963

Minority: European

Executive

Notable service in cabinet

André Kerherve, Minister of Industry and Mines
René Mahe, Minister of Economic Affairs

Costa Rica

Women

Right to vote: November 17, 1949
To stand for election: November 17, 1949

Executive

Astrid Fischel Volio, First Vice-President, May 8, 1998–present. President of a pharmaceutical firm and a historian, as well as secretary of planning and programs for the United Social Christian Party, Volio was elected on that party's ticket along with Miguel Angel Rodriguez as president. When he assumed office, Rodriguez gave his vice-president an additional appointment as Minister of Culture.

Elizabeth Odio Benito, Second Vice-President, May 8, 1998–present. A two-time former minister of justice (1978–1982, 1990–1994), Benito was serving as a justice on the International Court of Justice in the Hague when selected as a vice-presidential candidate. She was also elected on the United Social Christian Party ticket of Miguel Angel Rodriguez. When he assumed office, Rodriguez gave Benito an additional appointment as Minister of the Environment and Energy.

Power past

Victoria Garrón de Doryan, Second Vice-President, May 8, 1986–May 7, 1990. A former educator, Doryan was elected on the ticket with Nobel Prize–winning President Oscar Arias.

Rebeca Gryspan Mayufis, Second Vice-President, May 8, 1994–May 7, 1998. Mayufis was elected on the National Liberation Party ticket of President José Maria Figueres.

First appointed to cabinet

Estela Hernández Quesada Niño, Minister of Education, 1958

Notable service in cabinet

Mónica Blanco, Minister of Justice
Laura Chinchilla Miranda, Minister of Security, Government, and Police
Maureen Clarke, Minister of the Interior

Maria Eugenia Dengo Obregon de Vargas, Minister of Public Education
Muni Figueres, Minister of Foreign Commercial Programs
Astrid Fischel Volio, Minister of Culture
Aida de Fishman, Minister of Culture and Youth
Hilda Gomez Ramirez, Minister of Culture, Youth, and Sports
Rebeca Gryspan Mayufis, Minister of Housing
Estela Hernández Quesada Niño, Minister of Labor
Yolanda Ingianna, Minister of Women's Situation
Mercedes Lopez-Gordienko, Minister of Culture
Monica Nagel Berger, Minister of Justice
Carmen Naranjo, Minister of Culture
Elizabeth Odio Benito, Minister of Justice; Minister of the Environment and Energy
Florisabel Rodriguez, Minister of Information
Marina Volio, Minister of Culture

First appointed ambassador

Angela Acuña Braun, Ambassador to the Organization of American States, 1958

First provincial governor

In San Jose province, 1970. During the period 1990–1994, five of the seven Costa Rican provinces had female governors.

Legislative

First appointed to national legislature (Asamblea Legislativa, Legislative Assembly)

Ana Rosa Chacòn Gonànlez, National Liberation Party
Estela Hernández Quesada Niño, National Liberation Party
Maria Teres Obregòn Zamora, National Liberation Party

All appointed November 1953

Head of national legislature

R. M. Karpinsky Dodero, Legislative Assembly, 1986–1987

Judicial

First appointed to supreme court

Ana Maria Breedy, 1975

Minority: Afro-Latinamerican

Executive

First woman appointed to cabinet

Maureen Clarke, Minister of Justice, 1994

First woman elected governor

Marta Johnson, Port Limón province, 1994

Religious Minority: Jewish

Executive

First appointed to cabinet

German Weinstok, Minister of Health, 1994

Legislative

First elected to national legislature (Asamblea Legislativa, Legislative Assembly)

Sandra Piszk
Saul Weisleder

Both elected 1994

Côte d'Ivoire

Women

Right to vote: 1952
To stand for election: 1952

Executive

First appointed to cabinet

Jeanne Gervais, Minister of Women's Affairs, 1976

Notable service in cabinet

Danielle Bon-Claverie, Minister of Communications
Leopoldine Coffie, Minister for the Family and the Promotion of Women
Henriette Dangri Diabate, Minister of Culture
Albertine Ghanazan-Hepie, Minister for the Family and the Promotion of Women
Claire Therese Elisabeth Grah, Minister for the Promotion of Women
Jacqueline Lohoues-Oble, Minister of Justice
Safiatou Françoise Ba N'daw, Minister of Electric Power and Transport
Yaya Ouattara, Minister of Social Affairs

First appointed ambassador

Liliana Marie-Laure Ba, Ambassador to Denmark, Finland, and Norway, 1996

Legislative

First elected to national legislature (Assemblée nationale, National Assembly)

Three women, November 7, 1965

Croatia

Women

Right to vote: August 11, 1945
To stand for election: August 11, 1945

Executive

Notable presidential candidate, 1992

Savka Dabčevic-Kučar, founder and candidate of the Croatian People's Party; placed third with 6 percent of the vote. A former head of the regional Communist Party, she was removed in 1971 from her post in the League of Croatian Communists by president Tito due to her liberal views. She accepted the removal rather quietly, even issuing a resignation statement worded in groveling terms. When Croatia became independent in the early 1990s, she hoped for a comeback in the political arena. Dabčevic-Kučar formed a political party to contest the first free legislative elections, but she didn't fare well; her party placed third. The reason was her seventeen years of silence, in addition to the fact that she hadn't been jailed, as were many other Croatian nationalists in the 1980s. That meant that the general public either had forgotten Dabčevic-Kučar or didn't think that she had suffered as much as many of the others then on the forefront of the political scene.

Ex–power behind the scene

Ankica Tudjman, 1990–2000. Wife of president Franjo Tudjman. Ankica made news in 1998 when it was revealed that she possessed bank accounts containing close to half a million dollars. This was doubly surprising since her husband had declared his family's assets only a month earlier, claiming that his wife's only possession was a car. His political advisers attempted to brush off the revelation with the explanation that cash did not have to be stated as "personal assets." Croatians were surprised by the revelation of the first lady's wealth. Ankica had always been presented as a pensioner, one who headed children's charities and kept a relatively low profile. A far different view suddenly emerged of a woman with eleven bank accounts just in Zagreb, Croatia's capital. Naturally, speculation immediately mounted that Ankica was the money broker for the presidential family. The ensuing furor over the disclosure of her sudden wealth is expected to have an impact on the next parliamentary elections, scheduled for 2000. The scandal may well cost Tudjman's Croatian

Democratic Union control of Parliament. The president has been ailing for several years, and political analysts consider the scandal to be only the latest example of a man who is losing control of his political lieutenants and a political party that is losing its direction. The largest women's magazine in Croatia, in a readers' poll, voted the female bank clerk who revealed Ankica's accounts as its "Woman of 1998." Ankica herself received only 246 votes for the distinction, compared to the bank clerk's more than 22,000 votes.

First appointed to cabinet

Vesna Girardi Jurkic, Minister of Education, 1992

Notable service in cabinet

Marina Dropulic, Minister of Construction, Town Planning, and Housing
Ljerka Mintas-Hodak, Deputy Prime Minister; Minister of Domestic Policy and European Integration
Ljilja Vokic, Minister of Education and Sport
Milena Zic-Fuchs, Minister of Science and Technology

First appointed ambassador

Vesna Girardi Jurkic, Ambassador to France, 1995. In 1992, **Anamarija Besker** was appointed as ambassador to the UN office in Vienna.

Legislative

First elected to national legislature (Zastupnicki Dom, House of Representatives)[15]

Snjezana Biga-Friganovic, Social Democratic Party
Katarina Fucek, Croatian Democratic Union
Vesna Girardi Jurkic, Croatian Democratic Union
Savka Dabčevic-Kučar, Croatian People's Party
Mira Ljubic Lorger, Dalmatian Action Party
Milanka Opacic, Social Democratic Party
Vera Pivcevic Stanic, Croatian Democratic Union
Gordana Turic, Croatian Democratic Union

All elected August 2, 1992

[15]Women from Croatia were previously elected to the Parliament of Yugoslavia.

Head of national legislature

Katica Ivanisevic, House of Representatives, 1993–1997

Historical Note

While Croatia was still part of Yugoslavia, **Ema Derossi-Bjelajac** served as president of the presidency of the Socialist Republic of Croatia, 1985–1986.

Cuba

Women

Right to vote: January 2, 1934
To stand for election: January 2, 1934

Executive

Power behind the scene

Vilma Espin Guillois Castro, 1958–present. Engineering graduate from MIT, wife of General Raul Castro, fervent revolutionary, and third family member of the ruling Castro communist troika. Vilma joined the Cuban revolution when it was still fighting in the Sierra Maestra mountains, helping to organize underground activities. After Fidel Castro's rebels assumed power in 1959, his brother Raul, who had grown quite fond of Vilma, asked her to stay with them and play a larger role in governing the country. Raul and Vilma were married shortly thereafter, and since brother-in-law Fidel's marriage had ended in divorce (and since Fidel's other female relationships were of an ambiguous nature), Vilma became the de facto first lady of Cuba. When Fidel established the Federation of Cuban Women, Vilma was appointed to head it. She was also added shortly thereafter to the Central Committee of the Cuban Communist Party. Now, forty years later, she still serves in both positions. Vilma is a well-known figure on the communist circuit, due to her frequent attendance at international gatherings, where she continues to spout the now-stale slogans of Fidel's revolution. Husband Raul is first vice-president of the Council of State and has been designated as Fidel's heir.

Power past

Celia Sanchez, 1958–1980. Secretary, and probable mistress, to Fidel Castro. Serving with Fidel since the Sierra Maestra days, Celia's official title was "Secretary to the Presidency." Her actual role was to be his closest female companion, and, as a result, she became one of the most powerful women in Cuba. Celia's influence on Fidel—with respect to policy, politics, and family—was notable, yet conducted largely out of the limelight. Following her death from cancer in 1980, she was honored by having a revolutionary brigade named after her.

First appointed to cabinet

María Gómez Carbonell, Minister Without Portfolio
Julia Eugenia Consuegra Rudriguez, Minister Without Portfolio

Both appointed 1952

Notable service in cabinet

Barbara Castillo Cuesta, Minister of Domestic Trade
Elena Mederos de Gonzalez, Minister of Social Welfare
Rosa Elena Simeon Negrin, Minister of Science, Technology, and the Environment

First appointed ambassador

Blanca Díaz Collazo, Ambassador to Colombia, 1962

Legislative

First elected to national legislature (Senate and National Assembly)

María Gómez Carbonell
Alicia Hernández de la Barca

And four other women, all 1936

Religious Minority: Jewish

Executive

First appointed to cabinet

Oscar Ganz, Prime Minister, 1948

Cyprus

Women

Right to vote: August 16, 1960
To stand for election: August 16, 1960

Executive

First appointed to cabinet

Stella Souliotou, Minister of Justice, 1960

Notable service in cabinet

Claire Angelidou, Minister of Education and Culture
Stella Souliotou, Attorney General

First appointed ambassador

Myrna Cleopas, Ambassador to the People's Republic of China, 1993

Legislative

First elected to national legislature
(Vouli Antiprosopon, House of Representatives)

Rena Katselli, Democratic Party, May 1981

First elected to communal chamber (Turkish)

Kadriye Ahmet Houlousi, National Front, 1960

Political Entity: Turkish Republic of Northern Cyprus

Executive

First appointed to cabinet

Onur Bomar, Minister of Economy and Finance, 1994

Judicial

First appointed to supreme court

Gönul Eroren, 1994

CZECH REPUBLIC[16]

Women

Right to vote: 1920
To stand for election: 1920

Executive

Notable presidential candidate, 1993

Marie Stiborva. Candidate of the Communist Party of Bohemia and Moravia. Stiborva contested popular Czechoslovakian president Vaclav Havel's bid to become head of the new Czech Republic (after Slovakia decided to split off on its own). The Czech president is elected by Parliament, and Stiborva placed second in the balloting, with 49 out of 200 votes.

First appointed to cabinet (of Czechoslovakia)

Ludmila Jankovcová, Minister of Industry, 1947

Notable service in cabinet

Nasta Baumrukova, Minister of Labor and Social Affairs
Olga Keltosova, Minister of Labor, Social Affairs, and the Family
Vlasta Parkanova, Deputy Prime Minister; Minister of Justice
Zusana Roithova, Minister of Health
Eva Slavkovska, Minister of Education and Justice
Vlasta Stepova, Minister of Trade and Tourism

First appointed ambassador

Rita Klimova, Ambassador to the United States, 1990
Pailine Rznickova, Ambassador to Spain, 1990
Hanna Seveikova, Ambassador to Denmark, 1990
Magda Vasaryova, Ambassador to Austria, 1990

---

[16]Czechoslovakia, independent since 1918, split into the Czech Republic and Slovakia on January 1, 1993.

Legislative

First elected to regional legislature (Bohemian Diet)

Bozena Kunětická-Viková, National Liberal Party, June 13, 1912. Kunětická-Viková was elected but never seated. Prince Frantisek Thun, the governor of Bohemia, a region of the Austro-Hungarian Empire, refused to accept her election because she was a woman. She appealed to the interior minister in Vienna, the empire's seat, but he refused to override the governor. Thus, she was denied a certificate of election, and with it her seat.

First members of national assembly (National Czechoslovak Committee)

Bozena Ecksteinova, Social Democrat Party
Luisa Landova-Stychova, Czechoslovak Socialist Party

Both seated July 1918

First delegated (by indirect election) to national legislature of Czechoslovakia (Czechoslovak Revolutionary National Assembly)

Anna Chlebounova, Republican Rural Party
Bozena Ecksteinova, Social Democrat Party
Frantiska Kolarikova, Social Democrat Party
Bozena Kunětická-Viková, Czechoslovak National-Democratic Party
Luisa Landova-Stychova, Czechoslovak Socialist Party
Alice Masarykova, Slovak Club
Ludmila Zatloukalova, Republican Rural Party
Frantiska Zeminova, Czechoslovak Socialist Party

All delegated November 1918

First elected to national legislature of Czechoslovakia

Franziska Blatny, German Election Union
Anna Chlebounova, Agrarian Party
Marie Deutch, German Election Union
Betty Karpiskova, Social Democrat Party
Irene Kirpal, German Election Union
Luisa Landova-Stychova, Czechoslovak Socialist Party
Anna Mala, Social Democrat Party
Ludmila Pechmanova, Czechoslovak Socialist Party
Otilie Podzimkova, Czechoslovak Socialist Party
Eliska Purkynova, National Democratic Party
Josefa Rosolova, National Democratic Party
Augusta Rozypalova, People's Party
Frantiseka Skaunicova, Social Democrat Party

Anna Sychravova, Social Democrat Party
Frantiska Zeminova, Czechoslovak Socialist Party

All elected April 1920 to Chamber of Deputies

Bozena Ecksteinova, Czechoslovak Social-Democratic Labor Party
Emma Herzig, German Election Union
Anna Perthen, German Social Democratic Party

All elected March 1920 to Senate

First elected to national legislature of the Czech Republic (Poslanecka Snemovna, Chamber of Deputies)

Drahoslava Bartoskova, Civic Democratic Party
Petra Buzkova, Czech Social Democratic Party
Kvetsolava Celisova, Communist Party of Bohemia and Moravia
Milada Emmerova, Czech Social Democratic Party
Eva Fischerova, Czech Democratic Party
Jana Gavlasova, Czech Democratic Party
Zdenka Hornikova, Civic Democratic Party
Vlasta Hruzova, Republican Party
Tatiana Jirousova, Communist Party of Bohemia and Moravia
Pavla Jurkova, Christian Democratic Union–Czechoslovak People's Party
Milena Kolarova, Civic Democratic Party
Kvetoslava Korinkova, Czech Social Democratic Party
Jitka Kupcova, Czech Social Democratic Party
Hana Marvanova, Civic Democratic Party
Marie Noveska, Czech Social Democratic Party
Radomira Nyvltova, Republican Party
Hana Orgonikova, Czech Social Democratic Party
Jana Peskova, Republican Party
Jana Petrova, Civic Democratic Party
Ivana Plechata, Civic Democratic Party
Laura Rajsiglova, Republican Party
Anna Röschova, Civic Democratic Party
Zuzka Rujbrova, Communist Party of Bohemia and Moravia
Olga Sehnalova, Czech Social Democratic Party
Hana Skorpilova, Communist Party of Bohemia and Moravia
Michaela Sojdrova, Christian Democratic Union–Czechoslovak People's Party
Vlasta Stepova, Czech Social Democratic Party
Alena Svobodova, Communist Party of Bohemia and Moravia
Jindriska Zachardova, Czech Social Democratic Party
Blanka Zajlicova, Republican Party

All elected 1996

Head of national legislature (Czech Republic)

Libuse Benesova, Senate, 1998–present

Head of national legislature (Czechoslovakia, Chamber of Nations)

Sona Pennigrová, 1969–1984

Minority: Roma (Gypsy)

Legislative

First elected to national legislature (of Czechoslovakia)

Tomás Holmek, Communist Party. Records seem to indicate that Holmek was elected to the federal chamber rather than a regional chamber. Two members of the Roman Civic Initiative Party were also elected in 1990. Attempts to determine if their seats were in the federal or regional legislatures have thus far been unsuccessful.

First woman elected to national legislature (Poslanecka Snemovna, Chamber of Deputies)

Monika Horáková, Freedom Union, 1998

Religious Minority: Jewish

Legislative

First elected to national legislature (of Czechoslovakia)

Two persons, 1929

Denmark

Women

Right to vote: 1908; June 5, 1915
To stand for election: 1908; June 5, 1915[17]

Royalty

Margrethe II Alexandrine Thorhildur Ingrid Slesvig-Holsten-Sonderburg-Glücksburg and Bernadotte, Queen, January 15, 1972–present. The first queen regnant in Denmark's thousand-year-old monarchy, Margrethe succeeded her father, Frederik IX, on his death. Aside from her royal duties, she is also well known as a painter, illustrator, scenic designer, translator, and amateur archaeologist. As head of state, Margrethe is expected to remain above everyday politics. This has not prevented her from expressing her views to the Danes on ethical and moral questions of the day when she so chooses. Margrethe mixes quite freely among the citizens of Denmark, which has caused some of the more regal European royal houses to sneer at her as being one of the "bicycling" Scandinavian monarchs.

Executive

First appointed to cabinet

Nina Bang, Minister for Education, 1924

Notable service in cabinet

Else Winther Andersen, Minister of Social Affairs
Jytte Andersen, Minister of Labor
Yvonne Herløv Andersen, Minister of Health
Dorte Koch Bennedsen, Minister of Ecclesiastical Affairs; Minister of Education
Riit Bjerregaard, Minister of Education
Helle Degn, Minister of Development
Lone Dybkjær, Minister of the Environment
Pia Gjellerup, Minister of Trade and Industry

---

[17]The right to vote in and stand for election to local authorities was granted to women in 1908.

Eva Gredal, Minister of Social Affairs
Anne Lisbeth Groes, Minister of Trade, Industry, and Shipping
Jytte Hilden, Minister of Research; Minister of Cultural Affairs
Britta C. S. Holberg, Minister of the Interior
Mimi Jakobsen, Deputy Prime Minister; Minister of Industry and Trade; Minister of Culture
Marianne Jelved, Deputy Prime Minister; Minister of Economic Affairs and Nordic Cooperation
Fanny Jensen, Minister Without Portfolio
Karin Jespersen, Minister of Social Affairs
Bente Juncker, Minister of Social Affairs
Bodil Koch, Minister of Ecclesiastical Affairs[18]
Ingerlise Koefoed, Minister of Health
Elsebeth Kock-Petersen Larsen, Minister of Social Affairs
Ester Larsen, Minister of Health
Camma Larsen-Ledet, Minister of the Family
Naama Latasi, Minister of Health, Education, and Community Service
Agnethe Lausten, Minister of Housing
Nathalie Lind, Minister of Social Affairs
Tove Lindbo-Larsen, Minister of Ecclesiastical Affairs
Anne Lundholt, Minister of Industry
Mette Madsen, Minister of Ecclesiastical Affairs
Sonja Mikkelsen, Minister of Transport
Grethe Fenger Møller, Minister of Labor
Elsebeth Gerner Nielsen, Minister of Culture
Tove Nielsen, Minister of Education
Aase Olesen, Minister of Home Affairs
Lise Østergaard, Minister Without Portfolio
Helga Pedersen, Minister of Justice
Grethe Røstboll, Minister of Cultural Affairs
Margrethe Vestager, Minister of Education and Ecclesiastical Affairs
Birte Weiss, Minister of the Interior and Health; Minister of Ecclesiastical Affairs

First appointed ambassador

Bodil Begtrup, Ambassador to Iceland, 1955

---

[18]Bodil Koch and her daughter, Dorte Koch Bennedsen (see above), although they never served together in a cabinet, were the first mother and daughter to serve as ministers in any nation's cabinet.

Legislative

First elected to national legislature (Folketinget, Parliament)

Karen Ankersted, Conservative Party
Helga Larsen, Social Democratic Party
Mathilde Malling Hauschultz, Conservative Party
Elna Munch, Social Liberal Party

All elected April 22, 1918, to Folketing (Lower House)

Nina Bang, Social Democratic Party
Marie Christensen, Liberal Party
Marie Hjelmer, Social Liberal Party
Olga Knudsen, Liberal Party
Inger Gautier Schmit, Liberal Party

All elected April 30, 1918, to Landsting (Upper House)

Head of national legislature

Ingeborg Hansen, Landsting (Upper House), 1950–1953

Judicial

First appointed to supreme court

Bodil Dybdahl, 1953

Minority: Gay

Executive

Notable service in cabinet

Torben Lund, Minister of Health

Political Entity: Faeroe Islands

Executive

Power past

Marita Petersen, Prime Minister, January 18, 1993–September 15, 1994. Petersen, a member of the Social Democratic Party, headed a coalition government consisting of her party and two others. She was replaced after her party lost seats in the 1994 general election in the islands, but served for two years (1994–1996) as the speaker of the Logting, the Faeroes' legislative assembly.

First appointed to cabinet

Jóngerö Purkhús, Minister of Finance, Trade, and the Environment, 1984

Legislative

First appointed to legislature (Logting, Parliament)

Malla Samuelsen, Home Rule Party, 1964

First elected to legislature (Logting, Parliament)

Karin Kjølbro, Republican Party, 1978

Political Entity: Greenland

Executive

First woman appointed to cabinet

Johanne Davidsen, Minister of Social Conditions, 1983

Legislative

First woman in provincial legislature (Landsråd)

Elizabeth Johansen, 1953

First women in home-rule legislature (Landsting)

Else M. G. R. Høegh, elected 1975 as a "substitute" member, meaning that she sat as a member only on certain occasions. **Agnethe Nielsen** was elected in 1981 as a full member.

First elected to Danish national legislature (Folketinget, Parliament)

Augo Lynge
Frederik Lynge

Both elected 1953

First woman elected to Danish national legislature (Folketinget, Parliament)

Ellen Kristensen, Atassut Party, 1998

Djibouti

Women

Right to vote: 1946
To stand for election: 1986

Executive

First appointed to cabinet

Hawa Ahmad Yousouf, Minister-Delegate for the Promotion of Women, Family Well-being, and Social Affairs, 1998

First appointed ambassador

Not yet identified, with a strong indication that no woman has yet been appointed as an ambassador. The first female ambassador accredited to Djibouti was **Sanele Work Zewdie,** ambassador from Ethiopia, 1994.

Legislative

First elected/appointed to national legislature

No woman yet elected or appointed to the Assemblée nationale (National Assembly) since Djibouti's independence

Dominica

Women

Right to vote: July 1951
To stand for election: July 1951

Executive

Power past

Mary Eugenia Charles, Prime Minister, July 21, 1980–June 12, 1995. Charles first entered politics in 1968. Two years later she cofounded the centrist Dominica Freedom Party (DFP) and in 1975 was elected on its ticket to the colonial House of Assembly. The DFP won the 1980 general election, two years after independence, and Charles assumed office on July 21, 1980, as the Caribbean's first female prime minister. She achieved a measure of recognition in the United States in 1983, when she appeared on television at the side of U.S. president Ronald Reagan forcefully supporting the American-led invasion of neighboring Grenada. After winning reelection victories in 1985 and 1990, Charles retired shortly before the 1995 election to allow her party to choose a new leader.

Phyllis Shand Allfrey, 1958. A renowned poet and novelist, Allfrey founded the Dominica Labor Party in 1955, becoming its first president. She hoped by doing so to promote the concept of European-style democratic parties in the Caribbean. In 1958, the British formed the Federation of the West Indies, a political entity through which they hoped to administratively bind their smaller island colonies with the larger, more prosperous ones of Jamaica and Trinidad, then grant independence to the federation all at once. Allfrey was appointed to the federation's first cabinet as minister of labor and social affairs—the only woman, and the only white, so appointed. When the federation broke apart before its planned independence in 1962, Allfrey dropped her involvement in politics and returned to her writing.

First appointed to cabinet

Mary Eugenia Charles, Minister of Finance, 1980. **Mabel Moir James** had been appointed Minister of Home Affairs in 1966, when Dominica's status was that of an Associated State of the United Kingdom.

Notable service in cabinet

Alleyne Carbon, Minister of Communications and Works
Doreen Paul, Minister of Health and Social Services
Gertrude Roberts, Minister of Commercial Development and Women's Affairs

First appointed ambassador

Marciella H. Mukasa, Ambassador to the United States, 1985

Legislative

First elected to national legislature (House of Assembly)

Mary Eugenia Charles, Dominica Freedom Party
Judiana Henderson, Dominica Freedom Party

Both elected July 1980

First appointed to national assembly (Senate)

Bernie Didier, July 1980

Head of national legislature

Neva Edwards, House of Assembly, 1993–1995
Marie Davis-Pierre, House of Assembly, 1980–1988

Dominican Republic

Women

Right to vote: 1942
To stand for election: 1942

Executive

First appointed to cabinet

Altagracia Bautista de Suárez, Minister of Labor, 1966

Notable service in cabinet

Ligia Amada Melo de Cardona, Minister of Education, Fine Arts, and Public Worship
Ana de Molina, Minister of Public Finance
Ivelisse Prats de Perez, Minister of Education, Fine Arts, and Public Worship
Marithza Ruiz de Vielman, Minister of Foreign Relations
Alejandra Altagracia Guzman, Minister of Public Health and Social Welfare
Carmen Rosa Hernández, Minister of Presidential Administration
Jacqueline Málágon, Minister of Education, Fine Arts, and Culture
Anabella Marfin, Minister of Labor

First appointed ambassador

Minerva Bernardino, Ambassador to the United Nations, 1955

First appointed governor

In 1966, newly elected president Joaquin Balaguer appointed women as governors of all the provinces in the country. Political observers speculated that he did so to reward the overwhelming support provided to his campaign by the country's female voters.

Legislative

First elected to national legislature
(Cámara de Diputados, Chamber of Deputies)

Two women, 1946

Judicial

First appointed judge

Maria Matilda Luz Peña de Infante

Ecuador

Women

Right to vote: March 3, 1929; 1967[19]
To stand for election: March 3, 1929; 1967

Ecuador was the first country in South America to grant women the right to vote.

Executive

Power past

Rosalia Arteaga Serrano, President, February 9–11, 1997; Vice-President, August 10, 1996–February 9, 1997; February 11, 1997–March 30, 1998. When President Abdala Bucaram was dismissed for incompetence by the Ecuadorean National Congress in February 1997, a constitutional crisis quickly developed. Ecuador's constitution was unclear as to exactly who should succeed to the presidency. As vice-president, Arteaga proclaimed her right to the office. Congress intervened and immediately elected Fabian Alacon—one of its own—as the new president, but permitted Arteaga to assume office briefly before he was sworn in. Her two days as Ecuador's president gave her the shortest tenure thus far of any female head of state. When her minipresidency was over, Arteaga resumed her duties as vice-president. In March 1998, she resigned, as required under Ecuador's constitution, and sought the presidency in the elections later that year.

Notable presidential candidates, 1998

Rosalia Arteaga Serrano. Candidate of her self-formed party, the Independent Movement for an Authentic Republic, Arteaga placed fifth, with 6 percent of the vote, a disappointing finish for a former vice-president.

Maria Eugenia Lima. Candidate of the Marxist Popular Democratic Movement and former deputy in the National Congress, Lima placed sixth, with 2 percent of the vote.

First appointed to cabinet

Margarita Cedeños de Armijos, Minister of Social Affairs, 1979

[19]Between 1929 and 1967, voting was compulsory for men and optional for women; in 1967, it became compulsory for both sexes.

Notable service in cabinet

Rosangela Adoum, Minister of Education and Culture
Marianna Argudo, Minister of Social Welfare
Ana Lucia Armijos, Minister of Government, Police, and Municipality
Sandra Correa, Minister of Education and Culture
Edith Frias, Minister of Social Welfare
Yolanda Kakabadse, Minister of the Environment
Guadalupe Leon, Minister of Labor and Human Resources
Mariana Ordóñez, Minister of Communications
Juana Vallejo de Navarro, Minister of Information and Tourism
Flor Maria Valverde, Minister of the Environment
Rocío Vásquez, Minister of Tourism

First appointed ambassador

Amanda Pesantes Garcia, Ambassador to Denmark, 1975

First elected mayor

Elsa Bucaram, Guayaquil, 1988

Legislative

First elected to national legislature (Congreso Nacional, National Congress)

Fue Nela Martinez, 1956

First elected to national legislature (Senado, Senate)

Isabel Robelino, 1969

Minority: Arab-Ecuadorean

Executive

Jaime Jamil Mahuad Witt, President, August 10, 1998–January 22, 2000. Ecuador's second president of Arab descent is far different than the first. Mahuad, a former lawyer and professor who served two terms in Congress for the Popular Democratic Party, was elected to his post based on his strong performance as mayor of Quito, the capital. His master's degree in public administration from Harvard, combined with a reputation for honest, effective leadership, was just what the nation needed after the political uncertainty of the preceding years. Mahuad narrowly won his race against businessman Alvaro Noboa, who many feared was nothing more than a stalking horse for the exiled Abdalá Bucaram.

First to serve as president

Abdalá Bucaram Ortiz, 1996–1997. The son of Lebanese immigrants, Abdalá utilized his skill as a good athlete—in soccer—to secure upward mobility. He earned a law degree, then became mayor of Guayaquil, where he was accused of corruption because of his lavish lifestyle on an expensive estate. As candidate of the Partido Roldatista Ecuatoriana, he won the presidency by the narrowest of margins—a mere 20,000 votes. Six months into his presidential term, Abdalá found himself mired in controversy. He seemed to foster an erratic image, labeling himself El Loco (the Crazy One); on one occasion he released a compact disc on which he sang a song titled "A Crazy Man Who Loves." The political opposition in the national legislature seized upon all this and, with the support of massive street demonstrations calling for the president's ouster, removed him from office for "mental incapacity." Abdalá fled into exile, leaving the supreme court to sentence him to two years in jail for "slander" against two of his political rivals. He still swears he'll return one day, a possibility that should not be lightly dismissed, as temporary "exile" is often merely a rite of passage for Latin American politicians. Abdalá's removal from office did result in the brief tenure of Ecuador's only female chief executive (see above).

First elected mayor

Asaad Bucaram Elmhalin, Guayaquil, 1962

Minority: Asian-Ecuadorean

Executive

Notable service in cabinet

Guillermo Chang, Minister of Labor and Human Resources

Minority: Native Indian

Legislative

First elected to national legislature (Congreso Nacional, National Congress)

Luis Macas, Pachacutec Party, 1996

First woman elected to national legislature (Congreso Nacional, National Congress)

Nina Pacari, Pachacutec Party, 1998

Egypt

Women

Right to vote: June 23, 1956
To stand for election: June 23, 1956

Executive

Ex–power behind the scenes

Jehan Raouf Sadat, 1970–1981. Wife of assassinated president Anwar Sadat, Jehan was one of his closest advisers. Married to Sadat at age sixteen, Jehan grew into a formidable power in her own right after Anwar granted her the formal title of First Lady of Egypt in 1971. During their thirty-two-year marriage, she earned a bachelor's degree in Arabic language, then a master's degree in literature, and finally a doctoral degree. The fact that she defended her master's thesis on national television raised eyebrows in the Muslim country, causing many to feel that she had become too "prominent" a presence. Throughout her husband's presidential tenure, Jehan focused her energy on women's emancipation and education, reportedly helping choose the women who would run for Parliament under the ruling party's banner (and thus ensuring their election). After her husband's assassination in October 1981, Jehan came under fire from various Muslim elements in Egypt who felt that she had returned to her university work and social activities after too short a period of mourning. Shortly thereafter, Jehan moved to the United States, becoming a professor of international studies at the university level. In 1985, the Women's International Center established the annual Jehan Sadat Peace Award. Since Anwar's death, Jehan has continued her work as an activist for women's rights and peace, urging women to take their rightful place in the world's societies.

First appointed to cabinet

Hekmat Abu Zeid, Minister of Social Affairs, 1962

Notable service in cabinet

Nadia Makram Ebeid, Minister of Environmental Affairs
Venise Kamel Gouda, Minister of Scientific Research
Amal Abd ar-Rahim Othman, Minister of Social Insurance and Social Affairs

Aisha Rateb, Minister of Foreign Affairs; Minister of Social Insurance and Social Affairs
Karimah al-Sa'id, Minister of Education
Nawal al-Tatwi, Minister of the Economy
Marwat al-Tilawi, Minister of Social Security; Minister of Social Affairs

First appointed ambassador

Aisha Rateb, Ambassador to Denmark, 1979

Legislative

First elected to national legislature (Majlis, Assembly)

Rawya 'Atiya
Amina Shoukri

Both elected July 3, 1957

Religious Minority: Copt

Executive

Power past

Boutros Ghali Pasha, Prime Minister, 1908–1910. Boutros Ghali was a member of Egypt's largest Christian community—about 10 percent of the country's population—whose presence in Egypt dates back to the time of St. Mark. A former finance and foreign affairs minister who had successfully reorganized the country's judicial system after the British takeover, Boutros Ghali was appointed prime minister by Khedive Abbas II. He was assassinated in 1910 by a Muslim fanatic who was incensed that a Christian was presiding as head of the Egyptian government. Boutros Ghali was the grandfather of Boutros Boutros-Ghali, former secretary-general of the United Nations.

First appointed to cabinet

Boutros Ghali Pasha, Minister of Finance

Notable service in cabinet

Boutros Boutros-Ghali, Minister of Foreign Affairs
Youseef Boutros-Ghali, Minister of the Economy
Nagib Iskander, Minister of Public Health

Boutros Ghali Pasha, Minister of Foreign Affairs
Marqus Hanna Pasha, Minister of Public Works

Legislative

First woman elected to national legislature (Majlis, Assembly)

Leila Takla, 1973

El Salvador

Women

Right to vote: 1939
To stand for election: 1961

Executive

Notable vice-presidential candidate, 1999

Maria Marta Valladares, candidate of the left-wing Farabundo Martí National Liberation Front. A member of congress, she was better known by her nom de guerre, Nidia Diaz, acquired when she was a commander in the rebel army during El Salvador's civil war in the 1970s and 1980s. Valladares remains controversial, even though the war has ended and the rebels have joined in the democratic process, because of her reputed involvement in the murder of American military advisers in El Salvador.

Notable presidential candidate, 1994

Rhina Escalante. Escalante was candidate of the Christian Democratic Movement, a small splinter party.

First appointed to cabinet

Mirna Lievano de Márques Márquez, Minister of Planning and Coordination of Economic and Social Development, 1989. In 1974, **Maria Julia Castillo Rodas** was appointed as Undersecretary (Deputy Minister) of Health.

Notable service in cabinet

Maria Eugenia Brizuela de Avila, Minister of Foreign Affairs
Evelyn Jacir de Lovo, Minister of Education
Maria Cecilia Gallardo de Cano, Minister of Education
Ana Cristina Sol, Minister for State Modernization

First appointed ambassador

Ana Cristina Sol, ambassador to France, Belgium, Portugal, the European Economic Community, and UNESCO, 1989

Legislative

First elected to national legislature (Asamblea legislativa, Legislative Assembly)

Juana Caceres de Vides, Revolutionary Party for Democratic Unity
Margoth Muñoz de Burgos, Revolutionary Party for Democratic Unity

Both elected December 29, 1961

Head of national legislature

Gloria Salguero Gross, Legislative Assembly, 1994–1997
Maria Julia Castillo Rodas, Legislative Assembly, 1981–1989

EQUATORIAL GUINEA

Women

Right to vote: December 15, 1963
To stand for election: December 15, 1963

Executive

First appointed to cabinet

Cristina Djombe Ngani, Minister of Women's Plannification, 1978

Notable service in cabinet

Teresa Efua Asangono, Minister of Foreign Affairs and Cooperation
Teresa Avoro, Minister of Education, Science, and Francophone Affairs
Marcelina Oyo Ebule, Minister of Justice and Religious Affairs
Margarita Alene Mba, Minister of Women's Advancement and Social Affairs
Balbina Nchamanvo, Minister of Women's Promotion and Social Affairs
Purificaçion Angue Ondo, Minister of Women's Development

First appointed ambassador

Resureccion Bita, Ambassador to Morocco, 1998

Legislative

First elected to national legislature
(Cámara de Representantes del Pueblo,
House of Representatives of the People)

Cristina Macole, National Movement for Equatorial Guinea Liberation
Lorenza Matute, Party for the National Unity Movement

Both elected September 1968

Eritrea

Women

Right to vote: November 4, 1955
To stand for election: November 4, 1955[20]

Executive

First appointed to cabinet

Fozia Hashim, Minister of Justice, 1994
Worku Tesfamikael, Minister of Tourism

Notable service in cabinet

Askalu Monkerious, Minister of Labor

First appointed ambassador

Hibret Berhe, Ambassador to Sweden, Norway, and Finland, 1999
Hana Simon, Ambassador to Belgium and the European Union, 1999

Legislative

First elected to national legislature (Hagerawi Baito, National Assembly)

Twenty-two women, February 1994

[20]Until 1993, Eritrea was part of Ethiopia. The dates for female suffrage and the right to stand for election were granted during that period and carried over when independence was attained.

Estonia

Women

Right to vote: November 24, 1918
To stand for election: November 24, 1918

Executive

Notable presidential candidate, 1992

Lagle Parek, leader and candidate of the conservative Estonian National Independence Party. A former political prisoner of the Soviets, she finished fourth with less than 5 percent of the vote.

First appointed to cabinet (Estonian SSR)

Olga Lauristin, Minister of Social Security, 1944

Member of cabinet at declaration of independence (1990)

Siiri Oviir, Minister of Social Security

First appointed to cabinet (after restoration of independence)

Marju Lauristin, Minister of Social Affairs, 1992
Lagle Parek, Minister of Internal Affairs, 1992

Notable service in cabinet

Tiiu Aro, Minister of Social Affairs
Signe Kivi, Minister of Culture
Katrin Saks, Minister of Population
Andra Veidemann, Minister of European Affairs

First appointed ambassador

Senta Alas, Ambassador to Denmark, 1991

Valvi Strikaitiene, Ambassador to Lithuania, 1992
Leili Utno, Ambassador to Latvia, 1992

Legislative

Members of legislature during 1918 declaration of independence

Alma Anvelt-Ostra, Russian Social Democratic Worker's Party
Anna Leetsmann, Russian Social Democratic Worker's Party

First elected to national legislature (Constituent Assembly)

Alma Anvelt-Ostra, Estonian Social Democratic Worker's Party
Emma Asson, Estonian Social Democratic Worker's Party
Marie Aul, Estonian Social Democratic Worker's Party
Minni Kurs-Olesk, Estonian Social Democratic Worker's Party
Johanna Päts, Estonian Labor Party
Helmi Press-Jansen, Estonian Social Democratic Worker's Party
Marie Reisik, Estonian Labor Party

All elected April 1919

Ethiopia

Women

Right to vote: November 4, 1955
To stand for election: November 4, 1955

Royalty

Power past

Zauditu (Judith), Empress, September 25, 1916–April 1, 1930. Zauditu was the daughter of the great Menelik II, who dealt the Italians a crushing blow at the battle of Adowa in 1895 and therefore preserved Ethiopia as one of Africa's two independent states during the first half of the twentieth century. She was placed on the throne in place of her nephew Iyasu (Isaac), one of Menelik's grandsons, who was deposed because he had converted to Islam, shocking the predominantly Christian nation. The first woman on the Ethiopian throne since the legendary Queen of Sheba, Zauditu reigned but never ruled. Possessing only a rudimentary education from the Ethiopian Orthodox Church, many of whose members were themselves illiterate, and speaking no foreign languages, Zauditu led a solitary life. When she ascended to the throne, her distant nephew (and another of Menelik's many grandsons), Ras Tafari, was named as her regent and heir. Ruling the country in her stead, he was later better known as Emperor Haile Selassie II. After fourteen years of rule as a figurehead, Zauditu died of pneumonia complicated by diabetes.

Ex–partner in power

Menen Asfaw, 1930–1962. Empress and wife of Emperor Haile Selassie II. Menen was short in stature but otherwise formidable. She divorced her first husband in 1911 to marry the then-named Ras Tafari, by whose side she stood steadily for the next fifty-odd years as his most trusted adviser. And she was not loath to take up arms to defend her husband. Early in his reign, when an army revolt broke out and he was taken hostage, Menen commandeered a tank and drove it herself through the garrison's gates to free her husband. She accompanied him into exile after the Italian invasion in the 1930s, swearing an oath while they were abroad that if her husband were restored to his throne, she would never again wear a crown. That restoration came in 1941, with the help of British troops. Menen resumed her charitable works as a patron of the Ethiopian Red Cross and women's education, and continued to advise her husband on all aspects of his reign until her death in 1962. Selassie labored on alone until 1974, when an army mutiny, labor strikes, and student demonstrations, prompted by a horrific famine that had devastated the country, led to his overthrow.

Executive

First appointed to cabinet

Genet Zewde, Minister of Education, 1993

Notable service in cabinet

Membre Alemayehu, Minister of Labor and Social Affairs
Tadelech Michael, Minister of Women's Affairs

First appointed ambassador

Youdith Imre, Ambassador to Denmark, Finland, Norway, and Sweden, 1975

Legislative

First elected to national legislature (Chamber of Deputies)

Senedu Gebru, October 1957

Head of national legislature

Almaz Meko, House of Federation (upper chamber of Parliament), 1995

Fiji

Women

Right to vote: April 17, 1963
To stand for election: May 5, 1963

Executive

Power past

Adi Kuini Bavadra Speed. Onetime head of an opposition alliance, the Fijian Association Party, and widow of short-term former prime minister Timoci Bavadra, who was overthrown in a coup in 1987. Termed by many in the island country as the "Queen of Democracy," Speed has strong links to Fiji's traditional chiefly houses. Her selection as party head in mid-1989 was seen as a choice that would broaden the coalition party's links to both Indians and Fijians, overcoming the mutual distrust between the two ethnic groups. After marrying Clive Speed, a former prime ministerial press secretary, she resigned as party leader in 1991. She was back in power, with another political party, in 1999, however. After a predominantly Indian-based party won the parliamentary elections, she accepted the position of deputy prime minister. In September 1999, she was ousted as a leader in her new party but continued in her governmental post. Given her standing—both political and otherwise—in the country, it's not unlikely that Speed one day just might become the first female prime minister of Fiji.

First appointed to cabinet

Adi Litia Cakobau, Minister of Women and Culture, 1987. Cakobau was appointed in an interim administration, which only lasted a short while.
Taufa Vakatale, Minister of Education, 1992

Notable service in cabinet

Adi Losalini Dovi, Minister of Social Welfare
Adi Kaila Mara Nailatikau, Minister of Tourism and Transport
Irene Jai Narayan, Minister of Indian Affairs
Lavenia Padarath, Minister of Women, Culture, and Social Welfare
Adi Finau Tabakaucoro, Minister of Women, Social Welfare, and Culture

Adi Samanunu Cakobau Talakuli, Minister of Fijian Affairs
Seruwaia Hong Tiy, Minister of Health and Social Welfare
Taufa Vakatale, Deputy Prime Minister

First appointed ambassador

Adi Samanunu Cakobau Talakuli, High Commissioner (Ambassador) to Malaysia, also accredited to Thailand, 1999

Legislative

First elected to colonial legislature (Legislative Council)

Adi Losalini Dovi, 1966

First elected to national legislature (House of Representatives)

Adi Losalini Dovi, Alliance Party
Irene Jai Narayan, National Federal Party

Both elected 1970

First elected to a local council

Makin Karoro, Rubi Island Council, December 1996

Judicial

First appointed judge

Nazhat Shameen, 1999

FINLAND

Women

Right to vote: July 20, 1906
To stand for election: July 20, 1906

Notable First: On March 15 and 16, 1907, Finland became the first country in the world to elect women to its Parliament.

Executive

This almanac went to press too early to report the results of the January 2000 presidential election. It is safe to assume that the next president of Finland will be female, as four of the five main candidates in that contest are women. They are: Elisabeth Rehn (see below), Swedish People's Party; Tarja Halonen, Social Democratic Party; Heidi Hautila, Green Party; and Riita Uosukainen, Conservative Rally Party.

Notable presidential candidates, 1994

Eeva Kuuskoski-Vikatmaa. Running as an independent, Kuuskoski-Vikatmaa finished far back in the pack of contenders.

Elisabeth Rehn. Rehn, a former defense minister, was a candidate of the Swedish People's Party in Finland's first direct presidential election. A native Swedish speaker, she won 22 percent of the vote and placed second in the January 16, 1994, election, which qualified her for a runoff. In the second round of voting, she lost with 46 percent of the vote to Martti Ahtisaari. In her memoirs, Rehn revealed that during an official meeting in Syria with that country's defense minister, Mustafa Tlass, she was literally forced to swat away with her briefcase his unwanted sexual advances in the back seat of an automobile.

Notable presidential candidate, 1982

Helvi Silipä. Silipä ran unsuccessfully as an independent. She was also the first woman to serve as assistant secretary-general of the United Nations.

First appointed to cabinet

Miina Sillanpää, Minister of Social Affairs, 1926

Notable service in cabinet

Matti Ahde, Minister of the Environment
Eva Biaudet, Minister of Basic Services
Tarja Halonen, Minister of Foreign Affairs; Minister of Justice
Terttu Huttu, Minister of Health and Sports
Tytti Isohookana-Vikatmaa, Minister of Social Affairs and Health
Liisa Jaakonsaari, Minister of Labor
Anneli Jaatteenmaki, Minister of Justice
Hertta Elina Kuusinen-Leino, Minister Without Portfolio
Eeva Kuuskoski-Vikatmaa, Minister of Social Affairs and Health
Tyyne Leivo-Larsson, Deputy Prime Minister
Matti Lutiinen, Minister of Commerce
Sinikka Monkare, Minister of Social Affairs
Maija Perho, Minister of Social Affairs and Health
Sirpa Pietikäinen, Minister of the Environment
Hannele Pokka, Minister of Justice
Kaisa Raatikainen, Minister of the Interior
Elisabeth Rehn, Minister of Defense
Pirjo Rusanen, Minister of Housing
Suvi-Anne Siimes, Minister of Culture
Kaarina Suonio, Minister of Education
Anneli Taina, Minister of Defense; Minister of Housing
Pirkko Annikki Työläjärvi, Minister of Social Affairs and Health
Riita Uosukainen, Minister of Education

First appointed ambassador

Tyyne Leivo-Larsson, Ambassador to Norway and Iceland, 1958

Legislative

First elected to national legislature (Eduskunta-Riksdagen, Parliament)

Lida Aalle, Social Democratic Party
Eveliina Ala-Kulju, Old Finns Party
Hedvig Gebhard, Old Finns Party
Aleksandra Gripenberg, Old Finns Party
Lucina Hagman, Young Finns Party
Anna Maria Huotari, Social Democratic Party
Hilda Käkikoski, Old Finns Party
Mimmi Kanervo, Social Democratic Party
Jenny Maria Kilpiäinen (Nuotio), Social Democratic Party
Liisi Kivioja, Old Finns Party
Maria Sofia Laine, Social Democratic Party

Dagmar Neovius, Swedish People's Party
Alli Nissinen, Young Finns Party
Hilja Pärssinen, Social Democratic Party
Hilma Räsänen, Agrarian Union Party
Maria Raunio, Social Democratic Party
Aleksandra Reinholdsson (Lehtinen), Social Democratic Party
Miina Sillanpää, Social Democratic Party
Ida Vemmelpuu, Old Finns Party

All elected March 15–16, 1907, and seated May 23, 1907

Head of national legislature

Riita Uosukainen, Parliament, 1995–1999
Riita Uosukainen, Parliament, 1991–1995
Miina Sillanpää, Parliament, 1936–1947

Judicial

First appointed to supreme court

Maarit Saarni-Rytkölä, 1970

Minority: Gay

Executive

First appointed to cabinet

Pentti Holappa, Minister of Culture, 1972

France

Women

Right to vote: April 21, 1944
To stand for election: April 21, 1944

Notable First, 1979: **Simone Veil** became the first female president of the European Parliament.

Executive

Power past

Edith Campión Cresson, Prime Minister, May 15, 1991–April 2, 1992. Longtime Socialist Party member, former mayor (Thune, 1977), and first woman to serve as France's minister of agriculture (1981), Cresson was chosen as prime minister by French President François Mitterrand. Always known for being outspoken, she created a minor diplomatic flap while in office when during an interview she referred to the Japanese—because of their perceived work habits—as "ants." After a bumpy tenure in office, which saw her popularity sag rapidly, Cresson was removed by Mitterrand in favor of another socialist—this time a man. Cresson next moved into a wider circle of European politics: She was appointed European Union Commissioner for Research and Development. In 1999, all the EU commissioners—Cresson and her nineteen colleagues—resigned en masse after the eruption of a favoritism scandal in which many of the commissioners were charged with having appointed their cronies to lucrative positions within the EU. Cresson's name, unfortunately, was at the center of the affair.

Notable presidential candidates, 1995

Arlette Laguille. Persistent candidate of the small, far-left Workers Fight, Laguille placed sixth with slightly more than 5 percent of the vote.

Dominique Voynet. Cofounder of the French Green Party, Voynet was eliminated in the first round of the April 1995 voting, winning only 3.5 percent of the vote. She resurfaced in 1997 as minister of regional development and the environment in the cabinet of prime minister Lionel Jospin, who, after his Socialist Party won the national assembly elections that year, formed a coalition government that included both the Greens and the Communist Party.

Notable presidential candidate, 1988

Arlette Laguille. Candidate of the small, far-left Workers Fight, Laguille placed eighth with less than 2 percent of the vote.

Notable presidential candidates, 1981

Huguette Briand Bouchardeau. Candidate of the small, far-left United Socialist Party, Bouchardeau placed tenth with slightly more than 1 percent of the vote.
Marie-France Garaud. Running as an independent, Garaud, former councillor and adviser to President Georges Pompidou, placed ninth with less than 2 percent of the vote.
Arlette Laguille. Candidate of the small, far-left Workers Fight, Laguille placed sixth with slightly more than 2 percent of the vote.

Notable presidential candidate, 1974

Arlette Laguille. Candidate of the small, far-left Workers Fight, Laguille placed fifth with less than 3 percent of the vote. She was the first woman to run for president of France.

Notable Moment, 1936

Prime Minister Léon Blum, a member of the Radical Party who had been installed as head of a coalition government, appointed three women—**Suzanne Cécile Brunschvig, Iréne Joliot-Curie,** and **Suzanne Lacore**—as junior cabinet ministers in the education and health ministries at a time when French women had no political (that is, voting) rights.

Notable Moment, 1804

The Emperor Napoleon I appointed the twenty-four-year-old **Madame Marie Madeleine Sophie Armant Blanchard,** the best-known female aeronaut (balloonist) in Europe, as his chief air minister of ballooning. She was responsible for developing plans to launch an airborne balloon invasion of Europe for Napoleon's army.

First appointed to cabinet

Germaine Poinso-Chapuis, Minister of Public Health and Population, 1947. No woman served in a French cabinet after Poinso-Chapuis until Simone Veil was appointed minister of health and social security on May 28, 1974.

Notable service in cabinet

Martine Aubry, Minister of Employment
Edwige Avice, Minister of Cooperation and Development
Huguette Briand Bouchardeau, Minister of the Environment

Frédérique Bredin, Minister of Youth and Sports
Marie-George Buffet, Minister of Youth and Sports
Edith Campión Cresson, Minister of Agriculture; Minister of Industrial Redeployment and Foreign Trade
Hélène Drolhac, Minister of Penal Affairs
Georgina Dufoix, Minister of Social Affairs and National Solidarity
Françoise Giroud, Minister of Women's Affairs
Elisabeth Guigou, Minister of Justice
Catherine Lalumiere, Minister of Consumption
Corinne Lepage, Minister of the Environment
Annie Lesur, Minister of Education
Michele Alliot Marie, Minister of Youth and Sport
Monique Pelletier, Minister of Justice
Dominique Perben, Minister of Civil Defense, State Reform, and Decentralization
Nicole Questiaux, Minister of National Solidarity
Yvette Roudy, Minister of Women's Rights
Ségolene Royal, Minister of the Environment
Alice Saunier-Seité, Minister of Universities
Catherine Tasca, Minister of Francophony
Catherine Trautmann, Minister of Culture
Dominique Voynet, Minister of Town and Country Planning; Minister of the Environment

First appointed ambassador

Marcelle Campana, Ambassador to Panama, 1972. In 1646, **Renée du Bec** was accredited as ambassador to the King of Poland, the first French woman so designated.

Legislative

First to sit in parliamentary body

Marthe Simard, the only female member of the Free French Provisional Consultative Assembly, which met in Algiers in November 1943

First elected to national legislature (Assemblée nationale, National Assembly)

Denise Bastide, Communist Party
Madeleine Braun, Communist Party
Hélène de Suzannet, PRL
Germaine Degrond, SFIO
Marie Madeleine Dienesch, MRP
Eugenia Eboué, SFIO
Germaine François, Communist Party
Emilienne Galicier-Lallemand, Communist Party
Denise Ginallin, Communist Party

Lucie Guérin, Communist Party
Rose Guérin, Communist Party
Solange Lamblin, MRP
Irene Laure, SFIO
Marie Hélène Lefauchaeux, MRP
Francine Lefebvre, MRP
Rachel Lempereur, SFIO
Madeleine Léo-Lagrange, SFIO
Jeanne Leveille, Communist Party
Mathilde Mety, Communist Party
Raymonde Nédélec, Communist Party
Marie Oyon, SFIO
Mathilde Gabriel Péri, Communist Party
Germaine Peyrolles, MRP
Germaine Poinso-Chapuis, MRP
Rene Prévert, MRP
Gilberte Roca, Communist Party
Simone Rollin, MRP
Marcelle Rumeau, Communist Party
Hélène Solomon-Langevin, Communist Party
Alice Sportisse, Communist Party
Marie Texier-Lahoulle, MRP
Marie-Claude Vaillant-Couturier, Communist Party
Jeanette Vermeersch, Communist Party

All elected October 1945

Longest serving female member of national legislature

Marie Madeleine Dienesch, MRP. First elected in October 1945, she won the same constituency, Côtes-du-Nord, for eleven consecutive elections between 1945 and 1978.

Minority: African-French

Executive

First appointed to cabinet

Louis Aujoulet, Cameroon (French Equatorial Africa), Minister of Labor, September 1954

First woman appointed to cabinet

Lucette Michaux-Chevry, Guadeloupe, Secretary of State for the Francophonie, 1986

Notable service in cabinet

Felix Houphouet-Boigny, French West Africa, Minister of Public Health and Population; Minister of State

Legislative

First elected to national legislature (Assemblée nationale, National Assembly)

Blaise Diagne, Member from Senegal, 1914

First woman elected to national legislature (Assemblée constituante, Constituent Assembly)

Eugenia Eboué-Tell, Guadeloupe, SFIO, 1945. In 1946, she became the first black woman to be elected a senator of the French republic.

Head of national legislature (Sénat, Senate)

Gaston Monnerville, Senator from French Guiana, October 1958

Minority: Arab

Executive

First woman appointed to cabinet

Nafissa Sid-Cara, Algeria, Secretary of State for Algerian Affairs, 1958

Legislative

First women elected to national legislature (Assemblée nationale, National Assembly)

Kheira Bouabsa, Algeria
Rehiba Khebtani, Algeria
Nafissa Sid-Cara, Algeria

All elected 1958

Minority: Gay

Legislative

First elected to national legislature (Assemblée nationale, National Assembly)

Andre Laborrere, Socialist Party, 1997

Notable service in national legislature (Sénat, Senate)

Bertrand Delanoe, Socialist Party

Religious Minority: Jewish

Executive

First to serve as prime minister

Léon Blum, Radical Party, June 4, 1936

Gabon

Women

Right to vote: May 23, 1956
To stand for election: May 23, 1956

Executive

First appointed to cabinet

Antoniette Oliveira, Minister of Social Affairs and Women, 1980

Notable service in cabinet

Pascaline Mferri Bongo, Minister of Foreign Affairs
Victorine Lasseny-DuBoze, Minister of National Solidarity, the Family, and the Promotion of Women
Lucie Mba, Minister of Foreign Affairs, Cooperation, and Francophone Affairs
Paulette Moussavou Missambo, Minister of Civil Service and Administrative Reform

First appointed ambassador

Jeanne Nzao-Mabika, Ambassador to Senegal, 1987

Legislative

First elected to national legislature (Assemblée nationale, National Assembly)

One woman, February 12, 1961

Judicial

First appointed to supreme court

Marie Madeleine Mborantsuo

GAMBIA

Women

Right to vote: 1960
To stand for election: 1960

Executive

Isatou Njie Saidy, Vice-President, March 20, 1997–present. Saidy, a former teacher of French and English as well as a cabinet minister, was named as Gambia's vice-president by President Yahya Jammeh. He had seized power in a 1994 army coup and then won a disputed presidential election in September 1996. Several opposition leaders had faulted him because, although he had named a cabinet, the vice-presidential position remained empty. Opponents claimed that Jammeh was constitutionally required to fill the position, which he finally did with the Saidy appointment. It was rumored that Saidy was named only because the de facto vice-president at the time, Edward Singateh, was too young to meet the age requirement for the position.

First appointed to cabinet

Louise N'Jie, Minister of Youth, Sport, and Culture, 1982

Notable service in cabinet

Fatou Bensouda, Attorney General
Caumba Marenah Ceesay, Minister of Health, Social Welfare, and Women's Affairs
Santang Jow, Minister of Education
Ann-Therese Ndong-Jatta, Minister of Education
Louise N'Jie, Minister of Health and Social Welfare
Hawa Sisay-Sabally, Minister of Justice and Attorney General
Fatoumata C. M. Tambajang, Minister of Health, Social Welfare, and Women's Affairs
Susan Wafa-Ogoo, Minister of Information and Tourism

First appointed ambassador

Ruth Adjue Sowe, Ambassador to Belgium, France, Germany, Luxembourg, the Netherlands, and the European Union, 1991

Legislative

First elected to national legislature (House of Representatives)

Three women, May 1982

Georgia

Women

Right to vote: November 22, 1918
To stand for election: November 22, 1918

Executive

First appointed to cabinet (Georgian SSR)

Zinadia A. Kuadhadze, Minister of Trade, 1957

First appointed to cabinet (after independence)

Lia Andguladze, Minister of Education, 1990. **F. Tkebuchava** was appointed minister of communications in 1991.

Notable service in cabinet

Tamar Beruchasvili, Minister of Trade and Foreign Economic Relations
Nino Chkobadze, Minister of the Environment
Manana Dzozuashvili, Minister of Social Affairs and Health
Irena Sarishvili, Deputy Prime Minister

First appointed ambassador

Rusudan Lortkipanidze, Ambassador to Italy, 1998

Legislative

First elected to national legislature (Sakartvelos Parlamenti, Parliament)[21]

Lia Andguladze, Round Table–Free Georgia Party
Tamar Dekanosidze, Communist Party

---

[21]Women from Georgia were previously elected to the Supreme Soviet of the Georgian SSR and to the Parliament of the USSR.

Nino Djavaxishvili, Communist Party
Manana Dzozuashvili, Round Table–Free Georgia Party
Dali Firosmanishvili, Communist Party
Manana Gabashvili, Round Table–Free Georgia Party
Eter Gugushvili, Communist Party
Lia Kathcadze, Round Table–Free Georgia Party
Eter Khavelashvili, Communist Party
Maia Machavariani, Round Table–Free Georgia Party
Maia Natadze, Round Table–Free Georgia Party
Natela Qutelia, Round Table–Free Georgia Party
Mzeqala Shanidze, Communist Party
Irine Taliashvili, Round Table–Free Georgia Party
Maia Tomadze, Round Table–Free Georgia Party
Medea Tushmalishvili, Round Table–Free Georgia Party
Salome Zviadadze, Communist Party

All elected October 1990

GERMANY

Women

Right to vote: November 12, 1918
To stand for election: November 12, 1918

Executive

Power past

Sabine Bergman-Pohl, Head of State (German Democratic Republic), May 5–October 3, 1990. Bergman-Pohl, a parliamentarian, served temporarily after the collapse of the communist government in Berlin, stepping down when the German Democratic Republic dissolved itself and merged with the Federal Republic of Germany.

Ex–Red Queen, partner in power

Margot Honecker, 1963–1989. Wife of East German head of state Erich Honecker (1976–1989). Appointed education minister of the German Democratic Republic in 1963, Margot enthusiastically enforced one of the most inhumane policies of that regime—the deliberate orphaning of children. Those citizens caught attempting to flee their worker's paradise—and many who were simply declared enemies of the state—had their children seized and shuttled off to orphanages, from whence they were eventually transferred to "good" communist homes. Three years after the fall of East Germany, Margot and Erich were permitted to move to Chile—once the German courts determined that the former head of state had no legal responsibility for most, if not all, of the prosecutable offenses that had been committed by East German authorities during his tenure. The Honeckers joined a daughter who had married, naturally, a Chilean communist. Many of the children that Margot appropriated remain a source of anguish to their parents, who still have not been able to locate them. Erich died of cancer in 1994, while Margot the child snatcher still lives quietly in exile.

Notable presidential candidates, 1999

Uta Ranke-Heinemann, writer and candidate of the Party of Democratic Socialism. Daughter of socialist former president of West Germany Gustav Heinemann (1969–1974), she ran as the candidate of the renamed former Communist Party. Ranke-Heinemann placed third in the balloting.

Dagmar Schipanski, professor of electronics at the Technical University of Ilmenau in Thuringia, and candidate of the Christian Democratic Party. Schipanski was the first woman to chair the joint state-federal scientific advisory council, and the first "easterner" to seek the presidency after German reunification. She was notable because she did not belong to any political party, and her previous public service experience had been limited to membership in nonpartisan committees focused on scientific research.

Notable presidential candidate, 1994

Hildegaard Hamm-Brücher. Hamm-Brücher, the grande dame of Germany's third party, the Liberal Party, was a self-submitted candidate of that party in the presidential election.

Notable presidential candidate, 1984

Luise Rinser. Rinser was the Green Party's candidate.

Notable presidential candidate, 1979

Annemarie Renger. Head of the Bundestag (Federal Diet) and the Social Democratic Party. Renger lost the election (voted in the Bundestag, not among the general public) to Karl Carstens, the Christian Democratic Union candidate.

First appointed to cabinet

Elisabeth Schwarzhaupt, Minister of Health, 1961. In 1952, in the German Democratic Republic, **Else Zaisser** was appointed Minister of People's Education.

Notable service in cabinet

Hilde Benjamin, Minister of Justice (German Democratic Republic)
Christina Bergmann, Minister of Families
Herta Daeubler-Gmelin, Minister of Justice
Andrea Fischer, Minister of Health
Katherine Focke, Minister of Health, and Family and Youth Affairs
Gerda Hasselfeldt, Minister of Health
Margot Honecker, Minister of Education (German Democratic Republic)
Antje Huber, Minister of Health, and Family and Youth Affairs
Sabine Leutheusse-Schnarrenberger, Minister of Justice
Angela Merkel, Minister of the Environment, Nature Conservation, and Nuclear Safety
Claudia Nolte, Minister of Family Affairs, Senior Citizens, Women, and Youth
Brunhilde Peter, Minister of Labor, Health, and Social Affairs
Hannelore Rönsch, Minister of Family and Senior Citizens

Maria Schlei, Minister of Economic Cooperation
Irmgard Schwatzer, Minister of Environmental Planning, Building, and Construction
Käte Strobel, Minister of Health, and Family and Youth Affairs
Heidemarie Wieczorek-Zeul, Minister of Overseas Development
Dorothee Wilms, Minister of Education and Science
G. Wittowski, Deputy Prime Minister (German Democratic Republic)

First appointed ambassador

Eleonora Straimer, Ambassador from the German Democratic Republic to Yugoslavia, 1958
Ellinor von Puttkammer, Ambassador to the European Council, 1969
Margarette Hutten, Ambassador to El Salvador, 1972

First to head a state (as minister-president)

Heide Simonis, Social Democratic Party, Schleswig-Holstein, 1993

Legislative

First elected to national legislature (Nationalversammlung, National Assembly)

Lore Agnes, Independent Socialist Party
Marie Baum, Social Democratic Party
Gertrude Baumer, Social Democratic Party
Margarethe Behm, German National People's Party
Anna Blos, Social Democratic Party
Klara Bohm-Schuch, Social Democratic Party
Minna Bollmann, Social Democratic Party
Elisabeth Brönner, German Democratic Party
Hedwig Dransfeld, Christian People's Party
Wilhelmine Eichler, Social Democratic Party
Else Ekke, German Democratic Party
Friede Hauke, Social Democratic Party
Else Höfs, Social Democratic Party
Anna Hubler, Independent Socialist Party
Marie Juchacz, Social Democratic Party
Wilhelmine Kähler, Social Democratic Party
Katharina Klass, German Democratic Party
Frieda Lührs, Social Democratic Party
Ernestine Lutze, Social Democratic Party
Clara Mende, German People's Party
Agnes Neuhaus, Christian People's Party
Antonie Pfülf, Social Democratic Party

Johanna Reitze, Social Democratic Party
Elizabeth Röhl-Kirschmann, Social Democratic Party
Elfriede Ryneck, Social Democratic Party
Minna Schilling, Social Democratic Party
Käthe Schirmacher, German National People's Party
Maria Schmitz, Christian People's Party
Louise Schroeder, Social Democratic Party
Anna Simon, Social Democratic Party
Johanna Tesch, Social Democratic Party
Christine Teusch, Christian People's Party
Anna von Grierke, German National People's Party
Helene Weber, Christian People's Party
Marie Zettler, Christian People's Party
Louise Zietz, Independent Socialist Party

All elected January 19, 1919

Head of national legislature

Riita Sussmuth, Bundestag (Federal Diet), 1988–1994; 1994–1998
Annemarie Renger, Bundestag (Federal Diet), 1972–1976

Power past

Petra Kelly, 1983–1992. Cofounder of the Green Party and parliamentarian. Kelly, whose stepfather was an American serviceman, received her political training at an American university and while working for both the Robert Kennedy and the Hubert Humphrey presidential campaigns in 1968. She returned to Germany shortly thereafter, where she almost immediately cofounded the Green Party. In 1983, she and fellow party members were elected to the Bundestag. Although the party formally decried a structured leadership, Kelly's charisma, plus her youth, instantly made her a Green "star" in parliament. She served until October 1992, when she was killed by her lover, former general and fellow Green parliamentarian Gert Bastion, in an apparent murder-suicide. In September 1996, Kelly's hard work for the Green Party bore fruit; her former colleagues entered into a Red-Green alliance with the Social Democrats of Gerhard Schroeder to form a new government after the electoral defeat of longtime (four terms) Christian Democratic chancellor Helmut Kohl.

Judicial

First appointed to supreme court (German Democratic Republic)

Hilde Benjamin, 1949

Miscellaneous

Power past

Rosa Luxembourg, 1914–1918. One of the most prominent leaders of the international socialist movement, Luxembourg made her mark in Germany. Born in Poland, then a part of Russia, she fled to the less autocratic parts of Europe. She earned a doctorate in Switzerland, then migrated to Germany, where she became affiliated with the Social Democratic Party, a leading organization of international socialism. Luxembourg helped form a revolutionary faction within that party and worked to eventually transform it into the Communist Party of Germany. After World War I, which Luxembourg had vociferously opposed, she reluctantly took part in a 1918 uprising against the post-Kaiser regime. The revolt failed, and Luxembourg was arrested and murdered by German troops in January 1919. Until the fall of communism, she was celebrated throughout the Red world as one of the great martyrs of the people's struggle against capitalism.

Minority: Gay

Legislative

First elected to national legislature (Bundestag, National Diet)

Herbert Rusche, Green Party, 1983

First openly proclaimed gay elected to national legislature (Bundestag, National Diet)

Volker Beck, Green Party, 1994

Minority: Turkish-German

Legislative

First elected to national legislature (Bundestag, National Diet)

Cem Ozdemir, Green Party, 1994

First woman elected to national legislature (Bundestag, National Diet)

Leyla Onur, Social Democratic Party, 1994

GHANA

Women

Right to vote: 1954
To stand for election: 1954

Executive

Potential power

Nana Konadu Agyemang Rawlings. Wife of President Jerry Rawlings, Nana Konadu exerts considerable political power in her own right and is tipped to be a leading contender in Ghana's 2000 presidential race. As president of the Thirty-First December Women's Movement, Rawlings has facilitated the establishment of nursery and kindergarten facilities throughout Ghana, as well as of small processing factories, which brings Ghana's "market women"—the backbone of the country's small businesses—under the group's protection. The key to her success will be the endorsement of her husband's National Democratic Congress: He firmly controls the party, but observers are unsure whether he truly supports his spouse's bid for power. Ghana's women do have a fair measure of power, both political and economic. Two previous, but unsuccessful, presidential candidates recognized that fact; both of them had selected female running mates.

First appointed to cabinet

Susanna al-Hassan, Minister of Social Affairs, 1963. Mention has been made of an earlier woman in the cabinet, who served as minister of social welfare beginning in 1960.

Notable service in cabinet

Patience Addow, Minister for the Eastern Region
Christine Ama Ata Aidoo, Minister of Education
Christine Amoako-Nuamah, Minister of Education
Joyce Aryee, Minister of Information
Eunice Brookman-Amissah, Minister of Health
Margaret Clarke-Kwesie, Minister Without Portfolio
Aanna Naanna Enin, Minister of Mobilization and Social Welfare
Mary Grant, Minister of Education and Culture

Emma Mitchell, Minister of Trade and Industry
Gloria Amon Nikoi, Minister of Foreign Affairs; Minister of Finance
Esther Lily Nkansah, Minister for the Western Region
Nana Akuoko Sarpong, Minister of Health
Vida Amadi Yeboah, Minister of Tourism

First appointed ambassador

Bertha Amohoo-Neiser, Ambassador to Denmark, 1970
Amonno Williams, Ambassador to Luxembourg, 1972

Legislative

First elected to colonial legislature (Legislative Assembly of the Gold Coast)

Mabel Dove, 1954. Dove, later Mrs. Joseph Danquah, was the cousin of Constance Horton Cummings-Jones, another notable African female political pioneer (*see* Sierra Leone, First elected to office).

First appointed to national legislature (Parliament)

Susanna al-Hassan, Convention People's Party
Lucy Anin, Convention People's Party
Regina Asamany, Convention People's Party
Comfort Asamoah, Convention People's Party
Grace Ayensu, Convention People's Party
Ayanori Bukari, Convention People's Party
Sophia Doku, Convention People's Party
Mary Korateng, Convention People's Party
Victoria Nyarku, Convention People's Party
Christiana Wilmot, Convention People's Party

All appointed August 1960

First elected to national legislature (Parliament)

Lydia Azuele Akanbodiipo, National Alliance of Liberals
Catherine Katumi Tedam, Progress Party

Both elected August 1969

Judicial

First appointed to supreme court

Annie Jiagge, 1961

Greece

Women

Right to vote: January 1, 1952
To stand for election: January 1, 1952[22]

Royalty

Power past

Frederika, Queen, April 1, 1947–March 6, 1964. Frederika Louise of Hannover, Duchess of Brunswick and Queen of the Hellenes, full of German blood with nary a drop of Greek blood, always had a problem with the people of Greece. As one historian phrased it, "The Greeks can neither live with their kings, nor without them." When her husband, Paul I, of Danish-German descent, came to the throne in 1947, Greece was racked by a nasty communist insurgency, with the rebels perilously close to victory. The royal couple's effort to defeat the rebellion—assisted by British troops—played no small part in ensuring that Greece became the only Balkan nation not to fall under communist rule. Foregoing pomp and splendor, which had never been part of Greek royal tradition, they traveled widely throughout the country rallying their people behind them. In the years after the revolt was crushed, however, Frederika and Paul squandered much of the Greek people's goodwill toward them by relying too heavily on right-wing politicians, a strategy that would mark the balance of Paul's reign. Greeks felt that Frederika meddled too intensely—and too conspicuously—in public affairs, ostensibly seeking to protect the throne's interest. By the time Paul died in 1964, a bitter chasm had grown in Greek politics, with much of the Left's anger directed toward the royal family and with Frederika acting as an accommodating lightening rod. Her young and hapless son, Constantine II, managed to fall afoul of both the Greek Left and Right, and was forced into exile three years after succeeding his father. Frederika first joined her son and his wife abroad. Later, under the guidance of an Indian guru, she became a religious recluse, remaining so until her death in 1981.

Olga (Aspasia Manos), Regent, November 18–December 11, 1920. Olga assumed power when her husband, Alexander I (1917–1920), was bitten by a pet monkey and died from

[22]In 1930, a council of state expressed the opinion that women could have the right to vote in municipal and communal elections. In April 1949, a law was passed giving women the right to vote and the right to stand for office in municipal and communal elections. The new constitution, which went into effect on January 1, 1952, specifically established women's right to vote and stand for elections at the national level.

blood poisoning. Alexander's father, Constantine I, had abdicated in his favor after being accused of pro-German sympathies during World War I (his wife was the sister of Kaiser Wilhelm II). The king's death threw Greece, already unstable, into turmoil, and Olga, who had been married to Alexander for less than a year, became regent. This was seen as a temporary solution, because a general election had already been scheduled. In that election, the prime minister, who had opposed both kings, lost his mandate, and a plebiscite in early December 1920 showed that the Greeks were in favor of recalling King Constantine to the throne. As soon as he arrived back on the scene, Olga's regency ended. She lived quietly for another fifty years after her husband's bizarre death, one of the strangest ever to befall a ruling monarch.

Executive

Ex–power behind the scenes

Dimitra Liani Papandreou, 1989–1996. Dimitra was the second and much younger wife of socialist prime minister Andreas Papandreou. A former Olympic Airways hostess, she was credited with breaking up Andreas's marriage to his longtime American-born spouse, Margaret. After their marriage, the Greek tabloids delighted in splashing fully nude photos of Dimitra—occasionally with another woman—across their covers, which, while titillating to some, scandalized most Greeks. Papandreou's foes, inside and outside his party, claimed that Dimitra exerted undue influence over his political decisions. Due to the drastic difference in their ages (he was some fifty years her senior) and to Dimitra's propensity for flamboyant publicity, most astute political observers felt that it was only a matter of time until his long career in politics came to a sad end. Andreas outfoxed them all, dying in office in 1996 amid charges that young wife had tried to control the strings of the government while he was in his fatal coma. In January 1999, Dimitra was charged with fraud and embezzlement of public funds, which, if she is convicted, could lead to life imprisonment. She was accused of evading taxes on a multimillion-dollar house—nicknamed the Pink Villa—that she and Andreas had built in an exclusive Athens suburb. Dimitra claimed that it was Andreas who had handled all the financial transactions on the property, an allegation that tarnishes the image of her late husband, still revered by many Greeks.

Power past

Melina Mercouri, 1981–1994. Already an internationally acclaimed actress, Mercouri won new fame as the most outspoken and ardent foe of the right-wing junta that ruled Greece from 1967 to 1974. In retaliation for her criticism, the junta's leaders stripped Mercouri of her Greek citizenship; she retorted: "I was born Greek and I will die Greek. [They] were born fascist and will die fascist." When a left-wing socialist government won power in 1981, the new prime minister, Andreas Papandreou, a friend of Mercouri's, named her minister of culture, a post she held for almost eight years in several governments. During her tenure, she denounced "cultural imperialism," demanding the return of the Elgin marbles from London, where they had been carried almost a century before. After her death from cancer in 1994, Mercouri's lasting memorial has been the adoption of her idea that each year a different city in Europe should be designated as the "Cultural Capital of Europe."

First appointed to cabinet

Lina Tsaldaris, Minister of Welfare, 1956

Notable service in cabinet

Melina Mercouri, Minister of Culture
Vasso Papandreou, Minister of Development
Elisavet Papazoi, Minister for the Aegean
Marietta Yiannakou, Minister of Health, Welfare, and Social Services

First appointed ambassador

Elisavet Papazoi, Ambassador to Cuba, 1986

Legislative

First elected to national legislature
(Vouli Ton Ellinon, Greek Chamber of Deputies)

Eleni Scourti, Synagermos Party, 1953. She was elected in supplemental elections held after the regular ballot of November 1952.

Grenada

Women

Right to vote: August 1951
To stand for election: August 1951

Executive

Power past

Hilda Louisa Gibbs Bynoe, Governor, June 8, 1968–January 14, 1974. Bynoe, a native of Jamaica, was a practicing physician in Trinidad when she was named governor of the Associated State of Grenada in 1968, before the island achieved its independence. She was the first woman in the British Empire to hold the post of governor. After she left office, Bynoe returned to Trinidad with her husband and resumed her medical practice there. Since then, she has also published a book of poetry, which she has characterized as "social commentary in verse." Bynoe's father, T. J. Gibbs, also served as governor of preindependence Grenada.

Woman to watch

Joan Purcell, leader of the New Democratic Congress. Purcell has served in the cabinet and could be named prime minister if her party wins the legislative house or achieves a large enough membership to form a coalition cabinet with another party.

First appointed to cabinet

Cynthia Gairy, Minister of Social Affairs, 1972

Notable service in cabinet

Jacqueline Creft, Minister of Education
Clarice Modeste Curwen, Minister of Health and the Environment
Grace Duncan, Minister of Tourism, Civil Aviation, Women's Affairs, Cooperatives, and Social Security
Joan Purcell, Minister of Tourism, Civil Aviation, and Women's Affairs
Laurina Waldron, Minister of Housing, Social Security, and Women's Affairs
Joslyn Whitman, Minister of Tourism and Civil Aviation

First appointed ambassador

Marie-Jo McIntyre, Ambassador to the United Nations and Canada, 1976

Legislative

First elected to national legislature (Parliament, House of Representatives)

Nadia Benjamin, Grenada United Labor Party
Cynthia Gairy, Grenada United Labor Party
Waple Nedd, Grenada United Labor Party

All elected February 1972

First appointed to national legislature (Parliament, Senate)

Audrey Palmer, February 1972

Head of national legislature

Ann Peters, Senate, 1995–1999
Marcelle Peters, House of Representatives, 1992–1995
Margaret Neckles, Senate, 1990–1995

Judicial

Notable first: Monica Joseph was the first woman to serve on the supreme court of the Organization of Eastern Caribbean States.

Guatemala

Women

Right to vote: 1946
To stand for election: 1946

Historical Note: **Dona Beatriz de la Cueva de Alvarado** was the second wife of Pedro de Alvarado, Spanish conquistador, who conquered Guatemala and founded Guatemala City. When he died in 1541, Dona Beatriz had herself appointed royal Spanish governor of Guatemala in his place. Her rule was quite short—only two weeks. It ended when she was killed by an exploding volcano and earthquake. Even so, Dona Beatriz holds the distinction of being the only female Spanish colonial governor.

International Notable: **Rigoberta Menchú** won the 1992 Nobel Peace Prize.

Executive

Notable presidential candidates, 1999

Flor de Maria Alvarado de Solis. Candidate of the National Reconciliation Alliance Party, she received less than 0.5 percent of the vote.

Ana Catalina Soberanis Reyes. Former cabinet minister (Labor and Social Affairs), Reyes was a longtime member of the Democratic Christian Party. When her party failed to field a candidate, she ran on the New Guatemala Democratic Front ticket, but received less than 2 percent of the vote.

Ex–partner in power

Maria Cristina Vilanova Castro Arbenz, 1940–1954, wife of President Jacobo Arbenz Guzmán (1951–1954). Daughter of a wealthy Salvadorian coffee-growing family, Maria was always rumored to be more ambitious for her husband than he was for himself. She met the handsome military officer—he closely resembled 1940s actor Alan Ladd—at a Central American athletic competition, and they married shortly thereafter. Maria, who had broken with her family over her left-liberal views, immediately set about instilling new ideas in her husband's head. Most of these ideas were left-wing, fostered by her communist secretary (Maria Jerez de Fortuny, wife of the first secretary of the Guatemalan Communist Party) and other leftist friends. By 1945, Jacobo was minister of defense and a man on the rise. Maria backed her own strong beliefs with actions: It was rumored that she had connections to the group that assassinated one of her husband's prime conservative opponents in 1949. Jacobo succeeded anti-American Juan José Arévalo as president in 1951, and the country fell under the left-leaning, social reformist sway of the powerful couple. Although neither was a communist, Jacobo and Maria found communist support useful. A series of political blunders, plus their reliance on the communists, turned the United States firmly against the couple. The Americans encouraged an invasion by disgruntled right-wing army officers in 1954, and the Arbenzes fled abroad. For years they wandered in exile from Mexico and Switzerland to Czechoslovakia and onward to Moscow, ultimately ending up at Castro's side in Cuba. After Jacobo drowned in a bathtub in Mexico in 1971, Maria returned to El Salvador to make peace with her estranged family. When a left-wing guerrilla war erupted there in the late 1970s, she surprisingly moved to Paris rather than fight alongside the rebels.

First appointed to cabinet

Ruth Chicas Redón de Sosa, Minister of Welfare, 1978. The Guatemalan government cites María Eugenia de Putzeys, Minister of Education, 1980.

Notable service in cabinet

Marta Allodoguirre, Minister of Human Rights
Maria Luisa Beltranena de Padilla, Minister of Education and Culture
Arabella Castro Quiñonez de Comparini, Minister of Education
Anabella Morfin, Minister of Labor
Marithza Ruiz de Vielman, Minister of Foreign Affairs
Eunice Lima Schaul, Minister of Culture and Sports
Ana Catalina Soberanis Reyes, Minister of Labor and Social Affairs
Irma Luz Toledo Penate, Minister of Finance

First appointed ambassador

Francisca Fernandez Hall-Zuniga, Ambassador to Israel, 1959

Legislative

First elected to national legislature (Congreso de la Republica, Congress of the Republic)

Grace de Zirion, National Liberation Movement, 1965. The Inter-Parliamentary Union instead cites another woman as having been elected on March 1, 1956.

Head of national legislature

Arabella Castro Quiñonez de Comparini, Congress of the Republic, January 1994–January 1995

Ana Catalina Soberanis Reyes, Congress of the Republic, January 14, 1991–January 14, 1992

Minority: Native Indian

Executive

First appointed to cabinet

Alfredo Tay Coyoy, Maya-K'iche, Minister of Education, 1994

First elected mayor of a major city

Rigoberto Queme, Maya, Quetzaltenango, 1997

Legislative

First woman elected to national legislature
(Congreso de la Republica, Congress of the Republic)

Rosalinda Tuyuc Velásquez, Maya, Guatemalan New Democratic Front, November 1995

Guinea

Women

Right to vote: October 2, 1958
To stand for election: October 2, 1958

International Notable: **Jeanne-Martin Cisse** was the first female president of the United Nations Security Council, elected in 1972.

Executive

First appointed to cabinet

Camara Leffe, Minister of Social Affairs, 1961

Notable service in cabinet

Mariame Aribot, Minister of Social Affairs, Women's Promotion, and the Child
Aicha Bah, Minister of Primary, Secondary, and Vocational Education
Mariama Dielo Barry, Minister of Social Affairs
Makale Camara, Minister of Agriculture
Jeanne-Martin Cisse, Minister of Social Affairs
Ivonne Code, Minister for the Promotion of Women and Children
Saran Daraba, Minister of Social Affairs, Women, and Children
Sylla Koumba Diakite, Minister of Youth, Sports, and Civil Education
Josephine Leno Giulao, Minister of Works, Social Welfare, and Development

First appointed ambassador

Jeanne-Martin Cisse, Ambassador to the United Nations, 1972

Legislative

First elected to national legislature (Assemblée nationale, National Assembly)

Fourteen women, September 1963

GUINEA-BISSAU

Women

Right to vote: 1977
To stand for election: 1977

Executive

Notable presidential candidate, 1994

Antonietta Rosa Gomes. Gomes placed last (of eight candidates) with less than 2 percent of the vote.

First appointed to cabinet

Carmen Pereira, Minister of Health and Social Affairs, 1981

Notable service in cabinet

Ilia Barber, Minister of Foreign Affairs
Henriqueta Godhino Gomes, Minister of Public Health
Nharebat N'Incaia N'tchasso, Minister of Social Affairs and the Advancement of Women
Francesca Pereira, Minister of the Interior; Minister of Women's Affairs
Eugenia Saldanha, Minister of Health
Odette Semedo, Minister of National Education

First appointed ambassador

Not yet identified

First president of a region (provincial head)

Francesca Pereira

Legislative

First appointed to national legislature (Assemblea Nacional Popular, National People's Assembly)

Ten women, October 14, 1972

First elected to national legislature
(Assemblea Nacional Popular, National People's Assembly)

Twenty-two women, March 31, 1984

Head of national legislature
(Assemblea Nacional Popular, National People's Assembly)

Carmen Pereira, 1975–1980

Guyana

Women

Right to vote: 1953
To stand for election: 1945[23]

Executive

Power past

Janet Rosenberg Jagan, President, December 19, 1997–August 11, 1999; Prime Minister, March 17–December 19, 1997. Jagan, a U.S.-born former nurse and militant communist, is the widow of longtime Guyanese Marxist politician Cheddi Jagan, who had finally attained the presidency a few years before his death in 1997. Nine days after he died, his interim successor as president, Sam Hinds, who had been prime minister, named Janet to his old position. It wasn't Janet's first venture into a government position: Previously, she had served as agriculture and home affairs minister in several of Guyana's preindependence governments in the 1950s and 1960s. The constitution required that an election be held to fill the president's office permanently, and Janet, running as the candidate of the People's Progressive Party, founded jointly by her late husband and herself, won. Within hours of her victory, violent riots broke out as her opponents claimed fraud in the balloting. The disturbances continued until an agreement was reached in which she would end her presidential term earlier than normal and allow a new presidential election.

Viola Burnham, Vice-President and Deputy Prime Minister, August 15, 1985–July 7, 1991. Burnham was the wife of president Forbes Burnham, who died on August 6, 1985. He was succeeded by Vice-President and Prime Minister Desmond Hoyte. When Hoyte chose Hamilton Green as the new prime minister, Green immediately selected Viola as vice-president and deputy prime minister (with special authority for culture and social development).

First appointed to cabinet

Janet Rosenberg Jagan, Minister of Labor, Health, and Housing, 1957

---

[23]Women became eligible to sit on the British Guiana Legislative Council in 1945.

Notable service in cabinet

Agnes Bend-Kirton-Holder, Minister of Works, Transport, and Housing
Indra Chandrapal, Minister of Labor, Human Services, and Social Security
Winifred Gaskin, Minister of Education
Yvonne Harwood-Benn, Minister of Works, Transport, and Housing
Janet Rosenberg Jagan, Minister of Home Affairs; Minister of Labor, Health, and Housing
Urmia Johnson, Minister of Regional Planning; Minister of Cooperatives
Stella Odie-Ali, Minister of Home Affairs
Gail Teixeira, Minister of Culture, Youth, and Sports

First appointed ambassador

Winifred Gaskin, Ambassador to Barbados, 1973

Legislative

First elected to colonial legislature (British Guiana Legislative Council)

Jessie Burnham
Janet Rosenberg Jagan
Jane Philips-Gay

All elected April 1953

First elected to national legislature (National Assembly)

Seven women, December 1968

Head of national legislature

Lola Willems, 1973–1983

Judicial

First appointed to supreme court

Desiree Bernard, 1996. Bernard already held another record. In 1980, she was named as Guyana's first female judge.

Minority: Chinese-Guyanese

Executive

Power Past

Arthur Chung, President, March 17, 1970–October 6, 1980. A former judge on the supreme court of Guyana, Chung was elected for a six-year term to the largely ceremonial office of the presidency when Guyana became a republic in 1970. He was reelected in 1976 for an additional six-year term, but a new constitution was adopted in 1980 declaring the country a cooperative republic—although no one could define exactly what that meant. In any event, Chung's term was declared over, and he was replaced by Forbes Burnham, who had been serving as prime minister since the country's independence in 1966.

HAITI

Women

Right to vote: November 25, 1950
To stand for election: November 25, 1950

Executive

Power past

Claudette Werleigh, Prime Minister, October 23, 1995–February 7, 1996. Werleigh, a member of the Lavalas political group founded by Jean-Paul Aristide, was foreign minister when she was picked by President Aristide to be Haiti's prime minister. She served until the end of his term, at which time the new president replaced her with his own appointee.

Ertha Pascal-Trouillot, President, March 13, 1990–February 7, 1991. Pascal-Trouillot, the first female justice on Haiti's supreme court, was chosen to serve as interim president during a period of instability until new elections could be held. The interim presidency should have gone to one of the more senior justices on the court, but they all refused. Once Pascal-Trouillot accepted, the political situation in Haiti became so volatile that she went into hiding until her inauguration—primarily to evade the assassination squads that were sent after her. Her swearing-in ceremony was made notable by her comment: "I accept this heavy task in the name of Haitian women."

Ex–partner in power

Michéle Bennett Duvalier, 1980–1986. Wife of porcine Haitian president-for-life Jean-Claude (Baby Doc) Duvalier, Michéle was a shopaholic. She began with a $3 million wedding and reportedly had a monthly $50,000 standing order for flowers from Miami for the presidential residences. One shopping trip to New York was reputed to have cost $1.7 million. These extravagances occurred at a time when Haiti, a country that suffered 90 percent illiteracy, couldn't pay its oil import bills. Michéle particularly detested her mother-in-law, the formidable Simone (see below). Rumor had it that she taught a parrot obscenities, then placed the bird outside the older woman's bedroom to drive her away from the presidential palace and out of the couple's lives. Michéle often exercised political control, issuing orders and attending cabinet meetings because she was frustrated by the ineptness of her husband. During interviews with the couple, it was not unusual for Michéle to speak for him, which was understandable because the president often came across as inarticulate. Finally ousted from power in 1986 by the military, the Duvaliers, accompanied by family and retainers, left for exile in France aboard a fully loaded U.S. Air Force C-141 cargo plane. Reputed to have a fortune of some $400 million stashed abroad, the couple either squandered the fortune or saw it reclaimed by lawsuits. Once Jean-Claude lost the twin aphrodisiacs of power and money, Michéle left him. He still lives in exile, claiming to be in a state of penury, and avoids being seen in public. Her whereabouts are unknown.

Simone Duvalier, 1957–1986. Wife of Haiti's first president-for-life, François (Papa Doc) Duvalier, and mother of the second, Jean-Claude, Simone began life with a lowly status: She was born illegitimate. That didn't stop the determined lady; she managed to obtain a nursing degree, which eventually led to her marriage with Papa Doc. Frequently on the outs with her dictatorial, voodoo-loving husband, Simone moved in and out of periods of conjugal power with him. Whether in favor or out, Simone was regarded by many as the driving force behind her husband's brutal regime. He banished her several times, but she always managed to wiggle back into close proximity to him. Simone exercised even more power over her son after he took control of Haiti at age nineteen, on his father's death in 1971. She pulled Baby Doc's strings quite effectively, until his marriage in 1980 to Michéle Bennett (see above), avaricious daughter of a wealthy mulatto family. Simone and Michéle fought a continual, long-running battle to see who would control Baby Doc—and Haiti—with each woman winning different rounds. Like a good mother, Simone joined the Duvaliers in exile when they were forced out of power. After Michéle departed, Simone kept Baby Doc company until her death in 1998 at age eighty-four.

First appointed to cabinet

Rolande Chandler, Minister of Women's Affairs, 1988

Notable service in cabinet

Adeline Chancy, Minister of Literacy
Ginette Cherubin, Minister of Women's Affairs
Lise-Marie Dejean, Minister of Women's Affairs
Carole Denerville, Minister of Justice
Marie-Denise Fabian-Jean-Louis, Minister of Foreign Affairs
Mathilde Flambert, Minister of Labor and Social Affairs
Astride F. Gardere, Minister of Justice
Michaelle Amede Gideon, Minister of Public Health and Population
Thérese Guilloteau, Minister of Women's Affairs
Nonie Mathieu, Minister of Women's Affairs and Rights
Rosemarie Nazan, Minister of Women's Affairs
Maryse Pennete, Minister of Tourism
Marie-Michéle Rey, Minister of Finance and Economy
Claudette Werleigh, Minister of Foreign Affairs

First appointed ambassador

Lucienne H. Estine, Ambassador to Belgium, 1962

Legislative

First elected to national legislature (Chambre législative, Legislative Chamber)

Three women, May 12, 1961

Judicial

First appointed to supreme court

Ertha Pascal-Trouillot, 1986

Honduras

Women

Right to vote: January 25, 1955
To stand for election: January 25, 1955

Executive

Gladis de Arevalo, Third Vice-President, January 27, 1998–present. A former vice-minister in the Carlos Roberto Reina administration (1994–1998) and a lawyer, de Arevalo was elected on the Liberal Party ticket headed by Carlos R. Flores (see below). Since this was the third presidential election in a row in which a woman has appeared as one of the Designados (the term used for the vice-presidential slots), it may be assumed that it has become almost mandatory for party tickets to include a woman in hopes of capturing the female vote.

Power past

Guadalupe Jerezano Meija, Third Vice-President, January 27, 1994–January 27, 1998. Meija was elected on the presidential ticket of Carlos Roberto Reina of the Liberal Party. That election was notable because the opposition National Party ticket also included a female vice-presidential candidate.

Notable presidential candidate, 1997

Alba Nora Gúnera de Melgar. The widow of former president Juan Alberto Melgar (1975–1978), Nora ran as the candidate of the National Party, one of the country's two largest political parties. Nora was defeated by the Liberal Party candidate, Carlos R. Flores, on November 30, 1997, but still garnered almost 43 percent of the vote. The contest was characterized by charges on both sides of excessive American influence. Flores's wife is American, and the Nationalists claimed that she held undue sway over him. The Liberals took aim at Nora's chief campaign strategist, the notorious Dick Morris, longtime friend of American president Bill Clinton. Liberal Party critics complained about Morris's morals and their effect on Honduran politics, for it was during Morris's planning for Nora's campaign that a sex scandal implicated him in a long-term relationship with a Washington, D.C., prostitute. In 1985, Nora had been an unsuccessful candidate for vice-president on the National Party ticket; she had also served a stint as the appointed mayor of the capital city, Tegucigalpa, and mounted a futile campaign for the nomination as National Party presidential candidate in 1993 before dropping out of the race.

First appointed to cabinet

Alba Alonzo de Quesada, Minister of Labor, 1965

Notable service in cabinet

Sonia Canales de Mendieta, Minister of Culture, Tourism, and Information
Elizabeth Chilez Sierra, Procurator (Attorney) General
Rosa America Miranda de Galo, Minister of Labor
Silvia Xiomara Gomez de Caballero, Minister of Natural Resources and the Environment
Gabriela Nuñez, Minister of Finance
Alma Rodas de Fiallos, Minister of Public Education
Zenobia Rodas Gomez, Minister of Public Education

First appointed ambassador

Albertina Bernhard de Zelarya, Ambassador to Colombia, 1962

Legislative

First elected to national legislature (Congreso Nacional, National Congress)

Three women, 1957

Hungary

Women

Right to vote: 1918
To stand for election: 1918

Executive

First appointed to cabinet

Anna Ratko, Minister of People's Welfare, 1949

Notable service in cabinet

Katalin Botos, Minister Without Portfolio
Judith Csehak, Deputy Prime Minister; Minister of Privatization
Ibolya David, Minister of Justice
Anna Kethly, Minister of Social Affairs
Madga Kovavc Kosa, Minister of Labor

First appointed ambassador

Roza Bedy-Schwimmer, Minister to Switzerland, 1918. Bedy-Schwimmer was also the first woman in the world to hold the rank of ambassador-minister.

Legislative

First elected to national legislature (Provisional National Assembly)

Erzsebet Andics, Communist Party
Endrene Bajcsy-Zsilinszky, Smallholder's Party
Palne Botyanszky, Social Democratic Party
Karolyne Dobrentei, Communist Party
Jolan Majlat, Peasant's Party
Illesne Monus, Social Democratic Party
Ferencne Pollak, Social Democratic Party
Zoltanne Racz, Communist Party
Anna Ratko, Communist Party

Piroska Szabo, Communist Party
Julia Torok, Social Democratic Party

All elected 1945

Head of national legislature

L. Erdes, 1981
Vass Metzker Erzebet, 1963–1967

Minority: Roma (Gypsy)

Legislative

First elected to national legislature (Orszaggyüles, National Assembly)

Antonia Haga, Free Democrats
Aladar Horvath, Free Democrats
Tamas Peli, Free Democrats

All elected April 1990

Religious Minority: Jewish

Executive

First appointed to cabinet

Zsigmond Kunfi, Minister of Welfare, 1918. A Jewish Minister of War has also been cited as having been appointed during World War I to the Hungarian cabinet of the Austro-Hungarian Empire.

ICELAND

Women

Right to vote: June 19, 1915
To stand for election: June 19, 1915

Executive

Power past

Vigdis Finnbogadóttir, President, August 1, 1980–August 1, 1996. Finnbogadóttir, a member of the Althingi, Iceland's Parliament, and director of a theater group in the capital, Reykjavik, was elected in 1980 for a four-year term. After being comfortably reelected in 1984, 1988, and 1992, she announced that she would not stand again in 1996.

Notable presidential candidate, 1996

Gudrun Agnarsdóttir ran in the July 29, 1996, election to succeed Iceland's first female president; she placed third with slightly more than 26 percent of the vote. A practicing physician, Agnarsdóttir ran as an independent but was affiliated with the Women's Alliance, for whom she had served as a member of Parliament from 1983 to 1990. Another female candidate, **Gudrun Petursdóttir,** also an independent, withdrew from the election shortly before the voting; until then, she was polling at about 8 percent of the vote.

First appointed to cabinet

Audur Auduns, Minister of Justice and Ecclesiastical Affairs, 1970

Notable service in cabinet

Siv Fridleifsdóttir, Minister of the Environment
Ragnhildur Helgadóttir, Minister of Education; Minister of Health
Ingibjorg Palmadóttir, Minister of Health
Solveig Petursdóttir, Minister of Justice and Church Affairs
Johanna Sigurdardóttir, Minister of Social Affairs

First appointed ambassador

Sigridur A. Snævarr, Ambassador to Sweden and Finland, 1991

Legislative

First elected to national legislature (Althingi, Parliament)

Ingibjorg H. Bjarnason, Women's Alliance, July 8, 1922

Head of national legislature

Salome Thorkelsdóttir, Althingi (Parliament), 1991–1995
Gudrun Helgadóttir, United Althingi (Parliament), 1988–1991
Salome Thorkelsdóttir, Upper House, 1983–1987
Ragnhildur Helgadóttir, Lower House, 1961–1962; 1974–1978

Judicial

First appointed to supreme court

Guörun Erlendsdóttir, 1982

India

Women

Right to vote: January 26, 1950
To stand for election: January 26, 1950

International Notable: **Vijaya Lakshmi Pandit** was the first female president of the United Nations General Assembly, Eighth Session, 1953.

Executive

Power past

Indira Nehru Gandhi, Prime Minister, January 24, 1966–March 22, 1977; January 14, 1980–October 31,1984. Gandhi, no relation to Mohandas Gandhi, was the daughter of longtime Indian prime minister Jawaharlal Nehru. She came to power when Prime Minister Lal Bahadur Shastri died unexpectedly and the Congress Party voted her as its new leader—and prime minister. After a stormy term in office, she was ousted, then placed under house arrest. Once the government that had succeeded her fell apart, Gandhi triumphed in a new election and returned to power. Assassinated in office by several of her bodyguards, Sikhs who were angered by a military assault she had ordered against their holiest religious shrine, she died with her head cradled in the lap of her daughter-in-law Sonia (see below). Her son and successor, Rajiv Gandhi, was also assassinated a few years later, by Tamil separatists.

Power thwarted

Sonia Maino Gandhi, Italian-born wife of assassinated prime minister Rajiv Gandhi. Sonia's detractors call her the "Turin Shroud" for her frosty, unsmiling countenance, but many Congress Party notables felt that only another Gandhi at the helm could reverse the slippage of power the party has suffered since Rajiv's death. Sonia had always resisted political involvement, until the 1998 elections. Then, she went on the campaign trail, making speeches and winning a good measure of credit when the party held its own. In March 1998, after those elections, Sonia finally agreed to become leader of the Congress Party, and has been rewarded with nothing but trouble since. When the opposition coalition government collapsed in spring 1999, new elections were scheduled. Sonia was attacked—from both within and without the Congress Party—as being an "outsider" (i.e., a Roman Catholic) and a "foreigner." A minor faction split off from the party in protest against her, while the opposition also made much of her foreign birth. Sonia campaigned for election to two different seats—winning both—but would never definitely state whether she intended to become prime minister if the Congress Party won. That turned out to be a moot question, as she led the party to its worst defeat in fifty years. Sonia is now deeply mired in Indian politics, not the most suitable place for someone who has always claimed to be largely nonpolitical. She will most likely try and salvage what she can of the good family name for now, and then leave daughter Priyanka the task of full redemption as the fourth prime minister in the Nehru-Gandhi dynasty. Interestingly, Sonia speaks a half dozen languages, but critics charge that her Hindi isn't what should be expected of an Indian prime minister. During Sonia's 1998 campaign speeches, many Indians for the first time had the opportunity to hear her publicly speak the language, a prerequisite tongue for any Indian leader.

Woman to watch

Jayalalitha Jayaram. Film queen–turned–politician, Jayalalitha is often derided as the "Imelda Marcos of India." Leader of the Anna Dravida Munnetra Kazhagam Party, based in Tamil Nadu state, Jayalalitha gave up her movie career to become almost the perpetual bee in the bonnet of all Indian politicians. She ruled Tamil Nadu as chief minister (head of the local state government) for five years until trounced in local elections. Corruption charges alleging that she had salted away at least $19 million followed that defeat, along with the revelation that her wardrobe contained 10,500 saris and 350 pairs of shoes. These disclosures mattered not a whit to her many voting fans, who helped Jayalalitha go national in her politics and push her party into a coalition headed by the right-wing, Hindu-chauvinist Bharatiya Janata Party in 1997. Jayalalitha is flamboyant and volatile, a woman beholden to no one. In spring 1999, she withdrew from the already shaky coalition, then held talks with Sonia Gandhi and the Congress Party about supporting them in a new coalition government. That didn't work out, and India was forced to call a new national election, which the country neither wanted nor needed. The old coalition returned to power, slightly more powerful than before. Jayalalitha returned to Parliament, and, based on her past record, it seems only a matter of time until she'll be stinging someone again.

Woman to watch

Priyanka Gandhi Vadhera. Daughter of Rajiv and Sonia Gandhi, Priyanka wed a jewelry exporter in 1997, but pointedly kept her family name, obviously because of its political potency. Still in her mid-twenties and an educator, Priyanka continues to live in government-furnished housing with the benefit of a security detail, an understandable precaution considering that both her father and grandmother were assassinated. She joined the Youth Congress, an offshoot of the Congress Party, in early 1998, her first foray onto the political scene. Then, Priyanka went on the campaign trail to help her mother in the 1999 election. It was a wise move for both family members; Sonia won both of the seats she was contesting, and the people of India had a chance to see Priyanka close-up. Because that election was such a disaster for Sonia's leadership of the Congress Party, it is probably now Priyanka's turn to try to become the fourth prime minister of the Nehru-Gandhi dynasty. She already appears to be moving in that direction, by letting it be known after the election that she would "consider" serving in Parliament.

First chief minister of a state

Sucheta Kripalani, Uttar Pradesh, 1963

First appointed to cabinet

Rajkumari Amrit Kaur, Minister of Health, 1952

Notable service in cabinet

Uma Bharati, Minister of Human Resources and Development
Renuka Chowdhury, Minister of State for Health and Family Welfare
Indira Gandhi, Minister of Foreign Affairs; Minister of Defense; Minister of Atomic Affairs
Maneka Gandhi, Minister for the Environment and Forests[24]
Sheila Kaul, Minister of Education, Culture, and Social Welfare
Saroj Khaparde, Minister of Health; Minister of Textiles
Sarojini Mahishi, Minister of Tourism and Civil Aviation; Minister of Law, Justice, and Company Affairs
Jayanthi Natarajan, Minister of Civil Aviation; Minister of Parliamentary Affairs
Sushila Nayar, Minister of Health
Vasundhra Raje, Minister of External Affairs
Ratanamala Dhareshwar Savanoor, Minister of State for Planning and Program Implementation
Kanti Singh, Minister of Human Resource Development
Ursa Singh, Minister of Tourism
Kamala Sinha, Minister of State for External Affairs
Sushma Swaraj, Minister of Information and Broadcasting

First appointed ambassador

Vijaya Lakshmi Pandit, Ambassador to the Soviet Union, 1947. In 1949, Madame Pandit was posted as ambassador to the United States, the first female ambassador so accredited.

First governor of a state (postindependence)

Padmaju Naidu, West Bengal, 1956

---

[24]Widow of Sanjay Gandhi, youngest son of Indira Gandhi, Maneka was being groomed to eventually succeed her mother-in-law. After Sanjay's untimely death in a plane crash, Maneka and Indira had a political falling-out. Maneka has since cooperated with an opposing, basically anti-Gandhi faction in the Congress Party.

First governor of a state (preindependence)

Sarojinidevi Naidu, United Provinces, 1947

Legislative

First elected to national legislature
(Sansad, Parliament; Lok Sabha, House of the People)

Ansuyabai Borkar, Indian National Congress
Renu Chakravartty, Communist Party of India
Maragatham Chandrasekhar, Indian Congress Party
Ganga Devi, Indian National Congress
Minimata Agam Dass Guru, Indian National Congress
Subhadra Joshi, Indian National Congress
Anasuyabai Kale, Indian National Congress
Rajkumari Amrit Kaur, Indian National Congress
Bonily Khongmen, Indian National Congress
Sucheta Kripalani, Indian National Congress
Annie Mascarene, Independent
Sushila Ganesh Mavalankar, Indian National Congress
Indira Anant Maydeo, Indian National Congress
Shakuntala Nayar, Hindu Mahasabha
Sheoraj Vati Nehru, Indian National Congress
Uma Nehru, Indian National Congress
Ila Palchoudhri, Indian National Congress
Vijaya Lakshmi Pandit, Indian National Congress
Jayashri Raiji, Indian National Congress
Sushama Sen, Indian National Congress
H. H. Rajmata Kamlendu Mati Shah, Independent
Tarkeshwari Sinha, Indian National Congress
Ammu Swaminadham, Indian National Congress
Manibehn Vallabhbhai, Indian National Congress

All elected April 1952

First elected to national legislature
(Sansad, Parliament; Rajya Sabha, Council of States)

Violet Alva, Indian National Congress
Sharada Bharvava, Indian National Congress
Mayadevi Chettry, Indian National Congress
Pushpa Lata Das, Indian National Congress
Shoila Bala Das, Indian National Congress
Bukmini Devi, Independent
Mona Hensman, Indian National Congress

Chandrawati Lakhanpal, Indian National Congress
Lakshmi N. Menon, Indian National Congress
Lilavati Munshi, Indian National Congress
Savitri Nigam, Indian National Congress
Seeta Parmanand, Indian National Congress
Vijaye Raje, Janta Party
Begum Aziz Rasul, Indian National Congress
Angelina Tiga, Jharkhand Party

All elected April 1952

First head of state legislature

Sushila Nayar, Speaker, Delhi Legislative Assembly, 1952

First appointed to local legislature

Muthalaksmi Reddy, Madras Legislative Council, 1926

Judicial

First appointed judge

Anna Chandy, 1937

First appointed to state supreme court

Anna Chandy, Kerala, 1959

First appointed as state chief justice

Leila Seth, Himachal Pradesh, 1991

First appointed to national supreme court

Meera Sahib Fatima Beevi, 1989

Minority: Dalit

Executive

First woman to head state government

Mayawati, Uttar Pradesh, 1995

Religious Minority: Muslim

Executive

First elected president

Zakir Husain, 1969

First woman elected mayor

Zeenat Naaz, Deoband, Uttar Pradesh, 1996

Religious Minority: Sikh

Executive

First elected president

Zail Singh, 1982

Indonesia

Women

Right to vote: August 17, 1945
To stand for election: August 17, 1945

Executive

Megawati Sukarnoputri, Vice-President, October 28, 1999–present; daughter of the late President Sukarno (1945–1968) and leader of the Indonesian Democratic Party Perjuangan. A suburban housewife first elected to Parliament in 1987, Megawati developed into a highly vocal critic of the Suharto regime (1967–1998). When talk began that she would run for president in 1998, the government moved to undercut her authority: It simply took away her position by installing someone else as head of her party. After the forced resignation of President Suharto in 1998 in the aftermath of Indonesia's economic turmoil, Megawati was back on the campaign stump. Her party took the largest percentage—although not a majority—of the votes for the national legislature in 1999. It first appeared that that body might elect her as the nation's president when it convened. But Megawati doesn't speak freely, and she refused to move toward a coalition with the other parties that might have ensured her election. When the assembly finally voted in October 1999, she found herself outflanked by noted Muslim thinker Abdurrahman Wahid, who won 373 votes to her 313. Some of her followers rioted in the streets, but Wahid defused the situation quickly by choosing her as vice-president—and having the assembly confirm his choice. Wahid is nearly blind and has reportedly suffered two strokes. Although he's mentally alert, there are strong doubts about whether his health will permit him to serve a full five-year term. It's not unlikely that Megawati might still occupy her father's old presidential seat within a couple of years.

Power past

Siti Hardijanti Rukmana, 1968–1998. Eldest daughter of former president Suharto, Siti was active in both politics and business during his tenure. Tutut, as she is commonly known, headed a large business conglomerate, as did all of Suharto's children, and was chairwoman of the central board of her father's ruling Golkar Party. She was the most publicly visible of the former president's brood, all of whom possess great wealth. Like her siblings, Tutut implausibly claims that none of her money or power was due to special concessions made possible by her father's position. Her personal wealth has been estimated at $2 billion; the whole family's wealth has been estimated as $65 billion, or a staggering 20 percent of Indonesia's total resources. There were rumors that her father attempted to have Tutut, now in her late forties, named as his vice-presidential running mate in 1998, but the military brass squelched the idea. Suharto, to the surprise of many, appointed her minister for social welfare in March 1998, when he named his new cabinet for his seventh five-year presidential term. Before she could get a grip on her new position, however, the building housing the ministry was burned during the bloody riots that led to her father's forced resignation. Tutut's power now seems to have vanished for good. Her wealth might be the next to go.

Ex–partner in power

Siti Hartinah (Tien) Suharto, 1968–1996, wife of former president Suharto. Whereas the regime touted Indonesia's first lady as Ibu (Mother) Tien, her detractors caustically dubbed her "Madame Ten Percent" because of her involvement in building the family's powerful economic and political empire. A descendant of Javanese royalty, Tien was her husband's closest confidante during their fifty-two-year marriage, before her death in 1996.

First appointed to cabinet

Maria Ulfah Santoso, Minister of Social Affairs, 1946

Notable service in cabinet

Tutty Alawiyah, Minister of Women's Affairs
Andi Erna Anastasikia, Minister of Housing, Resettlement, and Regional Development
Yustika Syarfuddin Baharsjah, Minister of Agriculture; Minister of Women's Affairs
A. Moerpratomo, Minister of Women's Affairs
Kofiah Inder Parawangsa, Minister of Women's Affairs
Siti Hardijanti Rukmana, Minister of Social Welfare
Haryati Soebadio, Minister of Social Affairs
L. Soetanto, Minister of Women's Affairs
Mien Sugandhi, Minister of Women's Affairs

First appointed ambassador

Laili Rusad, Ambassador to Belgium and Luxembourg, 1959

Legislative

First appointed to national legislature
(Dewan Perwakilan Rakyat, House of Representatives)

Four women, February 1950

First elected to national legislature
(Dewan Perwakilan Rakyat, House of Representatives)

Thirty-three women, July 1971

Iran

Women

Right to vote: September 1963
To stand for election: September 1963

Royalty

Ex–partner in power

Farah Diba Pahlavi, Shahbanou (Empress), December 21, 1959–January 16, 1979. An architectural student in France when she first met Shah Mohammed Reza Pahlavi, Farah married the monarch in 1959. She was his third wife, but the first to bear him a male heir—the reason for his two previous divorces. Farah brought a softening woman's touch to the shah's often autocratic rule and was rewarded by being crowned empress in 1967, during a glittering ceremony in which the shah placed a crown on his own head à la Napoleon. The first woman in Iran's long history to be formally named as regent in her husband's absence or death, Farah exerted a strong feminine influence on her country. A devotee of the arts, she promoted Iranian culture and crafts, along with women's rights and literacy, throughout her husband's reign. When the Islamic revolution toppled Pahlavi in January 1979, Farah left Iran with her husband to join the rest of their family already in exile. Since Pahlavi's death from cancer in July 1979, Farah has lived quietly and out of sight, probably in the United States, rarely making public appearances or speaking out, most likely because she fears assassination by Iran's religious rulers. Her oldest son, Reza, has been proclaimed shah, but it is unlikely that the Pahlavi dynasty, or Farah's influence on Iran, will ever be restored.

Ex–power behind the scene

Princess Ashraf Pahlavi, 1941–1979, twin sister of Shah Mohammed Reza Pahlavi. Ashraf was rumored to be so strong-willed that the shah himself was terrified of her—her father was quoted as saying, "she should have been the man." Head of the Women's Organization of Iran and special ambassador to the United Nations, Ashraf was particularly disliked by the revolutionary forces that overthrew the monarchy. Her son, Shahrian, a captain in Iran's navy, was assassinated by the revolutionaries in 1979. Ashraf herself was also the target of an attempted assassination, when her Rolls-Royce was attacked by gunmen in the south of France.

Executive

Massoumeh Ebtekar, Vice-President, August 9, 1997–present. Ebtekar, who holds a Ph.D. in immunology, was appointed as one of seven vice-presidents in 1997 by newly elected moderate president Mohammed Khatami and given special responsibility for the environment. Although well known in Iran as the acting head of the Bureau of Women's Affairs and as the country's representative to the World Women's Conferences in Nairobi and Beijing, Ebtekar's appointment still came as quite a surprise in the Shia Muslim theocratic state. The appointment was undoubtedly meant as a reward to Iran's women, who had voted overwhelmingly in favor of Khatami and against his staunchly conservative opponent. Ebtekar certainly has the proper activist credentials from the Islamic revolution. She was then known as "Mary," the strident official spokesperson of the militants who occupied the U.S. embassy in Tehran in 1979. Appearing often in television clips shown around the world, "Mary" listed the crimes of America against Iran and denounced the hostages as "spies." Since assuming her new position, Ebtekar has tried to downplay mention in the foreign press of that earlier involvement in Iranian politics. Interestingly, her father was the revolutionary government's first minister of the environment, and she occupies the same office.

Thwarted presidential candidate, 1997

Azam Taleqani, former parliamentarian and daughter of deceased moderate Ayatollah Taleqani. Azam, who was a political activist before the Islamic revolution and was imprisoned by the shah's regime, announced her plans to run in Iran's 1997 presidential election. As soon as she did, the Council of Guardians, a group of hard-core Islamists charged with deciding who was "pure" enough to compete in the election, decreed that she was ineligible for the ballot. According to them, "only recognized statesmen committed to Iran's Islamic government" could be considered as candidates. Besides, they pointed out, the constitution of the Islamic Republic of Iran did not allow women to run for the office. Her ambition thwarted, Azam dropped from sight, but she soon resurfaced as a candidate for the Assembly of Experts, a quaint body with a semilegislative, semireligious standing.

Woman to watch

Faezeh Hashimi, member of Parliament and daughter of ex-president Hashimi Rafsanjani. The outspoken Faezeh is a supporter of moderate president Mohammed Khatami and is Iran's leading woman activist. Although Faezeh, mother of two, rejects the label "feminist," it's difficult to call her anything but that. Long an advocate of women's participation in sports, when her father was president she headed up the Islamic Countries Women's Sports Solidarity Games. Faezeh often traveled abroad with Rafsanjani on state visits and has even suggested that a woman could be president of Iran, but has denied that she wants the job. In 1998, Faezeh launched Iran's first women's daily newspaper, *Zan (Woman)*. She has used the newspaper as a forum in which to tout her views on women's rights and to assail Iran's more conservative elements. One of her targets pulled her into court, where her newspaper was charged with publishing "lies" over the alleged harassment of some of the country's more moderate figures. Does she want to be Iran's first female president? Surprisingly, this would not be an unlikely scenario, especially if Faezeh can merge the country's moderate males with the female vote.

Potential power

Maryam Rajavi. President of the National Council of Resistance of Iran (NCR), Maryam has been designated to become president of Iran should the NCR ever achieve power. An outgrowth of the leftist People's Mujahedin, which helped overthrow the shah, the NCR is headed jointly by Maryam and her husband, Massoud. The group now hopes, probably unrealistically, to oust the Shia Muslim mullahs who run Iran. Currently residing somewhere in the deserts of Iraq, Maryam controls an armed force of 30,000 soldiers (dubbed the National Liberation Army), 35 percent of whom are female, as are 70 percent of the officer corps. Saddam Hussein's Iraqi regime provides arms, money, and living space for Maryam's army, finding it a convenient proxy with which to threaten archrival Iran. It's highly doubtful that Maryam will ever be president of Iran, but she could be a power player if the clerical regime ever begins to suffer from the internal rumblings that toppled the shah.

First appointed to cabinet

Farrokhrou Parsa, Minister of Education, 1968

Notable service in cabinet

Mahnaz Afkhami, Minister of Women's Affairs
Massoumeh Ebtekar, Minister of the Environment
Aazam Nuri, Deputy Minister of Legal and Parliamentary Affairs

First appointed ambassador

Mehrangiz Dolatshahi, Ambassador to Denmark, 1976

First appointed mayor (after the 1979 Islamic revolution)

Zahra Sadrazam Noori, a district of Tehran, 1996

Legislative

First appointed to national legislature (Senate, Upper House)

Mehrangiz Manushehrian
Shamsolmoluk Mossahab

Both appointed September 1963

First elected to national legislature
(Majlis, National Assembly, Lower House)

Mehrangiz Dolatshahi, Progressive Center Party (later Iran Novin)
Nayereh Ebtehadj-Samie, Progressive Center Party (later Iran Novin)
Shokat-Malek Jahanbanii, Progressive Center Party (later Iran Novin)
Nezhat Nafissi, Mardom Party
Farrokhrou Parsa, Progressive Center Party (later Iran Novin)
Hadjar Tarbiat, Progressive Center Party (later Iran Novin)

All elected September 1963

Minority: Armenian

Legislative

First woman elected to national legislature
(Majlis, National Assembly, Lower House)

Emma Aghayan, 1974

Iraq

Women

Right to vote: 1958;[25] February 1980
To stand for election: 1958; February 1980

Executive

First appointed to cabinet

Dhia Jaher, Minister of Economics, 1949. Another source states that the first woman was appointed to the Iraqi cabinet in 1958, as minister of social action. Attempts will continue to find the definite answer.

First appointed ambassador

Not yet identified. Mention has been found of a female ambassador supposedly appointed in 1948.

Legislative

First elected to national legislature (Majlis Watani, National Assembly)

Sixteen women, June 1980

Judicial

First appointed judge

One woman, 1948

[25]Women were granted the right to vote and stand for election on March 26, 1958, under a constitutional amendment approved by the parliament of the Kingdom of Iraq. That regime was overthrown during the summer of 1958, before any elections with female participation took place.

Ireland

Women

Right to vote: June 2, 1918; July 2, 1928
To stand for election: June 2, 1918; July 2, 1928[26]

International Notable: **Mary Bourke Robinson** was appointed United Nations Commissioner for Human Rights in 1997.

Executive

Mary McAleese, President, November 11, 1997–present. McAleese, a member of the Fianna Fáil Party and a resident of Northern Ireland—but holder of an Irish passport, which entitled her to seek the Irish presidency—succeeded another woman, Mary Bourke Robinson, in the top spot. This marked the first instance anywhere in which one female elected president gave way to another (although a nonelected interim presidential commission separated their administrations). The October 30, 1997, election won by McAleese was notable because four out of the five contenders were female, with the lone male finishing last (see below).

Power past

Mary Bourke Robinson, President, December 3, 1990–September 12, 1997. Robinson, an attorney and member of the Labor Party, a small, left-of-center group in Irish politics, was a surprise victor in the 1990 presidential election. Once she occupied the high ceremonial office, Robinson achieved, and managed to maintain, strong popularity with the Irish public. She resigned early in order to accept a position with the United Nations.

Notable presidential candidates, 1997

Mary Banotti, candidate of the Fine Gael party and former candidate for the Irish Senate (1982) and Dáil (1983). Banotti was serving her third term in the European Parliament when she launched her presidential bid, in which she placed second with nearly 30 percent of the vote.

---

[26] Voting and electoral rights were granted to women over thirty years of age in 1918; in 1928, women were granted the same voting and electoral rights as men.

Adi Roche, candidate of the Labor Party, Democratic Left, and Green Party. A humanitarian noted for her work as executive director of the Chernobyl Children's Project, Roche finished fourth with 7 percent in the balloting.

Rosemary (Dana) Scallon, Independent, nominated by several county councils. An internationally known singer and winner of the 1970 Eurovision song contest, Scallon was living in the United States, working with the Charismatic movement and appearing in a television series broadcast on the U.S. Catholic Cable network, when she abruptly returned to Ireland and ran for president. Her position as a nonparty candidate touting traditional Christian values and morals won her third place, with almost 14 percent of the vote.

First appointed to cabinet

Countess Constance Gore-Booth Markiewicz was appointed minister of labor in the first cabinet of the Irish Free State in 1919; she did not actually serve, as she was in prison at the time due to her involvement in the struggle for Irish independence.
Máire Geoghegan-Quinn, Minister for the Gaeltacht, 1979

Notable service in cabinet

Niamh Bhreathnach, Minister of Education
Sile de Valera, Minister of Arts, Culture, and the Gaeltacht
Eileen Demond, Minister of Health and Social Affairs
Máire Geoghegan-Quinn, Minister of European Affairs
Mary Harney, Deputy Prime Minister; Minister of Enterprise and Employment
Gemma Hussey, Minister of Education
Enda Kerry, Minister of Tourism and Trade
Liz McManus, Minister of Housing and Urban Renewal
Liz O'Donnell, Minister of Overseas Development; Minister of Human Rights
Mary O'Rourke, Minister of Education
Nora Owen, Minister of Justice
Mary Wallace, Minister of Equality and Disability

First named ambassador

Josephine McNeill, Ambassador to the Netherlands, 1950

Legislative

First elected to national legislature (Dáil Éireann, House of Representatives)

Countess Constance Gore-Booth Markiewicz, 1919 (*see also* United Kingdom, Women, Legislative)

First elected to national legislature (Seanad Éireann, Senate)

Tras Honan, August 1977

Head of national legislature

Tras Honan, Seanad Éireann (Senate), May 13, 1982–February 23, 1983; 1987–1989

Judicial

First appointed to supreme court

Susan Denham, 1992

Minority: Gay

Legislative

First elected to national legislature (Seanad Éireann, Senate)

David Norris, Independent, 1987

ISRAEL

Women

Right to vote: May 15, 1948
To stand for election: May 15, 1948

Executive

Power past

Golda Mabovitch Meir, Prime Minister, March 17, 1969–June 2, 1974. Meir, a former foreign affairs and labor minister (and former U.S. citizen), became Israel's fourth prime minister on the death of Levi Eshkol in 1969. She guided Israel for five years, resigning in the aftermath of criticisms resulting from the barely successful 1973 Yom Kippur conflict against Israel's Arab neighbors.

First appointed to cabinet

Golda Meir, Minister of Labor, 1949

Notable service in cabinet

Shumalit Aloni, Minister Without Portfolio; Minister of Education; Minister of Communications; Minister of Arts and Sciences
Soshana Arbeli-Almozlino, Minister of Health
Sarah Doron, Minister Without Portfolio
Dalia Itzik, Minister of the Environment
Limor Livnat, Minister of Communications
Ora Namir, Minister of Labor and Social Affairs
Yuli Tamir, Minister of Immigrant Absorption

First appointed ambassador

Golda Meir, Ambassador to the Soviet Union, 1948

First elected mayor of a major city

Miriam Feierberg, Likud Party, Netanya, 1998

Legislative

First elected to national legislature (Knesset, Parliament)

Rachel Cohen-Kagn
Hasia Drori
Buba Eidelson
Faiga Ilanit
Chana Lamdan
Golda Meir
Ada Mimon
Devorah Netzer
Shoshana Parsitz
Esther Raziel-naor
Yehudit Simhoni

All elected January 1949

Minority: Arab

Executive

First appointed to cabinet

Nawaf Masalha, Deputy Foreign Minister, 1999

First woman elected mayor

Violet Khouri, town of Kafr Yassif

Legislative

First elected to national legislature (Knesset, Parliament)

Sif-Aladin al-Zoabi
Amin-Salim Jarjura
Tufik Tubi

All elected January 1949

First woman elected to national legislature (Knesset, Parliament)

Hussnia Jabara, Meretz Party, 1999

Judicial

First appointed to supreme court

Abdul Rahman Zuabi, 1998

Minority: Ethiopian-Israeli

Legislative

First elected to national legislature (Knesset, Parliament)

Addisu Messele, Labor Party, 1996

Minority: Lesbian

Executive

First elected to public office

Michal Eden, Meretz Party, Tel Aviv city council, November 1998

Religious Minority: Druze

Executive

First appointed ambassador

Walid Mansour, Ambassador to Vietnam, 1999

Legislative

First elected to national legislature (Knesset, Parliament)

Amel Nasser al-Din, Likud Party

Palestinian Authority

Executive

Notable presidential candidate, 1996

Samiha Khalil. A social worker and political activist, Khalil founded the Society of Imash el-Usrah in 1965, a family welfare group that provided Palestinian women with educational services and vocational training. Khalil was the sole opposition candidate to challenge Yasir Arafat for the position of executive of the Palestine National Authority. In losing, she did manage to garner more than 9 percent of the vote. Khalil was the first woman to run for the top executive position in a country or political entity in the Arab world.

First appointed to cabinet

Intissar al-Wazir, Minister of Social Affairs, 1994

Notable service in cabinet

Hanan Ashwari, Minister of Higher Education

First appointed diplomatic representative

Lailah Shaheed, accredited to France, 1994

Legislative

First elected to legislature (Palestinian Legislative Council)

Hanan Ashrawi, Independent
Dalal Abdul Hafeth Salameh, Fateh
Jamileh Ahmad Saydem, Fateh
Rawya al-Shawwa, Independent
Intissar al-Wazir, Fateh

All elected 1996

Italy

Women

Right to vote: February 1, 1945
To stand for election: February 1, 1945

Executive

Notable presidential candidate, 1999

Emma Bonino. Former European Union commissioner for humanitarian affairs, Bonino tried a novel tactic in her quest for the Italian presidency: She actually campaigned openly for the position. She publicly announced her candidacy, then appealed to Italians through a newspaper campaign to press their members of Parliament to name her as a candidate. The president, chiefly a ceremonial position, is elected by Parliament. By tradition, all campaigns are waged behind the scenes, and parties put forward the names of their candidates in private. Bonino, a former Radical Party president, does not shy away from unusual situations. In September 1997, she was arrested briefly by Taliban fighters in Afghanistan. On a visit there in her capacity as EU commissioner for humanitarian affairs, Bonino witnessed Muslim fanatics beat several members of her group after they were charged with taking photographs of Afghan women in a hospital.

Notable presidential candidates, 1992

Women who ran for president in 1992 included **Tina Anselmi,** former minister of education and social affairs; **Eleonora Chiavarelli Moro,** widow of murdered former prime minister Aldo Moro; and **Leonilde Iotti,** former head of the Chamber of Deputies and one of the first women in Italy elected to Parliament.

Ex–power behind the scene

Edda Mussolini Ciano, 1930–1944. Daughter of fascist dictator "Il Duce" Benito Mussolini and wife of his foreign minister, Count Galeazzo Ciano. Edda, the darling in her father's eye of his four children, was the most politically prominent of Benito's brood. As his most forceful child, she was undoubtedly the woman to whom he paid the most attention. Although her husband Ciano, as foreign minister, brokered the treaty that established Italy's alliance with Nazi Germany, Edda, who was even more pro-German and a close personal friend of the Hermann Goerings, always claimed that she was the moving force behind the pact. Her father didn't permit his fondness for Edda to stand in his way, however, when he was betrayed. After being dumped from office and imprisoned by war-weary plotters in his inner circle, and then freed by German rescuers, Mussolini promptly had Edda's husband executed along with three other coconspirators. The slaughter of his son-in-law was all for naught, however. When the war ended, Benito himself met with a similar fate: He was shot by partisans in 1945, and his body was strung up in a town square. Edda retreated to a private life, alternating her time between a home in Rome and a villa on Capri. She died in 1995 at age eighty-four, ignored by the Italians who had once so lustily cheered her father as the man "who made the trains run on time."

First appointed to cabinet

Tina Anselmi, Minister of Social Affairs and Health, 1976

Notable service in cabinet

Susanna Agnelli, Foreign Minister
Lara Balbo, Minister of Equal Opportunities
Katia Bellilo, Minister of Regional Affairs
Rosaria Bindi, Minister of Health
Franca Fallucci, Minister of Education
Anna Finocchiaro, Minister of Equality
Rosa Russo Jervolina, Minister of the Interior; Minister Without Portfolio
Giovanna Melandri, Minister of Culture and Sports
Livia Turco, Minister of Family and Social Affairs

First appointed ambassador

Graziela Simbolotti, Ambassador to the Republic of Korea, 1985. Mention might also be made of **Jolanda Brunetti Goetz,** who served in Burma in 1980 with diplomatic accreditation.

First elected mayor of a major city

Elda Pucci, Palermo, 1983

Legislative

Potential power

Alessandra Mussolini, 1992–present, parliamentarian and granddaughter of dictator Benito Mussolini. With her unusual pedigree (she is the daughter of Benito's youngest son, Romano, and actress Sophia Loren's sister), Alessandra first tried her hand in films. After a series of B movies, she switched to right-wing politics, joining the neofascist National Alliance Party. Alessandra has been elected to Parliament twice on that party's ticket and also ran twice (unsuccessfully) for mayor of Naples. Young—she's in her thirties—Alessandra could have a long, and possibly interesting, political future ahead of her if she makes a mark in the legislative chamber or finally wins city hall in Naples.

Passing fancy

Ilona Anna Staller, 1987–1994. Staller, a parliamentarian, is better known as Ciccolina ("little meaty one"), a nickname from her earlier career as a porn film star. The Hungarian-born Staller made quite a splash with her unconventional decision to forgo the world of paid sex for the world of politics. The move shouldn't have been completely unexpected, however. In 1979, she formed La Lista del Sol (the Sun Party), which she now claims was Europe's first "green" party. Her political career really kicked into high gear after she joined the Radical Party. In 1987, she was elected to her first term in the lower house of the Italian Parliament on the Radical ticket. Although she pushed an exotic mix of sex and environmental proposals, her parliamentary career was more noteworthy for its bizarre aspects. On one occasion, she offered herself to Iraq's Saddam Hussein if he would free Western hostages he'd taken shortly before the Gulf War broke out. Staller married American avant-garde artist Jeff Koons—they posed naked together atop their wedding cake—but the couple divorced two years later. In 1994, she decided against seeking reelection, thus ending one of the more unusual female parliamentary careers in any country.

First elected to national legislature (Constituent Assembly)

Adele Bei, Italian Communist Party
Bianca Bianchi, Italian Socialist Party
Laura Bianchini, Christian Democrat
Elisabetta Conci, Christian Democrat
Filomena Delli Castelli, Christian Democrat
Maria Federici, Christian Democrat
Angela Gotelli, Christian Democrat
Angela Maria Guidi Cingolani, Christian Democrat
Leonilde Iotti, Italian Communist Party
Teresa Mattei, Italian Communist Party
Angelina Merlin, Italian Socialist Party
Angiola Minella, Italian Communist Party
Rita Montagnana Togliatti, Italian Communist Party
Maria Nicotra, Christian Democrat
Teresa Noce Longo, Italian Communist Party
Ottavia Penna Buscemi, Uono Qualunque
Elettra Pollastrini, Italian Communist Party
Maria Maddalena Rossi, Italian Communist Party
Nadia Spano Gallico, Italian Communist Party

Vittoria Titomanlio, Christian Democrat
Maria de Unterrichter Jervolino, Christian Democrat

All elected June 1946

Head of national legislature

Irene Pivetti, Camera dei Deputati (Chamber of Deputies), 1994–1998
Leonilde Iotti, Camera dei Deputati (Chamber of Deputies), 1979–1992

Judicial

First appointed to supreme court

One woman, 1981

Minority: African-Italian

Legislative

First elected to office

Dacia Valent, Communist Party, European Parliament, 1989. In 1994, Valent ran unsuccessfully for the Italian Parliament on a "Rainbow Coalition of Citizen's Rights" ticket from Naples, hoping to become the first black to be seated there. Her opponent, and the winner, was the above-mentioned Alessandra Mussolini.

JAMAICA

Women

Right to vote: November 20, 1944
To stand for election: November 20, 1944

Executive

Failed bid for power

Portia Simpson, 1992. When Michael Manley resigned as prime minister due to ill health in 1992, Simpson, a cabinet member, was a leading contender to succeed him as both chief of the People's National Party and prime minister. In the end, she lost the party vote to Percival James Patterson but was named minister of labor, social security, and sports in his new cabinet.

First appointed to cabinet

Rose Leon, Minister of Local Government, March 1972. Leon had been the first woman appointed to a preindependence cabinet when she was made minister of health and labor in 1953.

Notable service in cabinet

Maxine Henry-Wilson, Minister Without Portfolio
Princess May Laws, Minister of Youth and Commercial Development
Lucielle Moir, Minister of Foreign Affairs
Portia Simpson, Minister of Labor, Welfare, and Sport

First appointed ambassador

Carmen Parris, Ambassador to France, 1975

Legislative

First elected to colonial legislature (Parliament)

Iris Collins-Williams, Jamaica Labor Party, North Western Saint James, December 14, 1944

First elected to national legislature (House of Representatives)

Enid Bennett, Jamaica Labor Party
Esmie Grant, Jamaica Labor Party

Both elected February 1967

First appointed to national legislature (Senate)

Venetia McDonald
Elsie Myrtle-Bennett

Both appointed February 1967

Head of national legislature

Violet Neilson, House of Representatives, 1997–present
Syringa Marshall-Burnett, Senate, 1996–present
Jeanette Grant Woodham, Senate, 1983–1989

Minority: Lebanese

Executive

First to serve as prime minister

Edward Seaga, Jamaica Labor Party, 1981

Japan

Women

Right to vote: December 12, 1945; February 24, 1947[27]
To stand for election: December 12, 1945; February 24, 1947

International Notable: **Sadako Ogata** is United Nations High Commissioner for Refugees.

Royalty

Michiko, Empress, January 7, 1989–present. The first commoner to wed into the Japanese royal family, Michiko virtually disappeared behind the layer of obscurity that traditionally shields the royal household. Her most notable moments have been when she and her husband, Emperor Akihito, travel abroad on state visits. Reportedly she lost her voice for a period of time in the mid-1990s. Rumors attributed the affliction to her frustration at living such a sheltered, confined life.

Potential power

Masako, Crown Princess. Married to Crown Prince Naruhito in June 1993, Masako could eventually be the catalyst that brings the Japanese royal family out into the open, since she's both a commoner and much more worldly than her mother-in-law. She speaks five languages, attended both Harvard and Oxford, and worked in the Japanese Foreign Ministry, where she showed great promise before deciding to forgo her career for a royal marriage. Her husband supposedly assured her that their life—once he ascended the throne—would be much freer than that of his parents. Masako's biggest disappointment to the Japanese thus far has been that after six years of marriage, she still has not budded an heir to the Chrysanthemum throne.

Executive

First appointed to cabinet

Masa Nakayama, Minister of Public Health and Social Welfare, 1960

---

[27]In 1945, women were granted the right to vote in elections for the House of Representatives (lower house of the Diet) and 1947 for the House of Councillors (upper house of the Diet).

Notable service in cabinet

Ryoko Akamatsu, Minister of Education
Wakako Hironaka, Minister of the Environment
Michiko Ishii, Minister of the Environment
Manae Kubota, Minister of Economic Planning
Mayumi Moriyama, Minister of the Environment; Minister of Education
Ritsuko Nagao, Minister of Justice
Seiko Noda, Minister of Post and Telecommunications
Sumiko Takahara, Minister of Economic Planning

First appointed ambassador

Nobuko Takahashi, Ambassador to Denmark, 1980

First elected mayor

Akagi Hisa, Uueno Mura, Ibaragi prefecture, 1947

First elected city governor

Kitamura Harue, Ashiya, Hyogo prefecture, 1991

Legislative

First elected to national legislature (Shugi-In, House of Representatives)

Hatsu Ando, Independent
Hatsu Imai, Liberal Party
Toshiko Karasawa, Communist Party
Shizue Kato, Socialist Party
Chiyo Kimura, Independent
Tsuruyo Kondo, Independent
Mitsu Koro, Independent
Haru Koshihara, Independent
Toshiko Matsuo, Socialist Party
Tenkoukou Matsutani, Independent
Hanako Miki, Independent
Kiyoko Miki, Independent
Hideko Mogami, Progress Party
Yone Moriyama, Progress Party
Kiyo Murashima, Progress Party
Tama Nakayama, Independent
Ito Niimatsu, Socialist Party
Misu Nomura, Independent
Kimi Ohashi, Independent

Yoshie Oishi, Independent
Tei Saito, Progress Party
Chiyo Sakakibara, Socialist Party
Hisa Sawada, Socialist Party
En Sugahara, Progress Party
Keiko Sugita, Liberal Party
Kiyo Takeda, Liberal Party
Shigeyo Takeuchi, Liberal Party
Utako Takeuchi, Independent
Tatsu Tanaka, Independent
Satoko Tokano, Independent
Fusa Tomita, Liberal Party
Haru Wazaki, Independent
Shizue Yamaguchi, Socialist Party
Harue Yamashita, Progress Party
Tsune Yamashita, Independent
Michiko Yamazaki, Socialist Party
Fumiko Yoneyama, Independent
Hisa Yoneyama, Socialist Party
Sei Yoshida, Independent

All elected April 1946

Head of national legislature

Takako Doi, House of Representatives, 1993–1997

Judicial

First appointed to supreme court

Hisako Nobuko Takahashi, 1994

Minority: Ainu

Legislative

First elected to national legislature
(Shugi-In, House of Representatives)

Shigeru Kayano, Social Democratic Party, 1994. Two years after his election, Kayano released the first comprehensive dictionary of the Ainu language; the Ainus are descended from the original inhabitants of the Japanese archipelago.

Minority: European

Legislative

First elected to municipal assembly

Marutei Tsurunen (Martti Turnen), Yugawara, Kanagawa prefecture, 1992. Tsurunen, a naturalized Japanese citizen born in Finland, has also made two unsuccessful attempts to win a seat in the House of Councillors, the upper house of the Japanese Parliament. He lost in 1995 by 30,000 votes but came closer to winning in 1998, losing by only 8,000 votes.

Minority: Korean

Legislative

First elected to national legislature (Shugi-In, House of Representatives)

Pak Ch'un-gŭm, 1932

Jordan

Women

Right to vote: 1974
To stand for election: 1974[28]

Royalty

Rania al-Yassin, Queen, February 7, 1999–present, wife of King Abdullah II. Rania's ultimate role in Jordanian politics will stem from her family background: She's a Palestinian. Since the country's population is equally divided between Jordanians and Palestinians, Rania will most likely become a symbol of the special relationship between the two peoples, helping to build their unity. Her husband is Western educated, has a Christian mother, and speaks weak Arabic; the fact that he has a Muslim Palestinian wife should factor as a plus for him in Jordanian political life.

Rania was born in Kuwait and lived there with her family until 1991, when, in the aftermath of the Gulf War, many Palestinian families were expelled on the suspicion that they had aided the Iraqi attackers. After relocating to Jordan, Rania married Abdullah in 1993. She has taken an interest in social issues such as helping battered and abused children.

Ex–partner in power

Noor (née Lisa Najeeb Halaby), 1978–1999. American-born (to a prominent family of Arab descent) fourth wife and widow of Jordan's King Hussein, Noor met her husband while working as a consultant for Royal Jordanian Airlines. Throughout their marriage, Noor worked with her husband to promote the country's culture, with a special personal emphasis on the steady betterment of conditions for the nation's women and children. The tireless efforts of the royal couple on behalf of their nation helped Jordan avoid much of the violence that has beset other Middle Eastern countries in recent decades. Often thought of as one of the more fragile monarchs in the Arab world—and likely to be toppled at any time, like his cousin King Faisal of Iraq in 1958—Hussein proved to be extraordinarily enduring. He died in 1999 of cancer. Shortly before his death, Hussein chose his eldest son, Abdullah (by his second, British wife, Muna), as his heir. After his ascension to the throne, Abdullah announced that his crown prince would be Hamzah, the eldest son of Hussein and Noor.

---

[28]Women actually exercised the right to vote and stand for election for the first time in 1989.

With her husband's death, Noor's influence over Jordan has receded, although she could again exert a measure of power if her son Hamzah indeed eventually follows his half brother Abdullah to the throne.

Executive

First appointed to the cabinet

Ina'am Mufti, Minister of Social Development, 1979

Notable service in cabinet

Rima Khalaf Hneidi, Minister of Planning
Hanna Owdeh, Minister of Finance
Leila Sharaf, Minister of Culture; Minister of Information

First appointed ambassador

Laurice Hlass, Ambassador to the United Nations, 1969

First elected mayor

Iman Fteimat, Kherbit al-Wahadneh, 1995

Legislative

First appointed to national legislature (Majlis al-Aayan, Senate)

Leila Sharaf, November 1989

First elected to national legislature (Majlis al-Nuwaab, House of Deputies)

Toujan Faisal, November 29, 1993

Judicial

First appointed judge

One woman, 1996

Kazakhstan

Women

Right to vote: January 31, 1924
To stand for election: January 31, 1924

Executive

First appointed to cabinet (Kazakh SSR)

Zaure S. Omarova, Minister of Social Affairs, 1966

First appointed to cabinet (after independence)

Akmoral Arystanbekova, Minister of Foreign Affairs, 1989

Notable service in cabinet

Zaure Kadyrova, Minister of Social Affairs
Zianulla Kaimzhanov, Minister of Revenues
Natalya Korzhova, Minister of Labor and Social Security

First appointed ambassador

Akmoral Arystanbekova, Ambassador to the United Nations, 1992

Legislative

First elected to national legislature (Parliament)[29]

Twenty-four women, March 1990

Head of national legislature

Zinayida Fedotova, Speaker of Parliament

---

[29]Women from Kazakhstan were previously elected to the Supreme Soviet of the Kazakh Soviet Socialist Republic and to the Parliament of the Soviet Union.

Kenya

Women

Right to vote: December 12, 1963
To stand for election: December 12, 1963[30]

Executive

Notable presidential candidate, 1997

Charity Kaluki Ngilu. Businesswoman and parliamentarian, Charity was elected to Parliament in 1992 on the Democratic Party ticket from Kitui Central, east of Nairobi. Charity belongs to the Kamba tribe, is married and the mother of three children, and owns several small businesses. She left the Democratic Party to run for president on the Social Democratic Party ticket, and she placed fifth with nearly 8 percent of the vote against President Daniel arap Moi, who was running for his fifth term. Despite her unsuccessful run, for which she had to give up her parliamentary seat, it's likely that Charity will continue to play a role in Kenyan politics at some level.

Ex–power behind the scene

Margaret Wambui Kenyatta, 1963–1978, daughter of Kenya's first president, Jomo Kenyatta. One of her father's closest advisers, Margaret never assumed an overly active role in Kenyan national politics, preferring to operate behind the scenes. Her public participation was more on the local level. She was a city councillor in Nairobi, then served as mayor of that city from 1970 to 1976. After her father's death in 1978, new president Daniel arap Moi treated her gingerly, and with some deference. He appointed her as ambassador to an agency of the United Nations, where she played a leading role during the UN Women's Conference held in Nairobi in 1986. Shortly after that, Margaret retired from an active role in Kenyan politics.

---

[30]The right to vote and stand for office had been given to European women in Kenya in 1919; in 1956, those rights were extended to African men and women under certain conditions related to educational level and property ownership. In 1963, all Kenyans, regardless of color and other previously restricting factors, were given the right to vote and stand for election.

First appointed to cabinet

Winifred Nyiva Mwendwa, Minister of Culture and Social Services, 1995

First appointed ambassador

Margaret Wambui Kenyatta, Ambassador to the United Nations Environmental Program, 1977

First elected mayor

Grace M. A. Onyango, Kisumu, 1965

Legislative

First elected to national legislature (Bunge, National Assembly)

Phoebe Asiyo, Kenya African National Union, December 1969

Minority: Asian

Legislative

First elected to national legislature (Bunge, National Assembly)

Krishna Guatama, 1979

First elected to office

Manibal A. Desai, Nairobi municipal council, 1917

Judicial

First appointed judge

Chunilal B. Madan, 1961

Minority: European

Executive

First appointed to cabinet

Bruce McKenzie, Minister of Agriculture and Animal Husbandry, 1963

Legislative

First elected to national legislature (Bunge, National Assembly)

Phillip Leakey, 1979

Religious Minority: Muslim

Legislative

First woman elected to national legislature (Bunge, National Assembly)

Marere Wamwachai, Kenya African National Union, 1997

Kiribati

Women

Right to vote: November 15, 1967
To stand for election: November 15, 1967

Executive

First appointed to cabinet

Tekarei Russell, Minister of Health, 1975

First appointed ambassador

No woman yet appointed

Legislative

First elected to colonial legislature (House of Representatives)

Tekarei Russell, 1971

First elected to national legislature
(Maneaba Ni Maungatabu, House of Assembly)

Fenua Tamuera, July 25, 1990. Tamuera was elected in a special by-election to replace her husband, who was lost at sea in an accident. The next woman in the legislature, **Koriri Muller,** elected in 1992, also won a special by-election. After winning these special elections, neither woman sought reelection in the next regularly scheduled election. It was not until September 30, 1998, that a woman (**Teima Onorio**) was able to win a seat during a regularly scheduled election.

Democratic People's Republic of Korea

Women

Right to vote: July 30, 1946
To stand for election: July 30, 1946

Executive

Ex–Red Queen, partner in power

Kim Song-ae, 1963–1994. Second (and possibly third) wife of longtime dictator, the "Great Leader" Kim Il-sung. Rumored to be a secretary to the dictator's security guards when they first met, Song-ae quickly improved her station in life. After marrying Kim, a position on the communist Korean Worker's Party Central Committee came her way, as did a seat in the pseudo-Parliament (the Supreme People's Assembly) and a leadership position in the Women's Union. The fly in her ointment was always her stepson, Kim Jong-il, whose mother had died when he was a small child. Kim Jong-il was twenty-one years old when his father remarried, and already quite a spoiled brat. Although Song-ae produced several children (rumors say three boys and a girl), she could never move them ahead of her stepson in her husband's eyes.

Her life with Kim Il-sung was certainly bizarre. His first (or second) wife, the mother of Kim Jong-il, was proclaimed a great national heroine in the mid-1970s; statues of her popped up across the country, while a national museum dedicated to her life was opened. It certainly must have been galling to Song-ae to see such lavish attention devoted to a woman she was trying to supplant in the affections of both her husband and the nation. When Kim Il-sung died in 1994, after having groomed Kim Jong-il to become the nation's "Dear Leader" and succeed him, tales swirled of palace intrigue and military plots to push the heir apparent aside in favor of one of Song-ae's children. In April 1998, she was not reelected as head of the women's group, and she was dropped four months later from her parliamentary seat. Given the ruthlessness of her stepson, one can only wonder what fate has finally befallen Song-ae and her children. One ominous sign is that statues of Kim Il-sung and his first wife continue to be unveiled, but no mention is ever made of his last wife.

First appointed to cabinet

Ho Chung-suk, Minister of Culture, 1948

Notable service in cabinet

Kim Pok-sin, Deputy Prime Minister
Pak Chong-ae, Minister of Agriculture
Pak Yong-sin, Minister of Culture
Yi Ho-hyok, Minister of Foodstuffs
Yi Yang-suk, Minister of Commerce
Yun Gi-jong, Minister of Finance

First appointed ambassador

Not yet identified

Legislative

First elected to national legislature
(Choe Ko In Min Hoe Ui, Supreme People's Assembly)

Sixty-nine women, August 1948

Republic of Korea

Women

Right to vote: July 17, 1948
To stand for election: July 17, 1948

Royalty

Continuing influence from the past

Min Ja-young (Myungsung), Empress/Queen, March 21, 1866–October 8, 1895. Twenty-fifth regent ruler of the Choson dynasty, Queen Min was one of the first vehemently anti-Japanese Korean politicians of modern times. Nineteenth-century Korea had no strong kings, only a series of child kings and weaklings controlled by queen dowagers and their clans. Such was Min's role. She was married at age sixteen to the vacillating, weak-willed Emperor Kojong (1863–1907), who was controlled first by his regent father and a previous dowager queen, then by his wife after she disposed of her rivals. Queen Min, along with her family clan and an assorted coterie of supporters, fiercely fought against foreign influences; they were opposed to most efforts at modernizing or Westernizing Korea, except when they served to help keep power in the clan's hands. The Mins were in the thick of the various court intrigues that revolved around the efforts of the great powers to exert influence over the peninsula. In 1895, when the Japanese realized they were on the verge of losing the Korean power game—against rivals China and Russia—they began to plot Queen Min's removal from the scene. Miura Goro, a Japanese minister resident in Korea at the time, was the ringleader. Using troops stationed in the country, ostensibly to help train the Korean army, the Japanese attacked Min's royal residence, Kyongbok Palace, stabbed the queen to death, then burned the body with kerosene, an immense sacrilege to Korean sensibilities. King Kojong huddled in fear in the Russian legation in Seoul for a period of time thereafter, but Russia's defeat in the 1905 Russo-Japanese War, fought largely in the vicinity of the Korean peninsula, proved that they would no longer be effective allies. Kojong somehow remained on his throne for another twelve years (and was succeeded by a son, who ruled for three years after that), but all the while Korean independence was gradually slipping away. By 1910, the sham was over. The new emperor was deposed and the country proclaimed a Japanese colony. Years later, Queen Min's death was avenged by Kim Yu, a Korean patriot, who assassinated the leader of her murder plot.

When Japan was defeated at the end of World War II and withdrew from Korea, a new power struggle was unleashed on the peninsula, this time between the communists led by the

North's Kim Il-sung and the regime of Syngman Rhee in the South. In 1948, Queen Min's avenger, Kim Yu, surprisingly emerged as a possible "third path" between these two, which might have led to an early reunification. But he too met the same fate as his queen: assassination by political enemies. Korea remains divided today, each half ruled by the successors of Kim Il-sung and Syngman Rhee. Both Koreas still harbor strong anti-Japanese feelings, much of which originated during the reign of Queen Min. Do Koreans still remember their last queen? Most certainly. In 1998, a big-budget musical extravaganza titled *The Last Empress,* celebrating Queen Min's life, opened in Seoul, London, and New York.

Executive

Notable presidential candidate, 1960

Yim Yong-sin Louise. Yim was the first female cabinet minister and first woman elected to Parliament in South Korea, and was a candidate for vice-president in 1954 on the ticket of a small left-wing party. She received less than 1 percent of the vote.

First appointed to cabinet

Yim Yong-sin Louise, Minister of Commerce and Industry, 1948

Notable service in cabinet

Cho Kyung-hee, Minister of Political Affairs
Hwang San-sung, Minister of the Environment
Joo Yang-ja, Minister of Health and Public Welfare
Kim Chong-rye, Minister of Health
Kim Jung-rye, Minister of Health and Social Affairs
Kim Kop-hyun, Minister of Political Affairs
Kim Mo-im, Minister of Health and Public Welfare
Kim Ok-kil, Minister of Education
Kim Sook-hee, Minister of Education
Kim Whal-ran, Minister of Information
Kim Young-jung, Minister of Political Affairs
Kim Yun-duk, Minister of Political Affairs
Lee Yun-sook, Minister of Political Affairs
Pak Hyon-suk, Minister Without Portfolio
Pak Yang-shil, Minister of Health and Social Affairs
Shin Nak-kyun, Minister of Culture and Tourism
Song Jeong-sook, Minister of Health and Social Affairs

First appointed ambassador

Lee In-ho, Ambassador to Finland, 1996. In 1948, **Mo Yun-suk,** as special ambassador, led a delegation to a UN General Assembly meeting in Paris. That delegation won official UN recognition that the Republic of Korea was an independent country and the only legitimate government on the Korean peninsula.

First elected mayor

Jeon Jae-hee, Kwangmyong

Legislative

First elected to national legislature (Kuk Hoe, National Assembly)

Yim Yong-sin Louise, 1949

Judicial

First appointed judge

Hwang Yoon-seok, Seoul district court, 1954

Minority: Lesbian

First elected to national legislature (Kuk Hoe, National Assembly)

Kim Ok-son, 1967[31]

[31]For details on the never-married, cross-dressing Kim Ok-son, see Chunghee Sarah Soh, *Chosen Women in Korean Politics* (New York: Praeger, 1991).

Kuwait

Women

Right to vote and to stand for election: According to the November 1962 constitution, only men have the right to vote and stand for election. During the Iraqi occupation of the country (1990–1991), the ruling family and many Kuwaitis fled abroad. The emir of Kuwait made vague pronouncements about seeking to rectify Kuwaiti women's inability to vote or stand for election as a reward for their suffering and participation in the struggle to reclaim the country once the Iraqis had been driven out. Although nothing immediately tangible in the way of voting rights came of these pronouncements, there was a start in promoting women to some positions of responsibility within the government. In March 1998, a parliamentary committee rejected a draft law, proposed by two of the chamber's more liberal males, that would have granted women the right to vote and run for Parliament.

In early May 1999, the ruling emir, Sheik Jaber al-Ahmad al-Sabah, dissolved the sitting Parliament and scheduled new elections. Then, on May 15, he issued an executive order for his government to grant women the same political rights as men, with that order to be confirmed by the new Parliament. Beginning in 2003, women would thus be able to vote and stand for election to Parliament. However, in November 1999, Parliament voted—by a two-vote margin—not to confirm the emir's decree, thus denying women the right to vote. Close observers of the situation believe that another vote (or votes) is expected.

Executive

First appointed to cabinet secretariat

Rasha al-Sabah, Undersecretary in the Ministry of Higher Education

Notable service in cabinet secretariat

Sara al-Duweisan, Undersecretary in the Planning Ministry
Siham Razoogi, Undersecretary in the Oil Ministry

First appointed ambassador

Nabila al-Mulla, Ambassador to South Africa and Zimbabwe, 1993

Legislative

Since women have not been allowed to vote or stand for office, they have been thus far excluded from Parliament, although it is quite possible that the first woman (or women) will be chosen in the elections scheduled for 2003.

Kyrgyzstan

Women

Right to vote: June 1918
To stand for election: June 1918

Executive

First appointed to cabinet (Kyrgyzstan SSR)

Sakin Bergmantrovna, Minister of Foreign Affairs, 1966

First appointed to cabinet (after independence)

Roza Otunbayeva, Minister of Foreign Affairs, 1994

Notable service in cabinet

Neliya Beyshenaliyeva, Minister of Justice
Mira Dzhangaracheva, Deputy Prime Minister
Larisa Gutchenko, Minister of Justice
Myrza Kaparov, Minister of Tourism and Sports
Shanyl Tummenbayeva, Deputy Prime Minister

First appointed ambassador

Roza Otunbayeva, Ambassador to the United States and Canada, 1992

Legislative

First elected in free elections to national legislature[32]

Sharipa Sadybakasova
Elected to Assembly of People's Representatives (Lower House), 1995

---

[32]Women from Kyrgyzstan were previously elected to the Supreme Soviet of the Soviet Socialist Republic of Kyrgyzstan and to the Parliament of the Soviet Union.

Rohat Achilova
Mira Jangaracheva
Alevtina Pronenko
Tokon Shaylieva

All elected to Legislative Assembly (Upper House), 1995

Laos

Women

Right to vote: 1958
To stand for election: 1958

Executive

First appointed to cabinet

Pany Yathotou, Governor of the Central Bank (a cabinet position in Laos), 1987

First appointed ambassador

Sengchanh Souklaseum, Ambassador to the Philippines, 1998

Legislative

First elected to national legislature
(Sapha Heng Xai, National Assembly)

Khampheng Boupha, Neo Lao Hak Sad Party, May 4, 1958

Latvia

Women

Right to vote: November 18, 1918
To stand for election: November 18, 1918

Executive

Vaira Vike-Freiberga, President, July 8, 1999–present. An unexpected choice for president, Vike-Freiberga won as a compromise candidate on a sixth parliamentary ballot, after all the leading candidates had dropped out or been rejected. She had fled Latvia as a seven-year-old when the Russian army invaded in 1945. Her family eventually emigrated to Canada, where Vike-Freiberga grew up, becoming an academic teaching and researching at Montreal's universities. One of her specialties was collecting Latvian folk songs into a computer database. Vike-Freiberga had only returned to Latvia, and given up her Canadian citizenship, about a year before her election. One of her first tasks will be to try and convince Latvia's sizeable Russian minority to integrate themselves to a greater degree into Latvian society. As an example to the Russians, many of whom have lived in Latvia for some fifty years without bothering to learn the local language, Vike-Freiberga took a novel approach: She quickly learned Russian herself, so as to be able to communicate better with her Russian constituents. She should have a relatively easy time explaining Latvian policy to the rest of the world, too, since she's also fluent in English, French, German, and Spanish, along with her native Latvian.

Notable presidential candidates, 1999

Vaira Paegle, candidate of the People's Party. Member of Parliament, People's Party executive board member, and former citizen of the United States, Paegle is also a former chairperson of the World Federation of Free Latvians. During parliamentary balloting, fifty-one out of a hundred votes are required for election; however, Paegle could not gather more than the twenty-four votes of her own party in the first two rounds. She was eliminated entirely in the fifth round of balloting, still stuck at twenty-four votes.

Ingrida Udre, Minister of the Economy and contender beginning in the third ballot. Udre never seemed to have much of a chance, and she was defeated in the fifth ballot, along with a male contender, by eventual winner Vaira Vike-Freiberga.

Notable presidential candidate, 1996

Ilga Kreituse. Candidate of the Democratic Party Saimnieks and former head of Parliament, Kreituse received 25 (of 100) parliamentary votes in the June 18, 1996, parliamentary election for president. She placed second to president Guntis Ulmanis, who was reelected to a second term.

First appointed to cabinet (before independence)

Valentina Pikkels, Minister of Social Affairs, 1961

First appointed to cabinet (after independence)

Vita Anda Terauda, Minister of State Reform, 1994

Notable service in cabinet

Silva Golde, Minister of Education and Science
Ingrida Labucka, Minister of Justice
Karina Petersone, Minister of Culture
Ingrida Udre, Minister of the Economy
Ramona Umblija, Minister of Culture

First appointed ambassador

Anna Zigure, Ambassador to Finland, 1991

Legislative

First appointed to national legislature (National Council)

Klāra Kalniņa, Social Democratic Worker's Party
Anna Rāmane-Kēniņa, Party of Latvian Democrats
Valērija Seile, Farmer's Party of Latgale

All appointed 1918

First elected to national legislature (Constituent Assembly)

Zelma Cēsniece-Freidenfelde, National Latvian Association
Klāra Kalniņa, Social Democratic Worker's Party
Valērija Seile, Farmer's Party of Latgale
Berta Vesmane, Social Democratic Worker's Party

All elected April 17–18, 1920

Head of national legislature (Seima, Parliament)

Ilga Kreituse, 1995

Religious Minority: Jewish

Legislative

First woman elected to national legislature (Seima, Parliament)

Marjaša Ruta, 1990

Minorities: Various

Legislative

The following minorities were appointed to the first National Council in 1918

Eight Germans
Six Jews
Four Russians

After elections were held on April 17–18, 1920,
the following minorities were elected to the Constituent Assembly

Six Germans
Six Jews
Four Russians
One Pole

Lebanon

Women

Right to vote: 1952
To stand for election: 1952

Executive

First appointed to cabinet

No woman yet appointed

First appointed ambassador

Samira Emile Hanna al-Daher, Ambassador to Japan, 1983. Mention should also be made of **Insaf Sultan,** who was appointed ambassador to Pakistan in 1997.

Legislative

First to serve in legislature (Majlis al-Nuwwab, National Assembly)

Mirna Emeel al-Bostaany (Myrna Boustani), 1964. Boustani was elected from a seat in the Shouf region in a special election to replace her father, independent deputy Emile Boustani, after his death in a plane crash. She did not stand for reelection to a full term in the next election (of April 1965).

First elected to national legislature (Majlis al-Nuwwab, National Assembly)

Bahaya al-Hariri (Bahia El Hariri)
Maha al-Khuri (Mahy El Khoury)
Nayla Moawad

All elected 1992

Judicial

First appointed judge

Rabee'ah Ameesh, 1994

Minority: Armenian

Executive

Notable service in cabinet

Shahe Barsoumian, Minister of Oil

Lesotho

Women

Right to vote: April 30, 1965
To stand for election: April 30, 1965

Royalty

Power past

'MaMohato Tabitha 'Masentle Lerotholi, Queen Regent, June 5–December 5, 1970; March 10–November 12, 1990; January 15–February 7, 1996. 'MaMohato Tabitha was the wife of King Moshoeshoe II and mother of present King Letsie III. She was called upon to assume a regency for the small African nation on three separate occasions. The first occurred when her husband was removed from the throne and went into exile in the Netherlands in 1970 during a political dispute with prime minister Leabua Jonathan. Moshoeshoe eventually returned to the country, after an agreement with Jonathan (and a new constitution) named him head of state but forbid his active participation in politics. All remained relatively quiet until a military coup in 1990 brought a group of officers to power who deposed Moshoeshoe and named his son Letsie as king, with his mother as regent again for a short time. Constitutional rule was restored in 1994, and Letsie abdicated in favor of his father, who resumed the throne in early 1995. King Moshoeshoe was killed in a car accident in January 1996, and his wife became regent a third time. Her final regency was the shortest, lasting only until Letsie could again be formally elected king.

Executive

Potential power

Deborah Khaulelo Ralitapole, 1999. A pharmacist, once exiled after being branded a communist, Ralitapole has emerged as one of the most important women in Lesotho politics. A former cabinet minister, she's also chaired the Independent Political Authority, an organization established to ensure free and fair elections. Ralitapole is tipped by many as a possible leader of the Basotho Congress Party and a potential prime minister should that party regain power.

First appointed to cabinet

Anna Matlelima Hlalele, Minister of Youth and Women's Affairs, 1986

Notable service in cabinet

'Mamoshebi Kabi, Minister of Women and Youth Affairs; Minister of Transport and Communications

Deborah Khaulelo Ralitapole, Minister of Health and Social Welfare

First appointed ambassador

Marion Likhapa Sehlabo, Ambassador to the United Kingdom, Austria, Belgium, France, West Germany, Italy, the Netherlands, Sweden, and Switzerland, 1977

Legislative

First appointed to national legislature (Senate)

Ellen 'Maposholi Molapo, MFP, April 1965

First elected to national legislature (National Assembly)

'Mamoshebi Kabi, Basotho Congress Party
Mats'eliso Moshabesha, Basotho Congress Party
Deborah Khaulelo Ralitapole, Basotho Congress Party

All elected March 1993

Head of national legislature (National Assembly)

Ntlhoi Motsamai, 1999

Liberia

Women

Right to vote: May 7, 1946
To stand for election: May 7, 1946

International Notable: **Angie Brooks** was president of the United Nations General Assembly's twenty-fourth session in 1969.

Executive

Power past

Ruth Sando Perry, Chairperson of the Council of State, September 3, 1996–August 2, 1997. Perry, a former member of Liberia's Senate, was sworn in as chairperson of the Council of State, a special body established to govern Liberia as part of a peace accord between warring factions in an attempt to end six years of civil war in the West African nation. In taking that position, Perry became the first female head of state in Africa.

Notable presidential candidate, 1997

Ellen Johnson-Sirleaf. Before her presidential run, Johnson-Sirleaf had a career of ups of downs. She was a former minister of finance and head of Liberia's development bank. After Samuel K. Doe and his People's Redemption Council overthrew President William Tolbert in 1980, the new rulers asked Johnson-Sirleaf to accept a position within the new government. She handled Liberia's negotiations with the World Bank and the International Monetary Fund, a perfect position for the internationally known and highly respected economist. By 1985, however, she was out of favor with Doe, who placed her under house arrest. Tried and convicted on sedition charges, Johnson-Sirleaf won a seat in Liberia's Senate from her prison cell. Granted clemency by Doe, she lived abroad during the chaotic years of anarchy that followed his own ouster from power. When Liberia finally made moves back toward democratic rule, Johnson-Sirleaf returned home to run for president, a race in which she was expected to do well. In Liberia's first truly free presidential election in years, Johnson-Sirleaf's result was disappointing: She placed a very distant second to victor Charles Taylor, winning less than 10 percent of the vote.

Ex–partner in power

Victoria David Tolbert, 1971–1980, wife of president William Tolbert. Along with her husband and their interlocking family connections among other descendants of American blacks, a class that had ruled Liberia for more than a century, Victoria lived a Marie Antoinette lifestyle that blatantly mocked the squalor of the nation. Using a business conglomerate, Tolbert Mesurado, the presidential couple (with their children and assorted relatives by blood and marriage) controlled a phenomenal amount of the country's wealth. Some sources estimate that they owned nearly 5 percent of Liberia's total land area. The rapacious Victoria was killed alongside her husband and twenty-six others in the executive mansion during a coup staged by dissident noncommissioned army officers in 1980.

First appointed to cabinet

Edith Mai Willes Padmore, Minister of Health and Welfare, 1972

Notable service in cabinet

Kate Bryant, Minister of Health and Welfare
Ellen Johnson-Sirleaf, Minister of Finance
Evelyn Kandaki, Minister of Education
Dorothy Musuleng-Cooper, Minister of Foreign Affairs
Victoria Reffell, Minister of Information
Amelia Ward, Minister of Planning and Economic Affairs

First appointed ambassador

Angie Brooks, Ambassador to the United Nations, 1968
Eugenia A. Wordsworth-Stephenson, Ambassador to Germany, 1978

Legislative

First elected/appointed to national legislature (House of Representatives)

Ellen Mills Scarborough, True Whig Party, 1960

Minority: Indigenous People

Executive

Power past

Henry Too Wesley, Vice-President, 1924–1928. Wesley, a Grebo, one of Liberia's original inhabitants, was elected on the True Whig ticket with Charles D. B. King. Until his election, all political power in the country had rested in the hands of the Americo-Liberian ruling class, a group of some 50,000 people descended from the freed American slaves who had founded the country in the 1840s. Wesley's inclusion on the ticket was strictly for show, an attempt to convince the country's native inhabitants that they too were considered Liberians. Wesley exercised absolutely no power, as witnessed by his being bumped off the ticket when King ran for reelection in 1928.

Libya

Women

Right to vote: 1963
To stand for election: 1963

Executive

First appointed to cabinet

Fatima Abd al-Hafiz Mukhtar, Minister of Education, 1989. There are also unsubstantiated reports of a female minister of agriculture, whose appointment began in 1978.

Notable service in cabinet

Salma Ahmed Rashed, Minister for Women's Affairs
Noura Han Abu-Sefrian, Minister for Women's Affairs
Fawziya Basheer Shalabi, Minister of Information, Culture, and Jamahiri Mobilization

First appointed ambassador

Fatima Magami, Ambassador to Ghana, 1992

Legislative

First elected/appointed to national legislature
(Mutamar Al Sha'ab Al Aam, General People's Congress)

As can best be determined, no woman ever served in the Parliament during the Libyan monarchy (1952–1969). With the establishment of the so-called People's Power in 1975, a structure of people's congresses was established. This structure involves pyramidal voting, where each level selects representatives to a higher level, with the General People's Congress at the apex. This body, which functions as a parliament, first met in January 1976. There was one female member in the seventh meeting (1984) of the congress. Efforts to determine her name and whether she was the body's first female member have thus far been unsuccessful.

Liechtenstein

Women

Right to vote: July 1, 1984
To stand for election: July 1, 1984

Liechtenstein was the last country in Europe to grant women the right to vote.

Executive

First appointed to cabinet

Cornelia Gassner, Minister of Construction and Traffic, 1993

Notable service in cabinet

Andrea Willi, Minister of Foreign Affairs

First appointed ambassador

Claudia Fritsche, Ambassador to the United Nations, 1990

Legislative

First elected to national legislature (Landtag, Diet)

Emma Eigenmann, Progressive Citizens Party, February 1986

Lithuania

Women

Right to vote: October 5, 1921
To stand for election: October 5, 1921

Executive

Power past

Irena Degutienë, Prime Minister, May 4–18, 1999; October 27—November 3, 1999. Following the abrupt resignation of Prime Minister Gediminas Vagnorius in 1999, Degutienë was chosen as acting prime minister. The forty-nine-year-old Irena was serving as minister of social care and labor at the time of her appointment. No new elections were needed because of her appointment, since she was a member of the Conservative Party, which held 68 of the 130 seats in the Lithuanian Parliament (Seimas). She was chosen again (for a three-day stint) as acting prime minister in the fall of 1999, after yet another prime minister (Rolandas Paksas) suddenly resigned.

Kazimiera Danutë Prunskienë, Prime Minister, March 17, 1990–January 10, 1991. Prunskienë, a former communist and attorney, became prime minister during the murky period when Lithuania was declaring its independence from the former Soviet Union. She resigned after a dispute with the chairman of the Supreme Assembly. Later, political rivals charged that she had served as an informer for the communists when she was younger. Prunskienë complained at a 1992 women's forum that she had been a victim of male power plays from both the right and the left during her tenure in office.

First appointed to cabinet

Elvyra Janina Kunevičienë, Minister of Finance, 1991

Notable service in cabinet

Laima Andrikienë, Minister of European Affairs
Irena Degutienë, Minister of Social Care and Labor
Rasa Rastauskienë, Minister of the Interior

First appointed ambassador

Halina Kobeckaite, Ambassador to Estonia, 1994. During 1918–1919, Lithuania had a de facto female ambassador in the person of **Jadvyga Chodakauskaite-Tubelienë,** who frequently substituted in Bern for the male ambassador to Switzerland.

Legislative

First appointed to national legislature (Seimas, Parliament)

Magdalena Galdikienë
Ona Muraskaite
Gabriele Petkevicaite
Emilija Spudaite-Gvildienë
Salomeja Stakauskaite

All appointed May 15, 1920

First elected to national legislature (Seimas, Parliament)[33]

Nijole Ambrazaityte
Laima Liucija Andrikienë
Irena Andriukaitienë
Ruta Gajauskaite
Miglute Gerdaityte
Romualda Hofertience
Vidmate Jasukaityte
Birute Nedzinskienë
Nijole Ozelyte-Vaitiekunienë
Kazimiera Danutë Prunskienë
Rasa Rastauskienë
Zita Slicyte
Valentina Suboc
Birute Valionyte

All elected 1990

Head of national legislature

Laima Liucija Andrikienë, 1992–1993

---

[33]Women from Lithuania were previously elected to the Supreme Soviet of the Soviet Socialist Republic of Lithuania and to the Parliament of the Soviet Union during the period that the country was under Soviet domination (1940–1990).

Religious Minority: Jewish

Legislative

First elected to national legislature (Seimas, Parliament)

Emanuelis Zingeris, Homeland's Union (Conservative faction), 1995

Luxembourg

Women

Right to vote: May 15, 1919
To stand for election: May 15, 1919

Royalty

Power past

Charlotte Aldegonde E'Lise Marie Wilhelmine, Grand Duchess, January 15, 1919–December 12, 1964. The second of two sisters to head Europe's only Grand Duchy, Charlotte succeeded to the throne when her older sibling abdicated. Determined to begin her reign with the people's assent, she insisted on a referendum, in which 80 percent of the population approved of her succession. When the Nazis invaded Luxembourg in World War II, Charlotte, remembering the problems her sister faced during that century's earlier German invasion (see below), wisely led her family and government into exile. After the war, she returned home to watch her country enjoy an era of unrivaled prosperity as it entered the European Economic Community. Finally, in her late sixties, and after an almost forty-five-year reign, Charlotte abdicated in favor of her eldest son.

Marie-Adèlaide, Grand Duchess, June 18, 1912–January 9, 1919. The eldest of Grand Duke William IV's six daughters, Marie-Adèlaide followed her father to the throne on his death; having no sons, he had convinced the nation's legislature to consent to changing the Grand Duchy's heredity laws to allow the accession of women. Marie-Adèlaide was unfortunate enough to be ruler when World War I broke out and the Germans invaded. Because her tiny country had virtually no defenses, the duchess, aged twenty, drove to the border and demanded that the Germans leave her country. When they refused, she simply accepted their presence, a wrongheaded move on her part. She displayed even less political aplomb by keeping her German advisers, receiving the kaiser on a state visit, and continuing to visit her own family and friends in Germany, none of which sat well with the pro-Allied sympathies of her subjects. Germany's defeat brought accusations of Marie-Adèlaide's pro-German activities, and she barely escaped having to abdicate by a narrow vote (twenty-one nay, nineteen aye, three not voting) in Luxembourg's Chamber of Deputies. One small but noisy public protest by her subjects in favor of abdication convinced Marie-Adèlaide that that would be the right thing to do after all, and she passed the Grand Duchy to her next oldest sister, Charlotte.

Maria Anna, Regent, March 19, 1908–June 18, 1912. Maria Anna was the wife of Grand Duke William IV, mother of their six daughters (and no sons), and a descendant of the Braganzas, the Portuguese royal family. She became regent during the final illness of her husband and continued to act in that role for her daughter Marie-Adèlaide for a few months after William's death.

Executive

First appointed to cabinet

Madeleine Frieden-Kinnen, Minister of Family, Education, and Youth Affairs, 1969

Notable service in cabinet

Anne Brasseur, Minister of National Education, Professional Training, and Sports
Mady Delvaux-Sterres, Minister of Transportation
Colette Flesch, Minister of Foreign Affairs, Trade, Cooperation, and Justice
Erna Hennicot-Schoepges, Minister of Education and Vocational Training
Marie-Josée Jacobs, Minister of Family
Lydie Polfer, Minister of Foreign Affairs

First appointed ambassador

Arlette Conzemius, Ambassador to the Council of Europe, 1993

First elected mayor

Collette Flesch, Luxembourg, 1970

Legislative

First elected to national legislature (Chambre des députés, Chamber of Deputies)

Marguerite Thomas-Clement, Social Democratic Party, April 1919

Head of national legislature

Erna Hennicot-Schoepges, Chamber of Deputies, 1989–1994; 1994–1995

MACEDONIA

Women

Right to vote: December 31, 1946
To stand for election: December 31, 1946

Executive

First appointed to cabinet

Gordana Sijanovska, Minister Without Portfolio, 1990
Sofija Todorova, Minister of Development, 1991

Notable service in cabinet

Milijana Danevska, Minister of Development
Radmila Kiprijanova, Vice–Prime Minister
Jane Miljovski, Vice–Prime Minister
Zlatka Popovska, Vice–Prime Minister
Merie Rushani, Minister of Science
Sofija Todorova, Minister of Education and Physical Culture

First appointed ambassador

Ljubica Z. Acevska, Ambassador to the United States, 1995

Legislative

First elected to national legislature (Sobranie, Assembly of the Republic)[34]

Ratka Dimitrova, Democratic Party of Macedonian Unity
Dosta Dimovska, Democratic Party of Macedonian Unity
Biljana Lazarovska, Democratic Party of Macedonian Unity
Gulistana Markovska, Alliance of Reform Forces
Slavjanka Stojanova, Social Democratic Union of Macedonia

All elected 1991

---

[34]Women from Macedonia were previously elected to the Parliament of Yugoslavia.

Head of national legislature

Before independence from Yugoslavia, a woman chaired the Assembly of the Socialist Republic of Macedonia (1984–1985).

Minority: Albanian

Executive

First woman appointed to cabinet

Eshtref Aliu, Minister of Culture, 1995

Minority: Roma (Gypsy)

Legislative

First elected to state Parliament

Abdi Faik, 1969. Faik was elected to the Parliament of the Socialist Republic of Macedonia, a constituent unit of the former Federal Republic of Yugoslavia.

First elected to national legislature (Sobranie, Assembly of the Republic)

Abdi Faik, 1998

MADAGASCAR

Women

Right to vote: April 29, 1959
To stand for election: April 29, 1959

Executive

First appointed to cabinet

Gisèle Rabesahala, Minister of Revolutionary Art and Culture, 1977

Notable service in cabinet

Ny Hasina Andriamanjato, Minister of Posts and Telecommunications
Lina Andriamifidimanana, Minister of Youth and Sports
Noeline Jaotody, Minister of Population, Women's Issues, and Childhood
Juliette Raharisoa, Minister of Tourism; Minister of Energy and Mines
Lila Ratsifandriamanana, Minister of Foreign Affairs; Minister of Scientific Research
Rahantalalao Henriette Ratsimbazafimaheta, Minister of Health
Alice Razafinakanga, Minister of the Civil Service, Labor, and Social Law
Colette Vaohita, Minister of the Environment

First appointed ambassador

No woman yet appointed

Legislative

First elected to national legislature (Parlement, Parliament)

Mrs. Jacob Achimo Fatima, Social Democratic Party, Senate
Elise Rasoamampionona, Social Democratic Party, National Assembly

Both elected August 1965

MALAWI

Women

Right to vote: 1961
To stand for election: 1961

Executive

Ex–partner in power

Cecilia Kadzamira, 1966–1994. Longtime companion of president-for-life Hastings Kamazu Banda, Cecilia was given the title "Official Hostess." As the niece of John Tembo, one of Banda's closest cronies, she stood beside the elderly president throughout almost all of his thirty-three-year reign. In deference to her, Banda banned the song "Cecilia" by the American pop duo Simon and Garfunkel, proclaiming it disrespectful to the woman he publicly called "Mama." After looting the country and stashing away a fortune estimated at hundreds of millions of dollars, Banda came to a sorry end. He was almost a hundred years old, deaf, and going blind when opposition forces finally united in 1994 and forced him to stand for election, which he lost. The new democratic government promptly arrested Banda, then tried him for complicity in the murder of four politicians. He was found innocent but confined to house arrest, with Cecilia naturally, in one of his former presidential palaces, where he remained until his death in 1997. Cecilia immediately fell into squabbles with Banda's family about who would inherit his vast fortune, with the new government taking the family's side.

Notable vice-presidential candidate, 1999

Febbie Nyirenda, candidate on the United Party ticket of presidential contender Bingu wa Mutharika. Evangelist, nurse, and bus company officer, Nyirenda was a forty-six-year-old widow by the time she got involved in politics. Her candidacy, a first for Malawi, did not impress the voters. The United Party received barely 22,000 votes out of the almost 2.5 million cast.

First appointed to cabinet

Fern Navere Sadyalunda, Minister of Community Development and Social Welfare, 1975

Notable service in cabinet

Mary Banda, Minister of Women, Youth, and Community Services
Edda Chitalo, Minister of Women and Children's Affairs
Lillian Patel, Minister of Women, Children's Affairs, and Commercial Development

First appointed ambassador

Two female ambassadors—Malawi's first—were appointed sometime between May 1994 and October 1997. **Julie Mphande,** ambassador to Belgium, Luxembourg, Germany, and other accreditations, was one, and the other was posted to Ethiopia.

Legislative

First elected to national legislature (National Assembly)

Rose Chibambo, Malawi Congress Party, April 1964

Minority: European

Executive

First appointed to cabinet

Colin Cameron, Minister of Works, 1964

MALAYSIA

Women

Right to vote: August 31, 1957
To stand for election: August 31, 1957

Executive

Woman to watch

Wan Azizah Ismail, wife of ousted deputy prime minister Anwar Ibrahim. When her husband was sacked by Prime Minister Mahathir Mohamad in late 1998 and then arrested on dubious sexual misconduct charges, Azizah moved rapidly to take up his cause of reforming Malaysian politics. At first appearance, it was an unlikely role for the middle-aged eye surgeon, who'd been married to Anwar for eighteen years. Actually, she was following a growing Asian tradition of women picking up the political banner for their husbands or male relatives, set by Benazir Bhutto of Pakistan, Corazon Aquino of the Philippines, and others. Known as "the Angel" even among her political enemies, Azizah soon came under fire from her husband's political rivals, especially after she accused the government of planning to inject him with the HIV virus while he was in detention, to make the charges of sodomy they had brought against him more credible. Azizah quieted somewhat after the government threatened to arrest her, but moved to spread her message over the Internet, a perfect medium for political protest in Malaysia, where television and newspapers are under firm government control. Since Anwar told her when he was arrested, "Azizah, if anything happens to me, you take over," she has already announced that she'll oppose Mahathir, maybe even in his own constituency, if he calls a snap election in an attempt to justify his ouster of his former heir apparent. In March 1999, it was announced that Azizah would head up a new political party, the National Justice Party. Since then, she has been steadily building a coalition with two other parties (the Islamic Party of Malaysia and the Democratic Action Party) to oppose Mahathir in the November 1999 election. She won a parliamentary seat for herself in that election, but her new party, along with its political partners, only fared modestly. The opposition coalition of parties did manage to almost double their number of parliamentary seats, but that still leaves Mahathir in control. Aziah Ismail will undoubtedly now carry her fight from the streets into the halls of Parliament, where she could prove a tough opponent for the prime minister.

First appointed to cabinet

Tan Sri Fatimah Hashim, Minister of Social Welfare, 1973

Notable service in cabinet

Seri Rafidah Aziz, Minister of International Trade and Industry
Zaleha Ismail, Minister of National Unity and Social Development
Napsiah Omar, Minister of Public Enterprise

First appointed ambassador

P. G. Lim, Ambassador to Yugoslavia, 1976

Legislative

First elected to colonial legislature
(Legislative Council of the Federation of Malaya)

Halimaton Abdul Majid, Alliance Party, 1955

First elected to national legislature
(Dewan Rakyat, House of Representatives)

Fatimah Hashim
Che' Khadijah Mohd Sidek

Both elected 1960

First appointed to national legislature (Dewan Negara, Senate)

Che' Aishah binti Haji Abdul Ghani, 1962

Judicial

First appointed judge

Siti Norma Taakob, 1983

Minority: East Indian

Legislative

First woman elected to national legislature
(Dewan Rakyat, House of Representatives)

Leela Rama, Malaysian Indian Congress, Selangor, 1995

Maldives

Women

Right to vote: 1932
To stand for election: 1932

Executive

First appointed to cabinet

Moomina Haleem, Minister of Health, 1977

Notable service in cabinet

Rashida Yoosuf, Minister of Youth, Sports, and Women's Affairs

First appointed ambassador

No woman yet appointed

Legislative

First elected to colonial legislature (Majlis, Citizen's Assembly)

Malim Fathumaa Fulhu
Fathmath Saeed

Both elected January 1, 1953

First elected to national legislature (Majlis, Parliament)

Aminaa Mohamed Amin, November 1979

MALI

Women

Right to vote: 1956
To stand for election: 1956

Executive

Ex–power behind the scene

Myriam Traore, 1968–1991, wife of ousted dictator Moussa Traore. Judged by some to be the fourth-poorest country in the world, Mali still proved to be lucrative for the Traores, albeit on a smaller scale when compared to some of Africa's other looting dictators. Estimates of the ruling family's "take" ranged from $350,000 to $100 million during Traore's brutal twenty-three-year rule. Overthrown in 1991, Traore was charged with crimes against humanity for having ordered troops to open fire on students protesting his government. Found guilty and sentenced to death, his sentence was later commuted to life imprisonment. In 1998, Myriam, Moussa, and Myriam's brother again found themselves in trouble. The charges this time—"economic crimes and illicit enrichment"—stemmed from the trio's embezzlement activities while in power and resulted in death sentences for all three. Moussa admitted taking kickbacks but claimed that the money was passed on to the government coffers. Myriam made the more unusual claim that the family's fortune was a gift from President Felix Houphouet-Boigny of Côte d'Ivoire. Swiss banks actually returned $2.7 million to Mali's treasury during the Traore trial, a first-ever return of plundered assets to an African country. The Traore family saga was back in the news by the fall of 1999. Mali's current president, in a televised speech, announced that he had commuted the trio's death sentences to life imprisonment.

First appointed to cabinet

Somine Dolo, Minister of Social Affairs and Health, 1965

Notable service in cabinet

Sy Maimouna Ba, Minister of Rural Development and Environment
Fatou Haidara, Minister of Industry, Artisanry, and Trade
Diallo Lalla, Minister of Employment and Civil Service

N'tji Idrissa Mariko, Minister of Arts and Culture
Diakhite Fatoumata N'Diaye, Minister for the Promotion of Women
Ascofare Ouleymatou, Minister of Communications
Sy Oumou Louise Sidibé, Minister of Public Health, Welfare, and Women's Affairs
Sy Kadiatou Sow, Minister of Foreign Affairs; Minister of Urban Development and Housing
Diarra Afsatou Thierno, Minister for the Promotion of Women, Child, and Family Affairs
Aminata Dramane Traore, Minister of Culture and Tourism

First appointed ambassador

Madina Ly-Tall, Ambassador to France and Spain, 1993

Legislative

First elected to colonial legislature

Aouna Keita, 1959

First elected to national legislature (Assemblée nationale, National Assembly)

Aouna Keita, 1964

MALTA

Women

Right to vote: September 5, 1947
To stand for election: September 5, 1947

Executive

Power past

Agatha Barbara, President, February 16, 1982–February 15, 1987. Before she became Malta's first female president, Barbara had already established several records: She was the first women elected to Malta's legislature (see below) and the first female cabinet member. A longtime associate of Dom Mintoff, head of Malta's Labor Party and a leading figure in gaining Maltese independence from Britain, Barbara served continuously in Parliament from 1947 to 1982 and held several cabinet portfolios (Education, Labor, Culture, and Welfare) in addition. In keeping with tradition, Barbara served only one term as head of state, a ceremonial position in Malta. Concurrent with holding the office of president, she was chancellor of the University of Malta.

First appointed to cabinet

Agatha Barbara, Minister of Education, 1955. She received the same portfolio in 1971, when she became the first woman to serve in a Maltese cabinet after independence.

Notable service in cabinet

Agatha Barbara, Minister of Labor, Culture, and Welfare
Helena Dalli, Minister of Women's Affairs
Giovanna DeBono, Minister for Gozo

First appointed ambassador

Alice Emo-Capodolisk, Ambassador to Portugal, 1970

Legislative

First elected to colonial legislature
(Il-Kamra Tad-Deputati, House of Representatives)

Agatha Barbara, Malta Labor Party, October 1947

First elected to national legislature
(Il-Kamra Tad-Deputati, House of Representatives)

Agatha Barbara, Malta Labor Party
Evelyn Bonaci, Malta Labor Party

Both elected 1966

Head of national legislature

Miriam Spiteri Debono, Malta Labor Party, House of Representatives, 1996

Marshall Islands

Women

Right to vote: May 1, 1979
To stand for election: May 1, 1979

Executive

First appointed to cabinet

Evelyn Konou, Minister of Health, 1995

Notable service in cabinet

Marie Maddison, Minister of Foreign Affairs

First appointed ambassador

Amatlain Kabua, Ambassador to Japan, 1997

Legislative

First elected to colonial legislature

Evelyn Konou, 1979

First elected to national legislature (Nitijela, Parliament)

Evelyn Konou, Voice of the Marshalls Party, November 1991

Mauritania

Women

Right to vote: May 20, 1961
To stand for election: May 20, 1961

Executive

First appointed to cabinet

Toure Aissanta Kane, Minister for Protection of the Family and Social Affairs, 1975

Notable service in cabinet

Diyé Bá, Minister of Health and Social Affairs
Ann Amadou Baraly, Minister of Industry
Khadijetou Mint Boubou, Minister of State (Civil Affairs)
Mintata Mint Hedeid, Minister of State (Women)
Sghair Ould M'Bareck, Minister of National Education

First appointed ambassador

No woman yet appointed. Attention might be paid to **Aicha Mint Mohamed Saleck Ould Marrackchi** as a potential future appointee, because in 1999 she was serving as a second counselor in Mauritania's embassy to the United States.

Legislative

First elected to national legislature (al-Jamiya al-Wataniya, National Assembly)

Fatma Lalla Zeina Mint Sbaghou, 1996

Mauritius

Women

Right to vote: 1956
To stand for election: 1956

Executive

First appointed to cabinet

Radhamanay Roonoosarny, Minister of Women and Consumer Affairs, 1975

Notable service in cabinet

Marie Claude Arouff-Parfait, Minister of Youth and Sports
Shirin Aumeeruddy-Cziffra, Minister of Women's Rights; Attorney General
Sheilabai Bappoo, Minister of Employment, Industrial Relations, Women's Rights, and Family Welfare
Marie-Théríese Minerva, Minister of Education, Science, and Technology
Indira Savitree Thacoor-Sidaya, Minister of Women, Family Welfare, and Child Development

First appointed ambassador

Ghislaine Henry, Ambassador to France, 1989

Legislative

First elected to national legislature (National Assembly)

Shirin Aumeeruddy-Cziffra, Mauritian Militant Movement
Ghislaine Henry, Mauritian Social Democratic Party
Vidula D. Nababsing, Mauritian Militant Movement

All elected December 1976

Mexico

Women

Right to vote: February 15, 1947[35]
To stand for election: October 17, 1953

Executive

Notable presidential candidates, 1994

Cecilia Soto Gonzalez. Candidate of the extreme left-wing Worker's Party, Gonzalez placed fourth with less than 3 percent of the vote in the election won by Ernesto Zedillo.
Marcela Lombardo. Candidate of the Socialist People's Party, Lombardo placed ninth with less than 0.5 percent of the vote.

Notable presidential candidate, 1982, 1988

Rosario Ibara de Piedra. Candidate of the Worker's Revolutionary Party, Ibara was the founder and director of the National Front Against Repression. As the first female presidential candidate in Mexico's history in 1982, Ibara wasn't very successful; her vote total was negligible. The same proved true in her 1988 race.

First appointed to cabinet

Rosa Luz Alegria Escamilla, Minister of Tourism, 1980

Notable service in cabinet

Silvia Hernández Enríquez, Minister of Tourism
Rosario Green, Minister of Foreign Affairs
Julia Carabias Lillo, Minister for the Environment, Natural Resources, and Fisheries
María Elena Vásquez Nava, Comptroller General
Norma Sananiego, Comptroller General
María de los Angeles Moreno Uruegas, Minister of Fisheries

---

[35]Women were permitted to vote in some local and state elections at an earlier date. Yucatán and San Luis Potosí were the first states to extend the franchise, in 1922 and 1923, respectively.

First elected governor of a state

Griselda Alvarez Ponce de León, Institutional Revolutionary Party, Colima, 1979. The next elected female governor was **Beatriz Elena Rangel Paredes,** Tlaxcala, 1986.

First appointed ambassador

Palma Guillén, Ambassador to Colombia, 1941

First elected to public office

Rosa Torres, President, Mérida Municipal Council, 1922

Legislative

First appointed to national legislature (Cámara de Diputados, Chamber of Deputies)

Aurora Jiménez Palacio, Institutional Revolutionary Party, Baja California, April 1954

First elected to national legislature (Cámara de Diputados, Chamber of Deputies)

Maria Guadalupe Asúa, Institutional Revolutionary Party, Jalisco
Remedios Albertina Ezeta, Institutional Revolutionary Party, México
Marcelina Galindo, Institutional Revolutionary Party, Chiapas
Margarita Garcia Flores, Institutional Revolutionary Party, Nuevo León

All elected July 1955

In 1924, **Elvira Carrillo Puerto** (see below) was elected to a seat in the Chamber of Deputies from San Luis Potosí, but the chamber refused to recognize her credentials and did not admit her.

Head of national legislature

Maria Moreno Uriegas, Chamber of Deputies, 1994–1997
Laura Alicia Garza Galindo, Chamber of Deputies, 1993
Silvia Hernández, Senate, 1993
Lucia Carrasco Xochipa, Senate, 1992
Graciela Larios Rivas, Chamber of Deputies, 1987
Hilda Anderson Nevarez, Chamber of Deputies, 1976
Maria Lavalle Urbina, Senate, 1965

First elected to state legislature

Elvira Carrillo Puerto
And three other women, all Yucatán, 1923

Judicial

First appointed to supreme court

Mária Christina Salmorán de Tamayo, 1961

Minority: Gay/Lesbian

Executive

First appointed ambassador

Pedro Joaquin-Coldwell, Ambassador to Cuba, 1998. Joaquin-Coldwell was described in some news reports as being an "open" bisexual. He had previously served stints as governor of Quintana Roo and as federal minister of tourism.

Legislative

First elected to national legislature
(Cámara de Diputados, Chamber of Deputies)

Patria Jimenez, Democratic Revolution Party, 1997

Religious Minority: Jewish

Executive

First appointed to cabinet

Arturo Waxman, Minister of Agrarian Reform, 1994

Legislative

First woman elected to legislature

Esther Kole Teniuk, Mexico City city council, 1994

Federated States of Micronesia

Women

Right to vote: November 3, 1979
To stand for election: November 3, 1979

Executive

First appointed to cabinet

Andrea Hillyer, Attorney General, 1995

First appointed ambassador

No woman yet appointed

Legislative

First elected to national legislature (Congress)

No woman yet elected to the unicameral Congress

Moldova

Women

Right to vote: April 4, 1978
To stand for election: April 4, 1978

Executive

Notable presidential candidates, 1996

Veronica Ambraciuc, Iuliana Gorea-Costin, and **Marcica Leteischi** ran either as candidates of minor parties or as independents, and all three received only an infinitesimal number of votes.

First appointed to cabinet (Moldavian SSR)

Olga V. Bykova, Minister of Social Affairs, 1962

First appointed to cabinet (after independence)

Claudia Melnic, Minister of Finance, 1990. Melnic appears to have served in some capacity as the finance minister. However, official Moldovan government sources credit **Alexandra Can,** appointed as minister of trade and industry in 1999, as the country's "first" female minister. In 1998, **Stela Scola** was charged with the functions of minister of transport and communication for an interim period.

Notable service in cabinet

Stela Scola, Minister of Transport and Communication

First appointed ambassador

Iuliana Gorea-Costin, Ambassador to the Council of Europe, 1997

Legislative

First elected to national legislature (Parlamentul, Parliament)[36]

Elena Balan
Nadeja Brinzan
Lidia Dicusar
Lidia Istrani-Ciobanu
Liudmila Lascionova
Svetlana Mislitkaia
Olga Ojoga
Valentina Podgornaia
Alexandra Raiu

All elected February 1990

Judicial

First appointed to supreme court

Raisa Botezatu
Vera Macinscala
Natalia Moldovanu
Anastasia Pascari
Valeria Sterbet

All appointed 1996

---

[36]Women from Moldova were previously elected to the Supreme Soviet of the Soviet Socialist Republic of Moldavia and to the Parliament of the Soviet Union.

Monaco

Women

Right to vote: December 17, 1962
To stand for election: December 17, 1962

Royalty

Ex–partner in power

Grace, Princess, April 19, 1956–September 14, 1982. Grace proved that fairy tales do come true: Little girls *can* grow up and marry princes. She found hers after moving from Philadelphia nouveau riche society, to acting on the stage and in films (as Oscar-winning Grace Kelly), and finally into the arms of a real European prince, Ranier III of Monaco. Although their principality was minuscule (New York's Central Park is larger), Grace's fame brought Monaco an updated image as something more than just a gambling mecca for the ultrarich. While her prince ruled as absolute monarch, Grace promoted charitable works and produced heirs, exactly as is expected from the consort of any sovereign. Her place at the prince's side was cut short when she suffered a fatal injury in an auto accident.

Executive

First appointed to cabinet

No woman yet appointed

First appointed ambassador

No woman yet appointed. Because of its small size, Monaco has relatively few ambassadors. The woman to attain the highest professional ranking in Monaco's diplomatic service thus far has been **Maguy Maccario-Doyle,** appointed consul-general to New York City in 1997.

Legislative

First elected to national legislature (Conseil nationale, National Council)

Roxanne Noat-Notari, February 1963

Mongolia

Women

Right to vote: November 1, 1924
To stand for election: November 1, 1924

Executive

Power past

Sühbaataryn Nemendeyn Yanjmaa, Chair (Acting) of the Presidium of the State Great Hural, September 23, 1953–July 7, 1954. Yanjmaa was the widow of the Mongol revolutionary hero Sühbaatar, a contemporary of Lenin's, who died in 1923. She was the vice-chairman of the Presidium when the incumbent, Gonchigiyn Bumstend, died suddenly in 1953. His death elevated her, in an acting capacity, to head the Presidium and become de facto leader of Mongolia. It's highly doubtful that she exercised much real power, for three reasons. First, she had originally been elected to the vice-chairmanship only as an honor to her dead husband; she was expected to do little and say even less. Second, Mongolia, until 1952, was under the despotic communist rule of Marshal Choibalsan. And third, the country was a complete satrapy of the Soviet Union. In 1954, at a party meeting, she was replaced with a male and quickly passed into obscurity.

Ex–Red Queen, partner in power

Filatova Tsedenbal, 1952–1984, wife of longtime communist dictator Yumzhayn Tsedenbal. An uneducated Russian who had left school at age sixteen, Filatova was chosen by the Soviet secret police to become her husband's spouse, because all Mongolians in the party hierarchy were required to marry Russian women. Tsedenbal was so much under the Russian thumb that the Soviet embassy was next door to his palace. Filatova, who spoke no Mongolian, was instructed by Elena Ceauçescu (*see* Romania) and Margot Honecker (*see* Germany) to help her husband by being more assertive, positioning herself as the "mother of her nation." Since Tsedenbal, unlike most communist dictators, shunned the spotlight, Filatova gladly became the publicly visible partner. She was soon notorious for meddling in everything—from the workings of the government to the courses taught in the university. Nothing escaped the attention of her shrewish tongue, from the cultural arts—television was a particular favorite of hers—to the factories. Along the way, she could not mask her lack of education or her utter contempt for the Mongols. It wasn't unusual for her white Mercedes to be stoned by children as she sped around tending to her Children's Welfare Fund, a charity to which everyone had to contribute but that produced little material results. Addicted to large earrings and pearls, Filatova was also medal crazy. It seemed to the Mongols that not a medal was awarded to anyone in the country without her also receiving one, much to their amusement. Both she and her husband seemed to detest Mongolia, so badly that they spent a considerable portion of each year basking in the warmer climate of the Black Sea resorts, often in the company of the Honeckers, the Ceauçescus, and other communist power couples. It was while they were on one of these holidays in 1984 that Tsedenbal was dumped from power. The Tsedenbals were pensioned off to a luxurious apartment in Moscow, where he died a few years later. By that time, their pension had already been cut and their car and driver taken away; Filatova was shrieking to anyone who would listen—few did—about how hard life was for them. Her husband was probably the least known of all the modern-day communist dictators, and Filatova's activities since his passing are unknown. Presumably, she still lives in Moscow, most likely ignored by Russia's current rulers.

First appointed to cabinet

D. Puntsag, Minister of Health, 1930

Notable service in cabinet

Badamhaamb, Minister of Labor
Myatauyn Lhaunsuren, Minister of Labor
Nyam-Osoryn Tuya, Minister of Foreign Affairs

First appointed ambassador

Ider Luvsandanzabgiin, Ambassador to UNESCO, with other accreditations, 1991. The library of the Mongolian Parliament credits the first female ambassador as being **Damdiny Baljinnyam,** appointed ambassador to the offices of the United Nations in Geneva sometime before 1991.

Legislative

First elected to national legislature (Ulsyn Ikh Khural, State Great Hural)

Fifty-nine women, June 1951

Head of national legislature

Sühbaataryn Nemendeyn Yanjmaa, 1953–1954

MOROCCO

Women

Right to vote: May 1963
To stand for election: May 1963

Executive

First appointed to cabinet

Amina Benkhadia, State Secretary of Energy and Mines
Aziza Bennani, State Secretary of Cultural Affairs
Nawal al-Moutawakil, State Secretary of Youth and Sports
Zoulikha Nacir, State Secretary of Social Affairs

All appointed August 1997

Notable service in cabinet

Aicha Belarbi, Special Minister of Cooperation
Nezha Chekrouni, Special Minister of the Handicapped

First appointed ambassador

Princess Lalla A'isha, sister of King Hassan, Ambassador to the United Kingdom, 1965

Legislative

First elected to national legislature (Majlis Nawab, House of Representatives)

Badia Skalli, Socialist Union of Popular Forces
Latifa Bennani Smires, Independence Party

Both elected June 1993

Religious Minority: Jewish

Executive

First appointed to cabinet

Serge Berdugo, Minister of Tourism, 1993

Political Entity: Saharawi Arab Democratic Republic

Executive

First appointed to cabinet

Nema Ould al-Joumani, Minister of Health, 1982

Mozambique

Women

Right to vote: June 25, 1975
To stand for election: June 25, 1975

Executive

Ex–partner in power

Graça Simbine Machel, 1975–1986, Widow of Mozambique's first president, Samora Machel, who died in a plane crash in 1986. In addition to being her husband's closest adviser, Graça was also Mozambique's first female cabinet minister. In 1995, she was awarded the United Nations' Nansen Medal for her outstanding contributions on behalf of refugee children. This distinction came soon after she had become intimately involved with South African president Nelson Mandela. When she and Mandela married in July 1998, Graça became the first woman since Eleanor of Aquitaine (in the twelfth century) to have been married to the heads of state of two different countries (*see* South Africa).

First appointed to cabinet

Graça Simbine Machel, Minister of Education, 1975

Notable service in cabinet

Alcinda A. De Abreu, Minister of Social Action
Acucena X. Duarte, Minister of Social Welfare

First appointed ambassador

Frances Victoria Velho Rodriguez, Ambassador to Austria, Belgium, France, Greece, the Netherlands, and the European Union, 1985. She had held the rank of ambassador in the foreign ministry since 1980.

First elected mayor

Laura Tamele, Frelimo, Manhica, 1998

Legislative

First elected to national legislature (Assembleia Popular, People's Assembly)

Alcinda A. De Abreu, Liberation Front of Mozambique
Maria Virginia Arruvaia, Liberation Front of Mozambique
Monica Chitupila, Liberation Front of Mozambique
Carlota Chiwanga, Liberation Front of Mozambique
Cecilia Miranda Chongo, Liberation Front of Mozambique
Celeste Vatatono Cossa, Liberation Front of Mozambique
Justina Gaspar, Liberation Front of Mozambique
Helena Maria da Gloria, Liberation Front of Mozambique
Melita João Guambe, Liberation Front of Mozambique
Maria Laice, Liberation Front of Mozambique
Rosinha Lisboa, Liberation Front of Mozambique
Graça Machel, Liberation Front of Mozambique
Celeste Manhica, Liberation Front of Mozambique
Isabel Martins, Liberation Front of Mozambique
Solome Moiane, Liberation Front of Mozambique
Felipa Muniveda, Liberation Front of Mozambique
Esperanca Muthemba, Liberation Front of Mozambique
Teresa Amuli Nhalingue, Liberation Front of Mozambique
Marina Pachinuapa, Liberation Front of Mozambique
Felizarda Paulino, Liberation Front of Mozambique
Maria Lizia Rafael, Liberation Front of Mozambique
Ana Sansão, Liberation Front of Mozambique
Leopoldina dos Santos, Liberation Front of Mozambique
Cristina Jeremias Tembe, Liberation Front of Mozambique
Teresa Romão Tembo, Liberation Front of Mozambique
Maria Teresa Veloso, Liberation Front of Mozambique

All elected December 4, 1977

Myanmar

Women

Right to vote: 1935
To stand for election: March 19, 1946

Executive

Victorious candidate for prime minister

Aung San Suu Kyi, 1989, daughter of the founder of modern Burma, the assassinated Aung San. Aung San Suu Kyi returned home from living overseas to care for her ailing mother and was promptly thrust to the head of Myanmar's struggle for democracy. Her party, the National League for Democracy, won more than 80 percent of the vote (and 392 of the legislature's 485 seats) in the first free elections held in Myanmar in more than twenty-five years. Shortly after the election, the ruling army junta annulled the results, placing Suu Kyi and many of her followers under house arrest. She was finally released from house arrest after six years, but the junta keeps her under close surveillance, curtailing many of her activities while refusing to either relinquish power or call new elections. Awarded the Nobel Peace Prize in 1991, Suu Kyi seems determined to wait out the junta, no matter how long it takes.

First appointed to cabinet

Daw Ba Maung Chien, Minister for the Karen State, 1952

First appointed ambassador

Daw Khin Kyi, Ambassador to India, 1960

First head of a state government

Daw Ba Maung Chien, Karen State, 1953

Legislative

First elected to colonial legislature (Legislative Council)

Daw Hnin Mya, 1937

First elected to national legislature (Constituent Assembly)

Daw Khin Hla
Daw Khin Pu
Daw Hla Shin
Daw Saw Shwe

All elected April 1947

Later in 1947, after their husbands were assassinated—in the same slaughter of government officials that claimed the life of Aung San Suu Kyi's father (see above)—the following three women were appointed to seats in the Constituent Assembly:

Daw Khin Khin
Daw Khin Kyi
Daw Khin Nyunt

Judicial

First appointed judge

Daw Pwa Hmi, Thambdi juvenile court, 1927

Namibia

Women

Right to vote: November 7, 1989
To stand for election: November 7, 1989

Executive

First appointed to cabinet

Libertine Amathila, Minister of Local Government and Housing, 1990

Notable service in cabinet

Pendukeni Ithana, Minister of Youth and Sports
Netumbo-Nandi Ndaitwah, Minister of Women

First appointed ambassador

Tonata Emvula, Ambassador to Sweden, Norway, Denmark, Finland, and Iceland, 1990

First provincial head

Claudia Uushona, 1999

Legislative

First elected to national legislature (National Assembly)

Libertine Amathila, South West Africa People's Organization
Margaret Barnes, Democratic Turnhalle Alliance
Michela Huebschle, South West Africa People's Organization
Pendukeni Ithana, South West Africa People's Organization
Pashukeni Shoombe, South West Africa People's Organization

All elected November 1989

Judicial

First appointed judge

Mavis Dorothy Gibson, 1996

Nauru

Women

Right to vote: January 3, 1968
To stand for election: January 3, 1968

Executive

First appointed to cabinet

Ruby Dediya, Minister of Finance

Notable service in cabinet

Nimes Ekewona, Minister of Education

First appointed ambassador

Millicent Aroi, Ambassador to Fiji, 1997

Legislative

First elected to national legislature (Parliament)

Ruby Dediya, December 1986

Nepal

Women

Right to vote: 1951
To stand for election: 1951

Executive

First appointed to cabinet

Dwarika Devi Thakurani, Deputy Minister of Health and Autonomous Government, 1959
Shusila Thapa, Minister of Health, 1975

Notable service in cabinet

Shailaja Acharya, Deputy Prime Minister; Minister of Water Resources
Vidya Bhandary, Minister of Population and the Environment
Lila Koirala, Minister of Women and Social Welfare
Mina Pandey, Minister of Women and Social Welfare
Sahana Pradhan, Minister of Industry and Commerce for Interior Government

First appointed ambassador

Brindheswari Shah, Ambassador to India, 1989

Legislative

First appointed to national legislature
(Shallakar Sammittee, Consultative Assembly)

Mangla Devi
Punya Prava Dhungana
Prativa Jha
Maya Devi Shah

All appointed 1952

First elected to national legislature (Pratinidhi Sabha, House of Representatives)

Dwarika Devi Thakurani, Nepali Congress Party, 1959

Head of national legislature

Lila Subha Shrestha, United Marxist-Leninist Party, Deputy Speaker, 1998

Minority: Dalit

Legislative

First elected to national legislature (Pratinidhi Sabha, House of Representatives)

Krishna Singh Pariyar, Nepali Congress Party, 1991

Netherlands

Women

Right to vote: August 9, 1919
To stand for election: November 29, 1917

Royalty

Beatrix Wilhelmina Armgard Orange-Nassau and Lippe-Biesterfeld, Queen, April 30, 1980–present. Third queen in a row to reign in the Netherlands, Beatrix has been regarded as one of Europe's most liberal monarchs. Her almost left-leaning positions fit the tradition of toleration among the Dutch people. Beatrix's marriage to a German diplomat in 1966, before she ascended the throne, was controversial, given the hard times the Dutch had suffered under Nazi occupation during World War II. Much of those hard feelings were eliminated the next year, however, when the couple had a son, the first male heir to the Dutch throne in more than a century.

Power past

Juliana Louise Emma Marie Wilhelmina Orange-Nassau and Mecklenberg-Schwerin, Queen, September 6, 1948–April 30, 1980. Juliana's reign was marked by alternating periods of controversy and calm. The Dutch East Indies (now Indonesia), a financial boon for the country, was lost soon after she ascended the throne. One of her four daughters was born near-blind, which led to a royal involvement with faith healers. The crown princess married a German, while another daughter wed a highly political claimant to the Spanish throne and became a Catholic, contrary to the Dutch traditions of noninvolvement by royalty in politics and rigid Protestantism. The head of one of Europe's wealthiest royal families, Juliana always appeared more like the chairman of the board of a successful corporation than a queen. Near the end of her reign, it was revealed that her longtime spouse had been involved in an unsavory financial matter. She took this disclosure as an indication that it was time for her to leave the throne. So, after forty-two years as monarch, Juliana followed her mother's example and abdicated in favor of her eldest daughter.

Wilhelmina Helena Pauline Maria Orange-Nassau and Waldeck-Pyrmont, Queen, November 23, 1890–September 4, 1948. Wilhelmina came to the throne as a child of ten, with her mother Emma acting as regent for the first eight years of her reign. During World War I she was able to protect her country's neutrality and even offered refuge to the German kaiser when he was forced to abdicate at the war's end. Wilhelmina was less fortunate with Hitler. After the Nazis invaded, she fled with her government to England and established a government-in-exile. To allay any fears that she had abandoned her people, she made regular broadcasts to the Dutch, always ending with the refrain, "Holland will rise again." At war's end Wilhelmina returned home to a ravaged land that was soon sapped by a nationalist revolution in its richest colony—the Dutch East Indies. After she decided that a younger hand was needed to steer her country through these troubled times, she abdicated after almost sixty years as queen in favor of her daughter.

Executive

First appointed to cabinet

Margaretha Klompé, Minister of Social Work, 1956

Notable service in cabinet

Els Borst-Eilers, Minister of Health, Welfare, and Sport
Hedy d'Acona, Minister of Welfare, Health, and Culture
Margreet de Boer, Minister of Housing, Planning, and the Environment
Evelien Herfkens, Minister of Development Cooperation
Annemarie Jorritsma, Vice–Prime Minister; Minister of Transportation and Public Works
Hanja Maij-Weggen, Minister of Transport and Public Works
Tineke Netelenbos, Minister of Transport and Public Works
Johanna Schouwenaar, Minister of Social Work
Winnifred Sorgdrager, Minister of Justice
Anne Vondeling, Minister of Finance; Minister of Agriculture

First appointed ambassador

Janine C. Ferringa, Ambassador to Ghana, 1975

Legislative

First elected to national legislature (Staten-Generaal, States-General)

Suzanna (Suze) Groeneweg, Social Democratic Labor Party, July 1918

Head of national legislature

Jeltje Van Nieuwenhoven, Second Chamber (Tweed Kamer), 1998–present

Minority: Lesbian

Legislative

First elected to national legislature (Staten-Generaal, States-General)

Evelien Eshius, 1982. Eshius was the first openly homosexual person in the world elected to a national office.

Netherlands Dependency: Netherlands Antilles

Executive

Susanne Camelia-Römer, Prime Minister, November 25–December 28, 1993; June 1, 1998–present. When Camelia-Römer assumed office in 1993, she succeed another woman, Maria Philomena Liberia-Peters, the first time that an elected female head of government succeeded another. After an election defeat, she returned to serve as minister of justice in the cabinet of another prime minister. Following an election in 1998 in which no party received a majority, Camelia-Römer was installed again as prime minister, heading a coalition government.

Power past

Maria Philomena Liberia-Peters, Prime Minister, September 18, 1984–January 1, 1986; May 17, 1988–November 25, 1993. Liberia-Peters was the leader of the People's Party, based on the island of Curaçao, and headed a coalition government.

Lucinda E. da Costa Gomez-Matheeuws, Prime Minister, 1977. Gomez-Matheeuws headed a coalition government that was in office for only a few short months in 1977.

First appointed to cabinet

Lucinda E. da Costa Gomez-Matheeuws, Minister of Health and the Environment, 1970

Political Entity: Aruba

Executive

First appointed to cabinet

Alicia Angela Tromp-Yarzagaray, Minister of Finance, 1993

Legislative

First elected to legislature (Parliament)

Digna Lacie-Herera, Aruba People's Party, 1986

New Zealand

Women

Right to vote: September 19, 1893
To stand for election: October 29, 1919

Executive

Helen Clark, Prime Minister, December 10, 1999–present. The first female leader of a New Zealand political party, Clark achieved that distinction in 1993 when she became head of the Labour Party. In Parliament since 1981, she has modified her original left-wing stance on many issues. In November 1999, Clark managed a smashing victory in defeating Prime Minister Jenny Shipley. Her government will obviously set New Zealand, once again, on a more leftist course than it had followed under her predecessor.

Power past

Jenny Shipley, Prime Minister, December 8, 1997–December 10, 1999. Shipley, a member of the National Party, was the only female cabinet minister in previous prime minister Jim Bolger's government. Even so, she managed to outwit her colleagues and lead an internal party coup, dumping Bolger from both the party leadership post and his position as prime minister. She managed to hold her right-wing coalition government together through several close no-confidence votes, and in the process had some success in office. In November 1999, Shipley campaigned in her first election as prime minister. She lost to Labour Party leader Helen Clark in the first election for head of a national government in a Western democracy between two women.

Catherine (Anne) Maclean Tizard, Governor-General, November 20, 1990–March 21, 1996. After a long and successful career as an instructor at Auckland University, Auckland city councillor (1971–1983), and finally mayor of Auckland (1983–1990), Tizard capped her life in public service by being appointed governor-general, the representative of the British monarch. Because of her outspokenness, she became one of New Zealand's most popular governors-general ever. As a sign of affection, she was commonly referred to as "Our Cath" during her term in office.

First appointed to cabinet

Mabel Howard, Minister of Health and Child Welfare, 1947

Notable service in cabinet

Margaret E. Austin, Minister of Internal Affairs; Minister of Arts and Culture; Minister of Civil Defense
Christine Fletcher, Minister of Women's Affairs; Minister of Youth Affairs; Minister of Local Government
Marie Hasler, Minister of Cultural Affairs
Margaret Anne Hercus, Minister of Social Welfare, Police, and Women's Affairs
Georgina te Heuheu, Minister of Courts and Women's Affairs
Annette King, Minister of Employment; Minister of Immigration and Youth Affairs
Robyn McDonald, Minister of Senior Citizens; Minister of Consumer Affairs
Deborah Morris, Minister of Youth Affairs
Katherine O'Regan, Minister of Consumer Affairs; Minister of Youth Affairs
Ruth Richardson, Minister of Finance
Margaret Shields, Minister of Women's Affairs; Minister of Statistics; Minister of Consumer Affairs; Minister of Customs
Jenny Shipley, Minister of Health; Minister of Women's Affairs
Whetu Tirikatene-Sullivan, Minister of Tourism; Minister of the Environment

First appointed ambassador

Barbara Angus, Ambassador to the Philippines, 1978. **Jean McKenzie** was New Zealand's first head of mission. In 1949, she was named chargé d'affaires, then promoted to minister, of the legation in France. McKenzie is noted in French records as being the first woman diplomat "accredited to France." When she retired in 1956, her successor at that station received the rank of ambassador. In 1968, Helen Hampton was appointed, with ambassadorial rank, permanent representative to the Office of the United Nations in Geneva.

First elected mayor

Elizabeth Yates, Onehunga, 1894. Yates was the first female mayor elected anywhere in the British Empire.

Legislative

First woman to cast a ballot in a parliamentary election

Katherine Sheppard, 1893

First elected to Parliament (House of Representatives)

Elizabeth Reid McCombs, Labour Party, September 13, 1933

Youngest woman elected to Parliament (House of Representatives)

Marilyn Waring, National Party, age twenty-two, 1975

Judicial

First appointed to high court

Sylvia Cartwright, 1993

First appointed chief justice of supreme court

Sian Elias, 1999

Minority: Maori

Executive

Notable power

Winston Peters, 1993–present. Deputy prime minister and treasurer since 1996, Peters, of part-Maori descent, is one of New Zealand's most controversial politicians. He began his career in the rightist National Party, left it to become an independent, then established the New Zealand First Party in 1993, which won two seats. In 1996, when his new party won seventeen seats in Parliament, he became New Zealand's most important power broker. Most observers thought that he would join a coalition government with the Labour Party. Unable to come to terms with them, he quickly signed up with the National Party to form a government. When they dumped prime minister Jim Bolger in favor of Jenny Shipley late in 1997, Peters threatened to bolt the coalition and proposed a new government with the Labour Party under Helen Clark. She refused to meet Peters's demands, so he returned to serving under Shipley for another round as deputy prime minister. Peters is regarded as a prickly figure, a person one does not take lightly. New Zealanders either like him intensely or dislike him with an equal fervor. With New Zealand's new voting system (a combination of both single constituencies and party lists), Peters might end up being a power broker for some time to come.

First woman appointed to cabinet

Whetu Tirikatene-Sullivan, Minister of Tourism, 1972

Legislative

First elected to Parliament (House of Representatives)

Tareha te Moananui
Frederick Nene Russell

Both elected April 1, 1868

First woman elected to Parliament (House of Representatives)

Iriaka Ratana, 1949

Minority: Asian–New Zealander

Legislative

First elected to Parliament (House of Representatives)

Pansy Wong, National Party, Chinese descent, October 12, 1996

Minority: Gay/Lesbian

Executive

First elected mayor

Jenny Rowan, Independent, Ingelwood, Taranaki, 1986

Legislative

First elected to Parliament (House of Representatives)

Chris Carter, Labour Party, Te Atatu, November 6, 1993

Notable service in Parliament

Tim Barnett, Labour Party, Christchurch Central

First woman elected to Parliament

Marilyn Waring, National Party, Waipa, 1975

Minority: Pacific Islander

Legislative

First elected to Parliament (House of Representatives)

Taito Phillip Field, Labour Party, November 6, 1993

Political Entity: Cook Islands

Executive

First appointed to cabinet

Fanaura Kingstone, Minister of Internal Affairs and Postmistress General, 1983

Legislative

First elected to colonial legislature (Legislative Assembly)

Marguerite (Margaret) Nora Kitimira Brown Story, 1965

Head of colonial legislature (Legislative Assembly)

Marguerite (Margaret) Nora Kitimira Brown Story, 1965–1979; 1983

Political Entity: Niue

Executive

First appointed to cabinet

O'Love Toveve Jacobsen, Minister of Education, Cultural and Ethnic Arts, Religion, Sports, and Youth Affairs, 1993. On March 19, 1999, Jacobsen was defeated in her bid to become prime minister of Niue by **Sani Lakatini** (National People's Party) by a vote of fourteen to six.

Legislative

First elected to colonial legislature (Legislative Assembly)

O'Love Toveve Jacobsen, 1993

Nicaragua

Women

Right to vote: April 21, 1955
To stand for election: April 21, 1955

Executive

Power past

Julia Meña Rivera, Vice-President, October 22, 1995–January 10, 1997. Meña, one of the leaders of the Liberal Independent Party, was selected to complete the last two years of the vice-presidential term when the incumbent, Virgilio Godoy, resigned to prepare for a run in the October 1996 presidential race.

Violeta Barrios de Chamorro, President, April 25, 1990–January 10, 1997. Chamorro, widow of newspaper publisher Pedro Chamorro, who had been assassinated by agents of President Anastasio Somoza, served in the Sandinista administration that pushed Somoza from power. She resigned soon after taking office, dismayed by the Sandinistas' own totalitarian tactics, and returned to publishing her family's newspaper. For years, she and her paper were the most vocal internal critics of the new Sandinista dictatorship. After the pro-communist government finally agreed to hold open elections in 1990, Chamorro contested the presidency as the candidate of a multiparty coalition. She won in a stunning upset, astounding the Sandinistas and their leftist supporters all over the world. In 1995, Chamorro's vice-president resigned over a disagreement with the president; his position was filled by a woman, Julia Meña Rivera (see below). For the first time in history, both the president and vice-president of a country were women. Chamorro went on to complete her term, then was succeeded by another democratic president. The Sandinistas have now lost two presidential elections in a row, driven from power, perhaps permanently, by a most determined woman.

Notable presidential candidate, 1990

Blanca Rojas Echaverry. Echaverry was leader and candidate of the small Nicaraguan Central American Union Party.

First appointed to cabinet

Olga Nuñez de Sassallow, Minister of Education, 1950

Notable service in cabinet

Lea Guido, Minister of Social Welfare
Marta Pereira, Minister of Health
María Helena de Perras, Minister of Education
Blanca Rojas Echaverry, Minister of Culture
Dona María Tellez Arguello, Minister of Health
Daysi Zamora, Minister of Culture

First appointed ambassador

Rita Delia Caso Montenegro, Ambassador to the United States and Canada, 1979

Legislative

First elected to national legislature (Asamblea Nacional, National Assembly)

Miriam Arguello Morales, Conservative Party
Selmira Gonzales, Conservative Party
Irma Guerrero, Liberal Party
Rosagio Guillen, Conservative Party
Lucidla Mantilla, Conservative Party
Olga Nuñez de Saballos, Liberal Party
Haydee Trana, Conservative Party
Alba Vallejo de Riva, Liberal Party

All elected February 1972

Head of national legislature

Miriam Arguello Morales, National Assembly, 1990–1991

Judicial

First appointed to Supreme Court

Vilma Mumez de Escoria, 1979. Some conflicting sources state that **Alba Luz,** 1982, was the first woman on the supreme court.

Minority: African-Nicaraguan

Judicial

First appointed to supreme court

Harlan Kent Henríquez Clair, 1995

NIGER

Women

Right to vote: 1948
To stand for election: 1948

Executive

Ex–partner in power

Aissa Diori, 1960–1974, wife of President Hamani Diori. A presidential wife who believed in using her spouse's position for material gain, Aissa amassed quite a large fortune, including many lucrative, quality buildings in the capital city, Niamey. A member of the Fulani tribe, she was particularly detested by Niger's militant students, who termed her "the Austrian" for their perception of her Marie-Antoinettish behavior and avarice. When the inevitable army coup overthrew her husband's corrupt regime on April 15, 1974, she was killed as she tried to fight off the force assaulting the presidential residence. Her husband survived; he was tried and convicted on corruption and embezzlement charges.

First appointed to cabinet

Aissata Moumouni, Minister of Social and Women's Affairs, 1989

Notable service in cabinet

Mariama Sambo Abdoulaye, Minister of Social Development, Population, and the Promotion of Women and Children
Mai Manga Boukar, Minister of Mines and Energy
Aissa Abdoulaye Diallo, Minister of Tourism and Crafts
Aissatou Foumakoye, Minister of Social Development, Women's Protections, and Children
Rabi Daddy Gaoh, Minister of Social Development, Population, and the Promotion of Women and Children
Maillele Mariama, Minister of National Education
Dodo Aichatou Mindaoudou, Minister of Foreign Affairs; Minister of Social Development, Population, and the Promotion of Women

First appointed ambassador

Not yet identified

Legislative

First elected to national legislature (Assemblée nationale, National Assembly)

Five women, all National Movement for the Development of Society Party, elected December 10, 1989. This party was founded and controlled by then-president General Ali Saibou.

NIGERIA

Women

Right to vote: 1958[37]
To stand for election: 1958

Executive

Almost–partner in power

Alhaja Kudirat Abiola, 1993-1996, senior wife of Moshood Abiola, winner of Nigeria's 1993 presidential election who was never allowed to take office. Married at age twenty-one and mother of seven children, Kudirat was a power in her own right. Although her husband was a millionaire businessman with interests from bread-making factories and telecommunications facilities to a chain of five newspapers, Kudirat made her own fortune by founding one of West Africa's leading pharmaceutical firms. When Moshood ran for president in 1993 under the banner of the Social Democratic Party, she coordinated his campaign in Nigeria's northern region. Moshood's victory in the election was annulled by the incumbent administration. When he proclaimed himself president anyway, the ruling military junta immediately imprisoned him. Kudirat picked up his banner, speaking in public and marching in demonstrations to draw international attention to her husband's plight. The military strongmen, led by General Sani Abacha, harassed her with threats and arrests, but they failed to still her voice. In 1996, as her car was stalled in traffic in Lagos, Kudirat was assassinated by six gunmen. Another Abiola wife, Titilayo, along with Kudirat's eldest daughter, picked up Kudirat's freedom campaign. Abacha's sudden death in 1998 brought a glimmer of hope that Moshood might be freed and perhaps even allowed to assume the presidency. It was not to be, however, for he, too, died unexpectedly, only a few weeks after the passing of his nemesis but while still in custody.

---

[37]Women in Nigeria's southern region were enfranchised in stages, beginning in 1950, whereas women in the northern region (predominantly Muslim) were not. Southern women voted and contested offices in the 1959 federal elections, but no northern women were allowed to do so. Northern women finally received their full electoral franchise (to vote and contest office) in 1976.

Notable presidential candidate, 1991

Sarah Jibril. Jibril was the first woman to run for president in Nigeria's turbulent, coup-ridden political scene. She didn't make it past the party primaries, but she did manage to make the women of Nigeria take notice that they too had a voice, however minor, in the nation's presidential politics.

First appointed to cabinet

Elizabeth Afadzwana Ivase, Minister of State Education
Janet Akinrinade, Minister of Internal Affairs
Ebun Oyegbola, Minister of National Planning

All appointed 1979

Notable service in cabinet

Rose Adunike, Minister of State Education
Onikedo Akande, Minister of Industries
Hajija Aishatu Ismaila, Minister of Women and Youth
Laraba Gambo Abdullahi, Minister of Women's Affairs
Flora N. Nwapa, Minister of Housing, Survey, and Urban Development
Princess A. O. Oguneye, Minister for the Federal Capital Territory
Hajo Sani, Minister of Women's Affairs
Udith Sefi Attah, Minister of Social Affairs

First appointed ambassador

R. T. Mohammed, 1977

Notable service in state government

Latifat M. Okunu, Deputy Governor, Lagos State
Pamela Sadauki, Deputy Governor, Kaduna State

Legislative

First appointed to national legislature (Senate)

Wuraola Esan, Western Region, 1960

First elected to national legislature (House of Representatives)

Esther Soyannwo, Western Region, 1964. Soyannwo's election provoked such controversy and violence that her party forced her to give up her seat before being sworn in.

First elected to national legislature (Constituent Assembly)

Janet Akinrinade, Oyo State, 1977

First appointed to national legislature (Constituent Assembly)

Faustina-Kariba Braide
Jummal Jarma
Toyin Olakunri
Abigail Ukpabi

All appointed 1977

First elected to national legislature (Federal House of Representatives)

Biola Babatope, Unity Party of Nigeria, Lagos State
Justine Eze, Nigeria People's Party, Anambra State
V. Nnaji, Nigeria People's Party, Anambra State

All elected 1979

First elected to regional legislature

Margaret Ekpo, Eastern House of Assembly, 1961

First elected to state legislatures

Five women, 1979

Notable first: **Sawaba Gambo** was the first Nigerian Muslim woman voted into public office, elected to the town council of Sabon Gari, Zaria, in 1976.

Judicial

First appointed judge

One woman, Lagos, 1943

Norway

Women

Right to vote: 1907; 1913
To stand for election: 1907; 1913[38]

International notable: **Gro Harlem Brundtland** was appointed director general of the United Nations World Health Organization in 1998.

Executive

Power past

Gro Harlem Brundtland, Prime Minister, February 4–October 14, 1981; May 9, 1986–October 16, 1989; November 3, 1990–October 25, 1996. Brundtland, a leader of Norway's Labor Party and a former minister of the environment, first led a short-lived interim government in 1981 before being voted out of office that same year. Five years later she was back, at the head of a more stable government. Voted out of office again, she returned to power a third time a little more than a year later. During part of her tenure as prime minister, Brundtland's husband served in the Stortinget, Norway's Parliament, but as a member of another party.

First appointed to cabinet

Kirsten Moe Hansteen, Minister Without Portfolio, 1945

Notable service in cabinet

Marit Armstad, Minister of Oil and Energy
Aus Inge Aure, Minister of Justice and Police
Grete Berget, Minister of Children and Family Affairs
Erna Bjartveit, Minister of Church and Cultural Affairs
Gro Harlem Brundtland, Minister of the Environment
Kristin Clement, Minister of Labor and Government Administration

---

[38]Women were granted the right to vote and stand for election in 1907, with special conditions related to private means, property, and income. Those restrictions were removed in 1913.

Grete Faremo, Minister of Justice; Minister of Development Cooperation
Kack Kullman Five, Minister of Trade and Shipping
Else Bugge Fougner, Minister of Justice and Police
Tove Strand Gerhardsen, Minister of Labor and Government
Kari Gjeseby, Minister of Justice; Minister of Trade and Shipping
Astrid Gjetsen, Minister of Consumer Affairs and Government Administration
Ragnhild Queseth Haarstad, Minister of Local Government and Labor
Valgerd Svarsrad Haugland, Minister of Children and the Family
Ann Holt, Minister of Justice and Immigration
Hilde Frafjord Johnson, Minister of International Development Aid and Human Rights
Magnhild Melteveit Kleppa, Minister of Social Affairs
Ase Kleveland, Minister of Cultural Affairs
Gete Knudsen, Minister of Trade and Shipping
Inger Kolstad, Minister of Consumer Affairs
Anne Enger Lahnstein, Minister of Culture
Ridbjoerg Loewe, Minister of National Planning and Coordination
Eldbjoerg Loewer, Minister of Labor and Government Administration
Annemarie Lorentzen, Minister of Consumer Affairs
Kristen Myklevoll, Minister of Consumer Affairs
Eldrid Norbo, Minister of Trade and Shipping
Kari Nordheim-Larsen, Minister of Development Cooperation
Gunhild Oyangen, Minister of Agriculture
Oddrunn Pettersen, Minister of Fisheries
Gudmund Restad, Minister of Finance
Mona Røkke, Minister of Justice
Ruth Ryste, Minister of Social Affairs
Wenche Sellaeg, Minister of Health and Social Affairs
Hill-Marta Solberg, Minister of Social Affairs
Solveig Sollie, Minister of Consumer Affairs
Inger Valle, Minister of Justice; Minister of Family and Consumer Affairs
Kristin Hille Valle, Minister of the Environment
Tove Vierod, Minister of Health and Social Affairs
Anne Vik, Minister of Agriculture

First appointed ambassador

Kirsten Ohm, Ambassador to the European Council, 1974

First elected mayor

One woman, 1925

Legislative

First to serve in national legislature (Stortinget, Parliament)

Anna Rogstadt, March 17, 1911. Rogstadt was elected as a *vara* (stand-in) on a party ticket; she replaced the duly elected member in 1912 and served until 1913.

First elected to national legislature (Stortinget, Parliament)

Karen Platou, Conservative Party, 1921

Head of national legislature

Kirsti Kolle Gröndahl, Stortinget, 1993
Ingerlise Gjøyv, Odelsting (Lower House), 1991–1993
Ashild Hauen, Odelsting (Lower House), 1985–1989
Liv Andersen, Odelsting (Lower House), 1981–1985
Magit Tøsdal, Odelsting (Lower House), 1977–1981
Ase Wind Lionæs, Odelsting (Lower House), 1973–1977
Torild Skard, Lagting (Upper House), 1973–1977

Judicial

First appointed to supreme court

Ragnhild Selmer, 1970

Minority: Gay/Lesbian

Executive

First appointed to cabinet

Ann Holt, Minister of Justice and Immigration

Legislative

Notable service in national legislature (Stortinget, Parliament)

John-Arne Balto
Anders Hornslien, Labor Party

Minority: Pakistani-Norwegian

Legislative

First elected to national legislature (Stortinget, Parliament)

Athar Ali, Red Caucus, 1993

OMAN

Women

Right to vote: 1997
To stand for election: 1997

Executive

First appointed to cabinet secretariat

Rajina bint Abdul Ameer bin Ali, by the Ministry of Development under the Ministry of the Economy
Thuwaibah bint Ahmad bin Isa al-Barwani, by the Ministry of Social Affairs under the Ministry of Social Affairs, Labor, and Vocational Training
Fawzia bint Nasir bin Juma al-Farsi, by the Ministry for General Education under the Ministry of Education

All appointed 1998

First appointed ambassador

Khadija bint Hassan bin Salman al-Luweti, Ambassador to the Netherlands, 1999. **Frances D. Cook,** ambassador of the United States, was posted in 1996 as the first female ambassador to Oman.

Legislative

First elected/appointed to advisory council (Majlis A'shura)

Shakouk bint Mohamed Ghamri
Taebah bint Mohamed Nawali

Both appointed 1997, after a special restricted election in which 50,000 selected Omanis, including women for the first time, elected a group a nominees for the council. The sultan then appointed eighty-two delegates from among the nominees so elected. Both women were reelected in the next election, which featured an expanded electorate.

First elected/appointed to state council (Majlis al-Dawlah)

Lamees bint Abdullah bin Mohammad al-Tael
Sameera bint Mohammad Ameen bin Abdullah
Shukoor bint Mohammad bin Salim al-Ghammari
Salma bint Mohammad bin Sulaiman al-Lamki

Pakistan

Women

Right to vote: August 1947
To stand for election: August 1947

Executive

Power past

Benazir Bhutto, Prime Minister, December 2, 1988–August 6, 1990; October 19, 1993–November 5, 1996. Bhutto, daughter of deposed president Zulfikar Ali Bhutto, became the first female head of government in a Muslim country when her party won the 1988 parliamentary elections. Her tenure was marked by unrest and shifting sentiments in Parliament, resulting in her removal from office by Pakistan's president in 1990. After a series of unstable governments, new elections returned Bhutto to power in 1993. However, in November 1996, she was again dismissed from office by presidential fiat. Bhutto, along with her entrepreneurial husband, faced charges of corruption, money laundering, and various other offenses, all of which she claimed were politically motivated. The couple was found guilty, sentenced to five years in prison, and levied an $8.6 million fine, and Bhutto was disqualified from public office. Bhutto is a relatively young woman, so there are more chapters to be written in her political career. A third term in office is not at all an unlikely prospect.

Notable presidential candidate, 1965

Fatima Jinnah. Sister of Mohammed Ali Jinnah, the founder and first governor-general of Pakistan (1947–1948), Fatima was popularly known as the "Mother of the Country." She became the candidate of a coalition of opposition parties (even listed on the ballot as "Combined Opposition Parties") when the original nominee died unexpectedly. During the campaign, Fatima became the first Pakistani politician to openly espouse the idea that her country should acquire a nuclear capability. She ran a surprisingly good race, drawing large crowds, and placed second in the presidential balloting to President Mohammed Ayub Khan, who was running for reelection. She carried the country's three largest cities—Karachi, Dacca, and Chittagong—and might have actually won the contest had the election not been controlled by an "electoral" college rather than by popular vote.

First appointed to cabinet

Mahmooda Saleem Khan, Minister of Education, 1962

Notable service in cabinet

Tahmina Daultana, Minister of Women, Social Welfare, and Special Education
Syeda Abida Hussain, Minister of the Environment and Women's Affairs; Minister of Education, Science, and Technology
Zahida Khaliquz Zaman, Minister of Health

First appointed ambassador

Ra'ana Liaquat Ali Khan, Ambassador to the Netherlands and Belgium, 1954. Khan has been recognized as the first Muslim woman in the world to hold the rank of ambassador.

First provincial governor

Ra'ana Liaquat Ali Khan, Sind, 1973

Legislative

First elected to national legislature (Constituent Assembly)

Shaista Suhrawardy Ikramullah
Jahanara Shah Nawaz

Both elected 1947. Ikramullah had been elected in 1946 to the joint Constituent Assembly of India, before Pakistan split off. Because of the ongoing partition debate, the Muslim League instructed its members not to take their seats in the assembly.

PALAU

Women

Right to vote: April 2, 1979
To stand for election: April 2, 1979

Executive

First appointed to cabinet

Dilmei L. Olkeriil, Minister of Community and Cultural Affairs, 1990

Notable service in cabinet

Ernestine K. Rengiil, Attorney General
Sandra Sumang Pierantozzi, Minister of Administration

First appointed ambassador

No woman yet appointed

Legislative

First elected to the national legislature (House of Delegates)

Akiko Catherine Sugiyama, Ngardmau State, 1975

First elected to national legislature (Senate)

Sandra Sumang Pierantozzi, 1997

Panama

Women

Right to vote: July 5, 1941; March 1, 1946
To stand for election: July 5, 1941; March 1, 1946[39]

Executive

Mireya Elisa Moscoso Arias Rodriguez, President, September 1, 1999–present. Mireya's second run for the presidency (see below) brought her the prize. She defeated Martin Torrijos, the son of the man who had ousted her husband from the presidency almost thirty years earlier. Her late husband, Arnulfo Arias de la Madrid, was elected president three times (1940, 1949, and 1968), and lost his office all three times in military coups. In fact, he served only eleven days of his third term before being overthrown by Omar Torrijos in 1968. Mireya, aged twenty-two at the time, married the near-octogenarian a year later, while he was in exile. She was a former government secretary, and she picked up Arias's political mantle when he died some nineteen years later. Mireya ran for president on the Arnulfista Party ticket, gathering almost 45 percent of the vote to defeat the junior Torrijos and a third candidate. She is a populist, and has promised a "new deal" for the Panamanian people. She will preside over the return of the Panama Canal from the United States during her first year in office. If Mireya manages to complete her five-year term, she will have served longer than all her late husband's stints in office put together.

Notable presidential candidate, 1994

Mireya Elisa Moscoso Arias Rodriguez. Mireya, the widow of three-time president Arnulfo Arias de la Madrid, was the candidate of the Democratic Alliance, of which her family's Arnulfista Party was a coalition member. She placed second with slightly more than 29 percent of the vote, coming in ahead of internationally known salsa singer Ruben Blades.

First appointed to cabinet

Maria Santa Domingo de Miranda, Minister of Social Welfare and Health, 1950

---

[39] A 1941 electoral law granted a limited franchise to women (to vote for and be elected to provincial bodies) if they held a university degree or had completed vocational training, a teacher's college, or secondary schooling. Full political rights were granted to women in 1946.

Notable service in cabinet

Edith de Bethancourth, Minister of Health
Leonor Calderon, Minister of Women, Youth, Family, and Childhood
Doris Rosa de Mata, Minister of Education
Aida Libia Moreno de Rivera, Minister of Health
Susana Richa de Torrijos, Minister of Education
Mariela Sagel, Minister of Government and Justice
Alba Esther Tejada de Rolla, Minister of Women, Youth, Family, and Childhood
Nitzia de Villareal, Minister of Commerce and Industry
Ivonne Young Vales, Minister of the Presidency

First appointed ambassador

Maria Lakes Bahas, Ambassador to Greece and Syria, 1979

Legislative

First elected to national legislature (Asamblea Legislativa, Legislative Assembly)

Esther Neira de Calvo, Liberal Party
Gumercinda Páez, Liberal Party

Both elected 1946

Head of national legislature

Balbina Herrera Araúz, Legislative Assembly, 1994–1999

Judicial

Notable service on supreme court

Marisol Vargas de Vasquez, Chief Justice

Minority: Chinese-Panamanian

Executive

First appointed ambassador

Carlos Yap, Ambassador to the Republic of China on Taiwan, 1990

Minority: Native Indian

Executive

First woman elected cacique *(tribal leader)*

Gabriela Caballero, Ngobe-Buglé tribe

Papua New Guinea

Women

Right to vote: February 15, 1964
To stand for election: February 27, 1963

Executive

First elected provincial governor

Josephine Abaijah, Milne Bay Province

First elected provincial premier

Enny Moaitz, Morobe Province, 1987

First appointed to cabinet

Nahau Rooney, Minister of Corrective Institutions and Liquor Licensing, 1977

Notable service in cabinet

Nahau Rooney, Minister of Justice; Minister of Decentralization

First appointed ambassador

Margareth Taylor, Ambassador to the United States, Canada, and Mexico, 1988

Legislative

First appointed to colonial legislature (House of Assembly)

Regina Booth, 1951

First elected to colonial legislature (House of Assembly)

Josephine Abaijah, Papua Besena Movement, 1972

First elected to national legislature (National Parliament)

Josephine Abaijah, Papua Besena Movement
Waliyato Clowes, Papuan Alliance
Nahau Rooney, Pangu Pati

All elected July 1977

Paraguay

Women

Right to vote: July 5, 1961
To stand for election: July 5, 1961

Paraguay was the last country in the Americas to grant women the right to vote and stand for election to office.

Executive

First appointed to cabinet

Maria Cynthia Prieto Conti de Alegre, Minister of Health, 1989

Notable service in cabinet

Maria Celsa Bareiro de Soto, Minister of Education and Culture
Haydee Carmagnola de Aquino, Minister of Women's Affairs
Carmen Frutos Albospino de Almada, Minister of Public Health and Social Welfare
Cristina Muñoz, Minister for Women

First appointed ambassador

Isabel Aurva Vallejo, Ambassador to Brazil, 1945

Legislative

First elected to national legislature
(Cámara de Representantes, Chamber of Representatives)

Two women, April 1, 1963

PERU

Women

Right to vote: September 7, 1955
To stand for election: September 7, 1955

Executive

Notable presidential candidate, 1995

Mercedes Cabanillas de Llanos de la Mata, candidate of the American Popular Revolutionary Alliance Party of discredited former president Alan García. She placed third, with slightly more than 4 percent of the vote, in the April 9, 1995, election. The victor in that contest was Alberto Fujimori (see below).

Notable presidential candidate, 1985

Dora Narres Valdivia de Castillo. She was the candidate of the Union Nacional Odrista Party.

First appointed to cabinet

Iida Iruzar, Minister of Health, 1987

Notable service in cabinet

Mercedes Cabanillas de Llanos de la Mata, Minister of Education
Elsa Carrera Cabrera de Escalante, Minister of Transportation, Communication, Housing, and Construction
Liliana Canale Novella, Minister of Trade, Industry, and Tourism
Blanca Nelida Colán, Attorney General
Maria Luisa Federici, Minister of the Presidency
Gloria Helfer, Minister of Public Education
Maria Cristina Rizo Patron, Minister of the Presidency
Miriam Schenome, Minister for the Promotion of Women and Human Development
Luisa Maria Cuculiza Torres, Minister for the Promotion of Women and Human Development
Maria Carlota Valenzuela, Minister of Justice

First appointed ambassador

Carmela Aguilar Ayanz, Ambassador to Portugal, 1980

First mayor of a major city

Anita Fernandini de Narajo, Lima

Legislative

First elected to national legislature (Senado, Senate)

Irene Silva de Santolalla, April 7, 1956

First elected to national legislature
(Cámara de Diputados, Chamber of Deputies)

Lola Blanco de la Rosa Sanchez
Alicia Blanco Montesinos
Maria Mercedes Colina Lozano de Gotuzzo
Carlota Ramos de Santolaya
Matilde Perez Palacios Carranza
Maria Silva Silva
Juana Ubillus de Palacios

All elected April 7, 1956

Head of national legislature

Martha Chávez Cossio de Ocampo, Congreso (Congress), 1995

Judicial

First appointed to supreme court

Elsi Landa Zapater, 1990

Minority: Chinese-Peruvian

Executive

First to serve as prime minister

Victor Joy-Way Rojas, 1998

First appointed to cabinet

Victor Joy-Way Rojas, Minister of Industry and Trade, 1991

Legislative

Head of national legislature

Victor Joy-Way Rojas, Congreso (Congress), 1996–1997

Minority: Japanese-Peruvian

Executive

Alberto Kenyo Fujimori Fujimori, President, July 28, 1990–present. Fujimori, the son of Japanese immigrants—there are some 50,000 Japanese-Peruvians—was a surprise victor in the April 1990 presidential elections. A college rector and onetime professor (he was a mathematician and head of the National Agrarian University), he had only sought office once before, a losing run for mayor of Lima the previous year. Novelist Mario Vargas Llosa was tipped to win the presidential race, but Fujimori, running a populist campaign, surprised everyone, except probably himself. A strong, decisive president, he smashed the guerrilla insurgencies that had plagued Peru for years, dismissed Congress in 1992, rewrote the constitution, established a new political party, then ran for reelection in 1995. In that contest, he bested another well-known personality: the former secretary-general of the United Nations, Javier Pérez de Cuéllar. Although Fujimori frequently sags in the opinion polls, he always pushes his agenda with a single-minded determination based on what he believes is right, usually to the consternation of everyone else, including his wife. The couple fell afoul of each other, separated, then divorced. Susana Higuchi Fujimori even mounted a short-lived, sputtering campaign for president herself in the 1995 election, before dropping out. Barred from what would be his third term, Fujimori has nevertheless been maneuvering to secure the right to run again. He's even rearranged Peru's supreme court in order to be declared eligible to seek reelection.

Notable service in cabinet

Daniel Hokama Tokashiki, Minister of Energy and Mines

Legislative

Head of national legislature

Jaime Yoshiyama Tanaka, Democratic Constituent Congress, 1992–1995

Minority: Native Indian

Executive

First elected president

Ramón Castilla, Quecha, April 1845

First appointed to cabinet

Ramón Castilla, Quecha, Minister of the Treasury, 1839

Religious Minority: Jewish

Executive

First appointed to cabinet

Efraín Goldenberg-Schreiber, Prime Minister, 1994

Philippines

Women

Right to vote: April 30, 1937
To stand for election: April 30, 1937

Executive

Gloria Macapagal Arroyo, Vice-President, June 30, 1998–present. Daughter of former president Diosdado Macapagal (1961–1965) and a senator, Arroyo ran on the LAKAS-NUC ticket headed by José de Venecia and endorsed by outgoing president Fidel Ramos. The Philippines allows split voting for its two highest offices; Arroyo outran her own running mate and topped the vote for Edgardo Angara, the vice-presidential choice of winning presidential candidate Joseph Estrada. She has moved to the forefront of Philippine politics and is a serious contender for the next presidential race in 2004. If Estrada stumbles badly in office, as some believe him capable of doing, she could move up to the presidential palace even sooner.

Power past

Corazon Cojuangco Aquino, President, February 25, 1986–June 30, 1992. Aquino, widow of assassinated politician and presidential aspirant Benigno Aquino, led the fight after her husband's death against the conjugal dictatorship of President Ferdinand Marcos and his wife, Imelda. She—and her coalition of allies—successfully pressured Marcos into calling a presidential election, then outwitted him at every turn. Before he could declare victory and effectively steal the election from her, Aquino claimed victory herself and had herself sworn in, then organized massive protests. The tremendous pressure, both internal and international, caused the Marcos duo to finally give up and flee the country, along with many of their cronies. After a rocky term in office, marked by several military revolts and pressure from separatist and other forces, Aquino wisely chose not to seek reelection to a second term, being contented with having restored democracy to the Philippines. Because of her remarkable feat in toppling one of the world's longest-ruling dictators almost by sheer force of will, she was chosen as *Time* magazine's Woman of the Year for 1986, only the third individual female selected for that honor.

Ex–partner in power

Imelda Marcos, 1972–1986. Wife (and widow) of longtime president Ferdinand Marcos, Imelda has been a cabinet minister and a governor, and is now a member of the House of Representatives. Known as the Iron Butterfly, Imelda has been accused of helping her husband loot the Philippines of untold billions during his twenty-odd years in power. When their conjugal dictatorship was toppled in 1986, they fled to exile in the United States, leaving behind Imelda's 3,000 pairs of shoes, 2,000 gowns, 200 girdles, and 500 bras. Still proclaiming her innocence, she was allowed to return to the Philippines in 1991 to bury her husband's body. She continues to fight a twenty-four-year jail sentence, along with myriad lawsuits filed by the government over the missing billions. Imelda ran for president in 1992, finishing fifth out of seven contenders. She still can't be counted "out" in politics, however. In 1995, she was reelected to the House of Representatives. When Imelda isn't pursuing her political interests, she spends time crawling down church aisles on her knees, praying for a happy outcome to her various legal problems. By 1998, Imelda's shoe was back in the presidential race once again. In April of that year, however, she abruptly dropped out, citing fears that violence would mar the voting.

Notable presidential candidate, 1992; 1998

Miriam Defensor Santiago. Santiago, who formerly headed a special presidential commission under Corazon Aquino, won nearly 20 percent of the vote to place second to Fidel Ramos in the May 1992 presidential race, in which she claimed that he cheated her of victory by rigging the ballot counting. In 1995, she was elected to a Senate seat but didn't make much of an impression in that chamber. Santiago launched another bid for the presidency in 1998 on her self-formed People's Reform Party ticket. In this election, Santiago appeared to be a spent force, winning only 2 percent of the vote to finish seventh among the candidates.

First appointed to cabinet

Asuncion Arnola Perez, Minister of Social Welfare, 1949

Notable service in cabinet

Emilia Boncodin, Secretary of Budget and Management
Nieves Confessor, Minister of Labor and Employment
Gemma Cruz Araneta, Secretary of Tourism
Corazon de Leon, Minister of Social Welfare and Development
Mina Gabor, Secretary of Tourism
Lina Liago, Secretary of Social Welfare and Development
Narzaline Lim, Minister of Tourism
Imelda Marcos, Minister of Human Settlements
Mita Pardo de Tavera, Minister of Social Welfare
Erlinda Perfianco, Secretary of Education, Culture, and Sports
Carmencita Reodica, Minister of Health

First appointed ambassador

Trinidad Fernandez Legarda, Ambassador to the Republic of Vietnam, 1962

First elected provincial governor

Guadelupe Carreon Adaza, Misamis province, 1937

Legislative

First to serve in colonial legislature (Philippine Assembly)

Hillary Clapp, 1931

First elected to commonwealth legislature (National Assembly)

Elisa Rosales Ochoa, November 1941

First elected to national legislature (House of Representatives)

Remedios Ozamis Fortica, 1946

First elected to national legislature (Senate)

Geronima T. Pecson, 1953

Judicial

First appointed judge

Natividad Lopez

First appointed to supreme court

Cecilia Muñoz Palma, 1973

Religious Minority: Muslim

Legislative

First elected to national legislature (Senate)

Haji Butu

Religious Minority: Protestant

Executive

First elected president

Fidel V. Ramos, 1992

Poland

Women

Right to vote: November 28, 1918
To stand for election: November 28, 1918

Executive

Power past

Hanna Suchocka, Prime Minister, August 8, 1992–October 14, 1993. Suchocka, a lawyer and former cabinet minister, was tapped as prime minister by president Lech Walesa. Within a short time, however, she learned that he was not averse to undermining her government. Suchocka struggled, but eventually lost this power game. Her fall led to a new general election, won by the ex-communists, which was surely not Walesa's intention when he first began feuding with his prime minister.

Notable presidential candidate, 1995

Hanna Gronliewicz-Waltz. Chairwoman of the Polish National Bank, Gronliewicz-Waltz made an independent bid for the presidency, supported by several right-wing and nationalist groups. She placed seventh with almost 3 percent of the vote.

First appointed to cabinet

Zofia Wasilkowska, Minister of Justice, 1956. In 1918, seven women, including **Irene Kosmowska,** vice-minister of social welfare, were appointed to various vice-ministerial positions in the Polish cabinet.

Notable service in cabinet

Franciszka Cegielska, Minister of Health
Izabella Czwinska, Minister of Culture and Arts
Teresa Kaminska, Minister of Social Affairs
Anna Kedzierska, Minister of Home Trade
Maria Milczarek, Minister of Labor
Anna Popowicz, Minister of Women's and Family Affairs
Hanna Suchocka, Minister of Justice
Joanna Wnuk-Nazarowa, Minister of Culture and Arts

First appointed ambassador

Maria Regent-Lachowicz, Ambassador to Sweden, 1983

Legislative

First elected to national legislature (Sejm, Diet)

Gabryela Balicka
Jadwiga Dziubinska
Irena Kosmowska
Maria Moczydlowska
Zofia Moraczewska
Zofia Sokolnicka

All elected January 26, 1919

Head of national legislature

Alicja Grzeskowiak, Senate, 1997–present

Judicial

First appointed to supreme court

Marion Mushkat, 1945

Minority: African

Executive

First elected to office

Anaclet Kalondji, Niedzialki village council, 1998

Minority: Ukrainian

Legislative

First woman elected to national legislature (Senate)

Halyna Levchanivs'ka, 1920

Portugal

Women

Right to vote: May 5, 1931; November 16, 1934; 1951; June 2, 1976
To stand for election: May 5, 1931; November 16, 1934; 1951; June 2, 1976[40]

Executive

Power past

Maria da Lourdes Pintasilgo, Prime Minister, August 1, 1979–January 3, 1980. Among the revolving minority governments that regularly rose and fell in the aftermath of Portugal's 1974 revolution was one headed by Pintasilgo. A chemical engineer by training, she had formerly held several cabinet portfolios, including minister of social affairs; she had been ambassador to UNESCO and had held a seat in Parliament; and she had authored three books. Pintasilgo was a founder of the Portuguese National Committee on the Status of Women. Her short-lived coalition government was in power only until new elections could be held. In 1986, perhaps having enjoyed her taste of power several years earlier, Pintasilgo ran for president (see below).

Notable presidential candidate, 1986

Maria da Lourdes Pintasilgo, Independent. A former prime minister (see above), Pintasilgo ran strongest in rural areas and, naturally, among women. That combination, however, wasn't strong enough to allow her to place higher than fourth (among the four primary candidates running).

First appointed to cabinet

Maria Teresa Lobo, Minister of Social Affairs, 1971

---

[40]In 1931, women were given the right to vote and stand for election, with the restriction that they had to have completed secondary or higher education (men only had to know how to read and write). All citizens who were literate were granted the right to vote and stand for election in 1934. Some restrictions on women, however, remained for election to certain local administrative bodies under a 1968 law. Full equality of the sexes with regard to the franchise and right of election to all bodies was achieved in 1976.

Notable service in cabinet

Elise da Costa Guimares Ferreira, Minister of the Environment
Teresa Gouveia, Minister of the Environment and Natural Resources
Manuela Ferreira Leite, Minister of Education
Maria Manuela Margado, Minister of Finance
Maria da Lourdes Pintasilgo, Minister of Social Affairs
Maria Rodrigues, Minister of Labor
Maria de Belem Roseira, Minister of Health

First appointed ambassador

Maria da Lourdes Pintasilgo, Ambassador to UNESCO, 1974

First appointed regional governor

Mariana Calhau, Évora

Legislative

First elected to national legislature (Assembleia da Republica, Assembly of the Republic)

Domitila de Carvalho, Accao Nacional Popular Party
Maria Guardiola, Accao Nacional Popular Party
Maria Candida Pereira, Accao Nacional Popular Party

All elected November 24, 1934, and seated January 11, 1935

Minority: African

Legislative

Notable service in national legislature (National Legislative Assembly)

Jamie Pinto Bull, from Portuguese Guinea province, 1964

QATAR

Women

Right to vote: 1999
To stand for election: 1999

In 1998, Qatar, one of the world's few remaining nations in which women were disenfranchised, announced that it would conduct its first real election on March 8, 1999. The contest was for a twenty-nine-member municipal council in Doha, the capital. According to diplomatic sources posted in the country, the municipal council election was to serve as a rehearsal for possible parliamentary elections in the near future. This assessment was based on the fact that the ruler, Emir Sheikh Hamad ibn Khalifa ibn Thani, had also appointed a committee of experts in November 1998 to draw up a permanent constitution for the country. That document, it was rumored, would provide for a directly elected Parliament.

The extension of the vote to women, and their right to stand for office, came about in an almost unannounced manner. No direct statement was ever made about the decision. It wasn't until preparations were almost complete for the municipal council election that the question even arose publicly. Once it did, the government confirmed that women would indeed be permitted to participate. Six women immediately stepped forward to offer themselves as candidates, along with more than 200 men. Back in June 1998, when open discussion about the election first began, conservative Muslim religious leaders had petitioned the emir to limit voting to men. Apparently, the emir simply chose to ignore their petition, perhaps swayed by his wife, Sheikha Moza. To encourage women's participation, she held several open meetings about the issue, inviting prominent women from other Persian Gulf nations to visit and discuss the matter.

In the March 8, 1999, event, most of the winners were well-known civil servants from prominent families. None of the six women won, and some expressed bitter disappointment. Still, women voting and running as candidates was a first for the Gulf region. Qatar's conservative neighbors were watching closely. And Qatar's first elected female officeholder will likely take her seat in the not-too-distant future.

Executive

First appointed to ministry position

Sheikha Ahmed al-Mahmoud, Undersecretary in the Ministry of Information and Culture, 1996

Legislative

First female candidates

Muza al-Malk (Moza al-Malik)
Jihan al-Mir
Wadha al-Suweidi
Nisya Darwish
And two other women, all 1999, Doha Municipal Council

Romania

Women

Right to vote: 1929; July 1946
To stand for election: 1929; July 1946[41]

Royalty

Ex–partner in power

Marie, Queen, October 10, 1914–July 20, 1927. Granddaughter of Queen Victoria and wife of Ferdinand I, Marie made her mark during World War I. She persuaded her pro-German husband—he was both a German *and* a Hohenzollern—to side with the Allies. Romania suffered terribly because of the couple's decision, but the conflict allowed Marie to shine. She worked as a Red Cross nurse, then oversaw a cholera camp, where she nursed the wounded and assisted in operations. Marie's reward came when the peace treaties at the war's end doubled Romania's population and territory. Additionally, she had gained worldwide fame for her activities as a wartime nurse. Whirlwind tours across Europe and to the United States followed. After Ferdinand's death, the shenanigans of Marie's son Carol—and his mistress—overshadowed her own good deeds, ruining the respect for the Romanian monarchy that she had worked so hard to achieve.

Ex–power behind the throne

Elena (Magda) Lupescu, 1923–1940. Largely forgotten now, the red-haired Magda was once considered the most notorious Jewish temptress since Delilah. A grand royal favorite in the mode of a du Barry or de Pompadour, she became involved in 1923 with Carol, crown prince of Romania, after his divorce from showgirl Zizi Lamparino. Within two years, he had renounced his right to the throne so that he could continue to cavort with Magda, but he changed his mind when his father died in 1927. After a brief period, Carol changed his fickle mind again, deciding to forgo becoming King Carol II and to let his small son rule instead. (Carol had actually made a legitimate "royal" marriage between his affairs with Zizi and Magda and sired a royal heir!) Three years later, Carol stormed back into Romanian politics, pushed his son aside, and seated himself on the throne, still in thrall to Magda. As

[41]Women were granted restricted electoral rights in 1929, and those under the same conditions as men in 1946.

fascism swept across Europe, Carol—along with Magda and a coterie of royal advisers hand-picked by her—viewed himself as a counterbalance to the movement's progress in Romania. He had judged himself wrongly, however, and was forced off the throne in 1940 as the country slipped under a pro-German militaristic dictatorship, although with Carol's son back on the throne as a figurehead. Magda departed with Carol to a rich, idle exile in Estoril, Portugal, where they sat out World War II. When the couple finally married in 1947, she was proclaimed "Princess" Elena, but was barely accepted by European royalty because of the couple's unsavory past. Carol died in 1953, leaving Magda to spend his millions alone until her death in Estoril in 1977.

Executive

Ex–Red Queen, partner in power

Elena Ceauşescu, 1965–1989, wife of dictator Nicolae Ceauşescu. Elena, despite her insufficient education, fancied herself a great scientist. She demanded and received accolades from all Romanian scientific institutes, and was wont to demand honorary degrees from foreign institutions, too. Her name appeared on many scientific papers and publications, due to her position and never to her intelligence. Elena's husband placed her on the Romanian politburo, the ruling council, and the couple made plans for their wastrel, drunken son Nicu to succeed his father one day. Elena grandly titled herself "Mother of the Country," but Romania's general populace had less favorable names for her, spoken in whispered tones to avoid the couple's wrath and their dreaded security establishment. Elena and Nicolae met the bloodiest fate of all the communist dictators unseated in the revolution that swept East Europe in the late 1980s. They were seized and tried by an ad hoc court in December 1989, which videotaped them alternately threatening, whining, and haggling about what was happening to them. Within minutes of the trial's end, Elena and Nicolae were executed, clinging to each other for support.

Ex–formidable power

Ana Rabinsohn Pauker, 1944–1953. Pauker, a Jew of Bessarabian descent, was part of a triumvirate than ran Romania after its takeover by communists. Although nominal power resided with Prime Minister Petru Groza (a dupe of the communists, though not communist himself), many regarded Pauker as the real ruler of the country. Named foreign minister in 1952, she was such a slavish follower of Moscow that Balkan wits accused her of carrying an umbrella in Bucharest when it rained in the Russian capital. Despite her unflagging adherence to the Red line, and to Stalin personally, Pauker was purged from power in 1953 and arrested the next year. She was luckier than many people purged under Stalin's instructions: She wasn't executed. Pauker was released after a short time in prison and ignored thereafter. She died in 1960, largely forgotten by Romanians.

First appointed to cabinet

Florica Bagdasar, Minister of Health, 1946

Notable service in cabinet

Maria Bobu, Minister of Justice
Elena Ceauşescu, Deputy Prime Minister
Lina Ciobanu, Minister of Light Industry
Constanţa Crăcium, Minister of Culture
Stella Enescu, Minister of Social Services
Cornelia Filipas, Deputy Prime Minister
Maria Flucsa, Minister of Light Industry
Suzana Gădea, Minister of Education
Alexandrina Gainuse, Minister of Labor
Ana Muresan, Minister of Domestic Trade
Ana Rabinsohn Pauker, Minister of Foreign Affairs
Paula Prioteasa, Minister of Food Industry and Collection of Agricultural Products
Aneta Spornic, Minister of Education and Instruction
Romica Tomescu, Minister of Waters, Forests, and Environmental Protection

First appointed ambassador

Elena Vacaresco, Ambassador to the League of Nations, 1924. The first woman appointed as an ambassador under the communist recgime was **Stana Dāgoi,** appointed ambassador to Denmark in 1978.

Legislative

First elected to national legislature (Marea Adunare Nationala, Grand National Assembly)

Florica Bagdasar, National Popular Party
Ana Bārbulescu, Plugarilor Front Party
Constanţa Crăcium, Communist Party
Maria Ilie Lazār, National Party
Elena Livezeanu, Plugarilor Front Party
Mihaela Manase, Social Democratic Party
Maria Marian, Social Democratic Party
Mariana Negurā, National Liberal Party
Ana Rabinsohn Pauker, Communist Party
Eugenia Rādāceanu, Social Democratic Party
Maria Rosetti, Independent
Jeaneta Safir, Social Democratic Party
Alexandra Sencovici, Communist Party

Maria Sevastru, Social Democratic Party
Alexandra Sidorovici, Communist Party
Elena Stoia, Communist Party
Olimpia Tenescu, Communist Party
Maria Tonsiulescu, Social Democratic Party

All elected November 19, 1946

Head of national legislature

Marie Gheorge, Grand National Assembly, 1983–1989
Alexandrina Gainuse, Grand National Assembly, 1978–1981

Minority: Hungarian

Executive

First to serve in national executive position

Ioan Cioabă, Provisional National Council, 1989

Notable service in cabinet

György Tokay, Minister Without Portfolio for Minority Affairs

Minority: Roma (Gypsy)

Legislative

First appointed to national legislature (Parlamental Romániei, Parliament)

Gheorghe Răducanu, Romani Democratic Forum, 1990

Religious Minority: Jewish

Legislative

First elected to national legislature

Four persons, 1931

Russia[42]

Women

Right to vote: June 1918
To stand for election: June 1918

Royalty

Power past

Alexandra, Czarina, October 20, 1894–March 15, 1917. Wife of Nicholas II, the last czar, Alexandra seemed cursed on all sides. She was a German in a land at war with her ancestral homeland, distrusted by the people her husband ruled, married to an inept, fearful, and indecisive man whom she deeply loved, and after having four daughters in a row finally produced a male heir to the throne who was plagued with hemophilia. Taken together, these factors in combination practically destined anarchy, an apt characterization of Alexandra's life and effect on Russia. She fell under the sinister presence of Rasputin, a dissolute mystic faith healer whose hold over her, in an era when the private lives of royals were shaded from view, was never understood by the Russian people. His escapades offended the sensibilities of the Russians, whether nobles or peasants, and Alexandra bore the brunt of their anger. Nicholas left her ostensibly in charge while he was away leading his troops—in his usual inept fashion—during World War I, which led to her being blamed even more vigorously when the conflict began to go badly for the Russians. The result of Alexandra and Nicholas's bungling was that the Romanov dynasty, which had ruled for more than 300 years, ended with the czar's abdication in 1917. Alexandra was murdered, along with Nicholas and all their children, by the communists in 1918. After the fall of the communist regime in 1991, the family members' bodies were recovered from a hidden grave, and they were laid to rest during a funeral ceremony in 1997.

Executive

Ex-power behind the scenes

Tatyana Dyanchenko, 1989–1999. Youngest daughter of President Boris Yeltsin, Tatyana is probably her father's closest political adviser, mainly because he tends to be reclusive and

[42]The information included here pertains both to Russia and to the former Soviet Union.

distrusts almost everyone else. Trained as a mathematician, she tracked missile trajectories at the Salyut Space Center before easing into a background role in politics. Tatyana managed her father's presidential campaign in 1996, bringing him to a second-term victory from a single-digit standing in the polls only months beforehand. When her father resigned the presidency on the last day of 1999, Tatyana lost all her power.

Ex–Red Queen, partner in power

Raisa Maksimovna Gorbachev, 1985–1991. Wife of reforming communist general secretary (later president) Mikhail Gorbachev, Raisa was a onetime lecturer in Leninist theology and also one of her husband's closest advisers. Reputed to be a dogmatic woman, she was known for a rivalry with her 1980s counterpart Nancy Reagan, wife of U.S. President Ronald Reagan. Rumors swirled that after one meeting, Nancy commented, "Who does that dame think she is?" After her husband's fall from power, Raisa attempted her own unsuccessful run for the Russian Parliament as the head of a minor women's ticket. She died in 1999 of leukemia and was buried with honors and quite a bit of grief from the Russian public. This was a surprise ending to her life, because the Russian people had been rather cool toward Raisa while her husband was in power.

First to sit on the Presidium of the USSR

Ekaterina Furtseva, 1956

First appointed to cabinet

Alekandra Mikhalovna Kollontai, Commissar of Propaganda and Agitation, 1919. In one of the short-lived 1917 prerevolutionary governments, **Countess Sofia Vladimirova Paina-Polovteseva** was appointed deputy minister of social affairs.

Notable service in cabinet

Ludmilla Bezlepkina, Minister of Social Security
Natalya L. Dementyeva, Minister of Culture
Oksana G. Dmitriyeva, Minister of Labor and Social Development
Tatyana B. Dmitriyeva, Minister of Health
Ekaterina Furtseva, Minister of Culture
Mariiya Kovrigina, Minister of Health
Valentina Matvienko, Deputy Prime Minister; Minister of Social Affairs; Minister of Labor Relations
Aleksandra Pochinok, Minister of Taxes and Levies

First president of a Soviet Socialist Republic

A. F. Nuortiva, Karelian Soviet Socialist Republic, 1924

First elected governor

Valentina Bronevich, Koryak Autonomous Region, 1996

First appointed ambassador

Alekandra Mikhalovna Kollontai, Ambassador to Norway, 1923. Some authorities have cited **Larissa Reisner** as the ambassador to Afghanistan in 1921, probably because she accompanied her father, noted orientalist Igor M. Reisner, on a special assignment there. The Russian State Library, however, confirms that Kollontai was the first formally appointed female ambassador.

Legislative

First elected to national legislature
(Verkhovnyi Soviet SSR, Supreme Soviet of the USSR)

Maria Aleksandrovna Spiridonova, 1922

Head of national legislature

Yadgar S. Nasriddinova, presiding officer of the House of Nationalities of the Supreme Soviet of the USSR, 1970 (*see also* Uzbekistan)

Judicial

First appointed to supreme court

Irina Yekaterina, 1951

Minority: Gay

Executive

First appointed to cabinet

Andrei Cherkizov, Minister of Culture, 1996

Minority: Japanese-Russian

Legislative

First elected to national legislature (State Duma, Parliament)

Irina Khakamada, Common Cause Party, 1993

Rwanda

Women

Right to vote: September 25, 1961
To stand for election: September 25, 1961; December 1978[43]

Executive

Power past

Agathe Uwilingiyimana, Prime Minister, July 17, 1993–April 7, 1994. Uwilingiyimana, a former minister of education and a compromise candidate for prime minister, was appointed by Hutu president Juvénal Habyarimana to bring balance into Rwanda's government between the underrepresented majority Hutu people and the long-dominant but minority Tutsis. After ethnic warfare broke out between the two groups in 1994, the violence quickly degenerated into genocide against the minority Tutsis. Uwilingiyimana was viewed as a traitor by many fellow Hutus and, as such, marked for extermination by Hutu extremists. She and her entire family were slain during the fighting by renegade Hutu soldiers, who had been encouraged in their rampage by a radical faction in the Hutu-dominated army.

Ex–power behind the scenes

Agathe Kanziga Habyarimana, 1973–1994. Wife of President Juvénal Habyarimana. When her husband, a moderate Hutu, decided to disband the one-party rule of his National Revolutionary Movement for Democracy and move toward accommodation with Rwanda's minority Tutsi inhabitants, opposition to his plans seemed to coalesce around his wife. A clique of top advisers especially close to her, known as the "clan de Madame," including three of her brothers-in-law, formed the backbone of Hutu extremism in Rwanda. They ordered the presidential guard to form a militia tasked with thwarting any steps toward moderation. This wasn't the first time Agathe had involved herself in politics; she had previously been part of a delegation to China seeking to purchase arms for the Hutu-dominated military. On April 6, 1994, an antiaircraft missile fired from the perimeter of the capital city's airport destroyed the president's plane, killing him and the president of neighboring Burundi.

[43]In September 1961, women were granted the right to stand for all offices except that of president of the republic; that restriction was removed in 1978.

Although the Tutsis were blamed for the attack, the area from which the missile was fired was in the secure grip of the presidential guard. Within forty-five minutes of the crash, the genocidal slaughter of Tutsis, as well as of moderate Hutus, began in Rwanda. The killing ended only when a Tutsi exile army invaded in late 1994 and took over the country, causing more than a million Hutus to flee to surrounding nations. The president's widow was among those who fled. In 1996, in a French court, she and her family sued three human rights organizations that had cited her role in encouraging the genocide. The suit was tossed out, with the plaintiffs being ordered to pay the defendants' court costs.

First appointed to cabinet

Madeleine Akinkamiye, Minister of Social Affairs, 1964

Notable service in cabinet

Aloysia Inyunba, Minister of Family and Women's Affairs
Immaculee Kayumba, Minister of Transport and Communication
Angeline Muganza, Minister of Gender and Women's Development
Marthe Mukamurenzi, Minister of Justice
Agnes Ntamabyaliro, Minister of Agriculture
Pauline Nyiramasuhuko, Minister of Family and Gender Affairs
Beatrice Sebatware-Panda, Minister of Internal Affairs, Communal Development, and Resettlement
Agathe Uwilingiyimana, Minister of Education

First appointed ambassador

Not yet identified

Legislative

First elected/appointed to national legislature (Assemblée nationale, National Assembly)

Unknown number of women, December 1965

SAINT KITTS AND NEVIS

Women

Right to vote: 1951
To stand for election: 1951

Executive

First appointed to cabinet

Constance Mitcham, Minister of Health and Women's Affairs, 1984

First appointed ambassador

Laurine Fenton, High Commissioner (Ambassador) to Canada, 1991. Fenton is the high commissioner from the Organization of Eastern Caribbean States, of which St. Kitts and Nevis is a member.

Legislative

First elected to national legislature (National Assembly)

Constance Mitcham, July 1984

Head of colonial legislature

Ada-Marie Edwards

Saint Lucia

Women

Right to vote: 1924
To stand for election: 1924

Executive

Calliopa Perlette Louisy, Governor-General, September 17, 1997–present. Louisy, a well-known St. Lucian educator, was selected as governor-general after a sixteen-day political crisis sparked by the resignation of her predecessor, Sir George Mallet.

First appointed to cabinet

Heraldine Rock, Minister of Social Affairs, Housing, Group Needs, Cooperatives, the Provident Fund, and Water, 1974

Notable service in cabinet

Margarita Alexander, Minister of Education and Cultural Affairs
Sarah Flood, Minister of Health, Human Services, Family Affairs, and Women's Affairs
Lorraine Williams, Minister of Legal Affairs and Women's Affairs; Attorney General

First appointed ambassador

Sonia Johnny, Ambassador to the United States and the Organization of American States, 1997

Legislative

First elected to colonial legislature (Legislative Council)

Marie Grace Augustin, 1954

First appointed to national legislature (Senate)

Beryl Edwards, Saint Lucia Labor Party

Francis Mitchell, Saint Lucia Labor Party

Both appointed July 1979

Elected to national legislature (House of Assembly)

No woman yet elected

Judicial

Notable service on supreme court

Suzie D'auvergne, 1990

Saint Vincent and the Grenadines

Women

Right to vote: May 5, 1951
To stand for election: May 5, 1951

Executive

First appointed to cabinet

Yvonne Francis-Gibson, Minister of Youth and Women's Affairs, 1989

Notable service in cabinet

Stephanie Browne, Minister of Health and the Environment

First appointed ambassador

Laurine Fenton, High Commissioner (Ambassador) to Canada, 1991. Fenton is the high commissioner from the Organization of Eastern Caribbean States, of which St. Vincent and the Grenadines is a member.

Legislative

First elected to national legislature (House of Assembly)

Valcina Ash, Labor Party
Ivy Joshua, People's Political Party

Both elected December 1979

Head of national legislature

Fatima Adams, 1989–1991

Judicial

First appointed to supreme court

Sylvia Bertrand

SAMOA

Women

Right to vote: October 1990
To stand for election: October 1990[44]

Executive

First appointed to cabinet

Fiame Naomi Mata'afa, Minister of Culture, Youth, and Sports, 1991. Her father was the first prime minister of independent Samoa, and her mother (see below) was the nation's first female ambassador.

Notable service in cabinet

Polataivo Fosi, Minister of Women's Affairs
Brenda Heather, Attorney General
Leniu Tofaeono, Minister of Women's Affairs

First appointed ambassador

Laulu Fetauimalemau Mata'afa, High Commissioner (Ambassador) to New Zealand, 1989. Her husband was the nation's first prime minister after independence, and their daughter (see above) was the first woman appointed to a cabinet position.

Legislative

First appointed to national legislature (Fono, Legislative Assembly)

Taulapapa Faimaaia Vaovasa-Manaia Filipo, 1970

First elected to national legislature (Fono, Legislative Assembly)

Fiame Naomi Mata'afa

---

[44]Universal suffrage was granted in 1990; prior to that, only the heads of Samoan clans had the right to vote and stand for election.

Matatumua Maimoaga Vermeulen

Both elected April 1991

Judicial

First appointed judge

Taulapapa Faimaaia Vaovasa-Manaia Filipo, 1994

San Marino

Women

Right to vote: April 29, 1959
To stand for election: September 10, 1973

Executive

San Marino, founded in the fourth century, claims to be the oldest continuous republic in the world. Every six months, two heads of state—titled captains-regent—are selected from a governing council (see below). For each of the terms of the women listed below, the co–captain-regent was a man.

Rosa Zafferani, Captain-Regent, April 1–October 1, 1999
Patricia Busignani, Captain-Regent, April 1–October 1, 1993
Edda Ceccoli, Captain-Regent, October 1, 1991–April 1, 1992
Gloriana Ranocchini, Captain-Regent, April 1–October 1, 1984; October 1, 1989–April 1, 1990
Maria Lea Pedini-Angelini, Captain-Regent, April 1–October 1, 1981

First appointed to cabinet

Clara Boscagli, Minister of Public Works, 1974

Notable service in cabinet

Clara Boscaglia, Minister of Finance
Emma Rossi, Minister of Territory and the Environment

First appointed ambassador

Savina Zafferani, Ambassador to Italy, 1989

Legislative

First elected to national legislature
(Consiglio Grande e Generale, Great General Council)

Four women, September 8, 1974

São Tomé and Príncipe

Women

Right to vote: July 12, 1975
To stand for election: July 12, 1975

Executive

Notable presidential candidate, 1996

Alda Bandeira. Former cabinet minister and candidate of the Party of Democratic Convergence, Bandeira placed third with 14 percent of the vote.

First appointed to cabinet

Alda da Graça do Espírito Santo, Minister of Culture and Education, 1975

Notable service in cabinet

Maria do Nascimento de Graça Amorim, Minister of Foreign Affairs
Alda Bandeira, Minister of Foreign Affairs
Maria das Neves Ceita Batista da Costa, Minister of Economics

First appointed ambassador

Maria do Nascimento de Graça Amorim, Ambassador to France and Portugal, 1975

Legislative

First elected to national legislature
(Assembleia Nacional, National Assembly)

Alda Bandeira
Alda da Graça do Espírito Santo
Julieta da Graça do Espírito Santo
Maria Aurora Lopes

Lurdes de Maria Lima Pires dos Santos
Maria Fernanda Pontifice J. Bonfim

All elected December 1975

Head of national legislature

Alda da Graça do Espírito Santo, National Assembly, May 12, 1980–March 2, 1991

Saudi Arabia

The right to vote does not exist in Saudi Arabia. There is no parliament, and political parties are forbidden. There is a consultative council, the Majlis as-Shura, which has ninety appointed members, but no woman has ever been appointed as a member.

In October 1999, an unusual thing—for Saudi Arabia—happened in regard to women's rights. First, the head of consultative council stated that there was *"no objection in principle"* to women being present at meetings of the council. According to him, *"Society and the council must benefit from the qualifications and experiences of women. There is absolutely nothing that prevents women from giving advice to the council."* Another member of the council echoed that sentiment, saying that allowing women to attend the council meetings *"gives them a clear recognition of their role in society, which is as important as men's role."* He went on to state that if women wanted to ask questions about the proceedings, or make suggestions, they should approach a council member before the meeting.

On the day following these two rather dramatic statements about women, it was announced that some twenty women had indeed attended a session of the consultative council, being allowed to follow the debates from a balcony overlooking the council chamber.

Previously, the crown prince had called for women to be allowed to contribute fully to society and take part in dialogue over their own future. Observers have also detected some recent movement toward granting women the right to drive automobiles in the country—undoubtedly with many restrictions.

Women's rights are now becoming an issue in the Persian Gulf countries. Therefore, closer scrutiny will be required to monitor how Saudi Arabia begins to treat this issue. Until now, after Afghanistan, Saudi Arabia had probably maintained the tightest restrictions in the world on its female citizens.

Senegal

Women

Right to vote: February 19, 1945
To stand for election: February 19, 1945

Royalty

Power past

Aline Sitoe, Queen of the Diola, Casamance, 1936–1943. Beginning in 1942, this youthful queen—she was in her early twenties—turned her people against their French overlords, making her name famous throughout French West Africa. Her battle cry, "The white man is not invincible," became a rallying point for all West Africans opposed to French rule. She encouraged a boycott of all French-made goods and fostered strong self-reliance among her people, especially among the women. French troops besieged the town that served as her power base and, after a lengthy battle, forced her to surrender. Aline Sitoe was sentenced to ten years' exile but died of scurvy shortly after surrendering. Her native Casamance region continues to clamor for self-rule, even though Senegal achieved independence from France in 1960. The area, south of the Gambia River, is a hotbed of secessionist agitation, requiring the Senegalese government in Dakar to pay close attention to the dreams that Aline Sitoe stirred up more than fifty years ago.

Executive

First appointed to cabinet

Caroline Diop Faye, Minister of Social Action, 1978

Notable service in cabinet

Marie-Loise Corea, Minister of Labor and Employment; Minister of Science and Technology
Mata Sy Diallo, Minister of Emigration, Literacy, and the Promotion of National Languages
Fambaye Fall Diop, Minister of Emigration
Mantoulaye Guene, Minister of Social Development

Maimouna Kane, Minister of Social Affairs
Therese King, Minister of Public Health
Abibatou Mbaye, Minister of African Economic Integration
Marie Sarr Mbodj, Minister of Technical and Professional Training
Aminata Mbengue Ndiaye, Minister of Family, Social Affairs, and National Solidarity
Ndioro Ndiaye, Minister of Women and Children's Affairs
Aissata Tall Sall, Minister of Information
Idrissa Seck, Minister of Trade, Crafts, and Industrialization
Aminata Tall, Minister of Literacy and the Promotion of National Languages

First appointed ambassador

Mme. Claude Absa Diallo, Ambassador to UNESCO, 1973

Legislative

First elected to national legislature (Assemblée national, National Assembly)

Caroline Diop Faye, UPS, December 1963

Minority: European

Executive

First appointed to cabinet

Jean Colin, Minister of Finance, 1964

Seychelles

Women

Right to vote: August 6, 1948
To stand for election: August 6, 1948

Executive

First appointed to cabinet

Rita Sinon, Minister of Internal Affairs, 1986

Notable service in cabinet

Noellie Alexander, Minister of Administration
Simone Testa de Comarmond, Minister of Education; Minister of Tourism and Transportation
Jacqueline Dugasse, Minister of Health
Sylvette Frichot, Minister of Information, Culture, and Youth
Sylvette Pool, Minister of Local Government, Youth, and Sports
Danielle de St. Jorre, Minister of Planning and External Affairs

First appointed ambassador

Geovinela Gonthier, Ambassador to the United States, 1983

Legislative

First elected to colonial legislature (Legislative Council)

M. H. Stevenson-Delhomme, December 1967

First appointed to national legislature (National Assembly)

Rita Savy, Seychelles Democratic Party, September 1976

First elected to national legislature (National Assembly)

Annie Athanasius, Seychelles People's Progressive Front

Lorna Camille, Seychelles People's Progressive Front
Marie Andrée Dingwall, Seychelles People's Progressive Front
Christie Fred, Seychelles People's Progressive Front
Jessy Freminot, Seychelles People's Progressive Front
Rita Gappy, Seychelles People's Progressive Front
Colette Payet, Seychelles People's Progressive Front
Helene Ragain, Seychelles People's Progressive Front

All elected June 1979

Sierra Leone

Women

Right to vote: April 27, 1961
To stand for election: April 27, 1961[45]

Executive

Notable presidential candidate, 1996

Jeridine Williams-Sarho. Candidate of the coalition Congress Party, and basically unknown, Williams-Sarho was the first woman to seek the office of president in Sierra Leone. She received less than 1 percent of the vote.

First appointed to cabinet

Ella Koblo Gulama, Minister Without Portfolio, 1962

Notable service in cabinet

Fama-Joka Bangura, Minister of Foreign Affairs
Alusine Fofanah, Minister of Foreign Affairs
Shirley Yema Gbujama, Minister of Social Welfare and Gender and Children's Affairs; Minister of Foreign Affairs
Amy Smythe, Minister of Gender and Children's Affairs

First appointed ambassador

Shirley Yema Gbujama, Ambassador to Ethiopia, 1972

First elected to office

Constance Horton Cummings-Jones, Freetown city council, 1933. Cummings-Jones was also the first woman in Africa elected to a city council seat, and was the cousin of another

---

[45]Well-to-do women (i.e., those who paid income tax or owned property) were granted the right to vote and stand for election in 1930.

pioneer African female politician, Mabel Dove (*see* Ghana, First elected to colonial legislature).

Legislative

First elected to colonial legislature

Ella Koblo Gulama, 1957

First elected/appointed to national legislature

Not yet identified

Judicial

First appointed judge

One woman, Freetown, 1943

SINGAPORE

Women

Right to vote: July 18, 1947
To stand for election: July 18, 1947

Executive

First appointed to cabinet

Seet Ai Mee, Minister of Community Development, 1991

Notable service in cabinet

Aline Wong, Minister of Health

First appointed ambassador

Jayalekshime Mohideen, Ambassador to Belgium, the Netherlands, Luxembourg, and the European Economic Community, 1989. In the same year, **Chan Heng Chee** was appointed ambassador to the United Nations.

Legislative

First appointed to colonial legislature (Legislative Council)

Elizabeth Choy Su Moi, April 10, 1951

First elected to colonial legislature (Legislative Council)

Mrs. Vilasini Menon, 1951

First elected to national legislature (Parliament)

Loh Miaw Gong, Socialist Front Party
Mrs. Devan Nair, People's Action Party
Chan Choy Siong, People's Action Party

All elected July 1963 and seated September 21, 1963

Judicial

First appointed to Supreme Court

Lai Siu Chiu, 1994

Minority: East Indian

Legislative

First woman elected to colonial legislature (Legislative Council)

Mrs. Vilasini Menon, 1951

First elected to national legislature (Parliament)

Mrs. Devan Nair, People's Action Party, 1963

SLOVAKIA[46]

Women

Right to vote: 1920
To stand for election: 1920

Executive

Notable presidential candidate, 1999

Magda Vasaryova. Independent, retired film actress *(Closely Watched Trains),* and former Czechoslovakian ambassador to Austria. She declared her candidacy for the presidency early in 1999, then obtained the necessary signatures via public petitions in a remarkably short period of time to formally enter the race. Opinion polls taken when she announced her candidacy placed Vasaryova in distant second place behind former president Michal Kovac. Slovakia's presidential election was originally due to be held in 1998 but was postponed (see below). By the time the election—now by popular vote instead of parliamentary vote—was held, Vasaryova's support had slipped to the point where she finished a distant third, with less than 7 percent of the vote.

Notable presidential candidate, 1998

Brigita Schmognerova. After President Michal Kovac's term expired in March 1998, under the Slovakian constitution, it was the duty of the Parliament to elect his successor. Although Prime Minister Vladimir Meciar (of the misnamed Movement for a Democratic Slovakia) headed the largest party, he was unable to force through any of his choices on four succeeding ballots. When the fifth ballot was taken on April 15, 1998, Schmognerova, from the Party of the Democratic Left (the second-largest in Parliament), placed second with forty-three votes. She and the front-runner were scheduled for a runoff vote on April 30, in which the winner would need a total of ninety votes, or a three-fifths majority of the members. When that vote was taken, again neither candidate was able to reach the required number of votes, although Schmognerova did gain an additional four votes. Another round of voting was then scheduled

[46]Czechoslovakia, independent since 1918, split into the Czech Republic and Slovakia on January 1, 1993. Because of that split, some information appearing under the Czech Republic in this almanac is replicated in this section.

for late May, but Schmognerova, because of her earlier losses, became ineligible. The presidential election finally was declared hopelessly deadlocked and was postponed until after new parliamentary elections. That election resulted in a new coalition of parties taking control of the government. One of the coalition's first acts was to mandate that the election of the president would henceforth be done by popular vote rather than by parliamentary election.

First appointed to cabinet (of Czechoslovakia)

Ludmila Jankovcová, Minister of Industry, 1947

First appointed to cabinet after independence

Katarina Tóthová, Minister of Justice, 1992

Notable service in cabinet

Olga Keltosova, Minister of Labor, Social Affairs, and Family
Zdenka Kramplova, Minister of Foreign Affairs
Maria Machova, Minister of the Privatization of National Property
Brigita Schmognerova, Deputy Prime Minister; Minister of Finance
Eva Slavkovska, Minister of Education
Katarina Tóthová, Deputy Prime Minister

First appointed ambassador

Klára Novotná, Ambassador to Sweden
Vera Stráznická, Ambassador to Poland and the European Council

Both appointed 1994

Legislative

First members of national assembly (National Czechoslovak Committee)

Bozena Ecksteinova, Social Democrat Party
Luisa Landova-Stychova, Czechoslovak Socialist Party

Both appointed July 1918

First delegated (indirect elections) to national legislature (Czechoslovak Revolutionary National Assembly)

Anna Chlebounova, Republican Rural Party
Bozena Ecksteinova, Social Democrat Party
Frantiska Kolarikova, Social Democrat Party
Bozena Kunĕtická-Viková, Czechoslovak National-Democratic Party
Luisa Landova-Stychova, Czechoslovak Socialist Party
Alice Masarykova, Slovak Club

Ludmila Zatloukalova, Republican Rural Party
Frantiska Zeminova, Czechoslovak Socialist Party

All delegated November 1918

First elected to national legislature (of Czechoslovakia)

Franziska Blatny, German Election Union
Anna Chlebounova, Agrarian Party
Marie Deutch, German Election Union
Betty Karpiskova, Social Democrat Party
Irene Kirpal, German Election Union
Luisa Landova-Stychova, Czechoslovak Socialist Party
Anna Mala, Social Democrat Party
Ludmila Pechmanova, Czechoslovak Socialist Party
Otilie Podzimkova, Czechoslovak Socialist Party
Eliska Purkynova, National Democratic Party
Josefa Rosolova, National Democratic Party
Augusta Rozypalova, People's Party
Frantiseka Skaunicova, Social Democrat Party
Anna Sychravova, Social Democrat Party
Frantiska Zeminova, Czechoslovak Socialist Party

All elected April 1920 to Chamber of Deputies

Bozena Ecksteinova, Czechoslovak Social-Democratic Labor Party
Emma Herzig, German Election Union
Anna Perthen, German Social Democratic Party

All elected March 1920 to Senate

First elected to national legislature
(Národná Rada Slovenskej Republiky, National Council)

Twenty-three women, June 1992

Minority: Hungarian

Executive

Notable service in cabinet

Pal Csaky, Minister of Minorities and Human Rights

Minority: Roma (Gypsy)

Executive

First to hold executive position

Emil Rigo, member of the Slovak Communist Party politburo, 1968

SLOVENIA

Women

Right to vote: August 10, 1945
To stand for election: August 10, 1945

Executive

Notable presidential candidates, 1992

Candidates included two women running as independents: **Darja Levarizar-Bebler,** who placed fifth with less than 2 percent of the vote, and **Alenka Zagar-Slana,** who placed sixth, also with less than 2 percent of the vote.

First appointed to cabinet

Katja Boh, Minister of Health and Social Security
Jozica Puhar, Minister of Labor

Both appointed May 16, 1990

Notable service in cabinet

Mitja Gaspari, Minister of Finance
Rina Klinar, Minister of Family and Social Affairs

First appointed ambassador

Katja Boh, Ambassador to Austria, 1992

Legislative

First elected to national legislature (Drzavni Zbor, National Assembly)[47]

Ljerka Bizilj, Independent
Polonca Dobrajc, Slovene National Party
Mateja Kouk, Associated List of Social Democrats

---

[47]Slovenian women had previously been elected to the Parliament of Yugoslavia.

Mihaela Logar, Slovene People's Party
Metka Karner Lukæ, Slovene People's Party
Irena Oman, Slovene People's Party
Breda Peèan, Associated List of Christian Democrats
Vika Potoènik, Liberal Democratic Party
Maria Pozsonec, Hungarian Ethnic Communities
Jana Primoie, Slovene Christian Democrats
Danica Simié, Democratic Party of Slovenia
Nada Skuk, Slovene Christian Democrats
Jadranka Sturm-Kocijan, Liberal Democratic Party

All elected December 1992

Head of legislature (Narodna Skubscina, People's Assembly of the Slovenian Socialist Republic, Yugoslavia)

Vida Tomsic, 1974–1978

Judicial

First appointed to supreme court

Marija Krisper Kramberger, November 1991

Minority: Hungarian

Legislative

First woman elected to national legislature (Drzavni Zbor, National Assembly)

Maria Pozsonec, Hungarian Ethnic Communities, December 1992

Solomon Islands

Women

Right to vote: 1978
To stand for election: 1978

Executive

First appointed to cabinet

Hilda Auvi Kari, Minister of Forests, the Environment, and Conservation, 1993

First appointed ambassador

No woman yet appointed

Legislative

First elected to colonial legislature (Legislative Council)

Lilly Ogatina, 1965

First elected to national legislature (Parliament)

Hilda Auvi Kari, People's Alliance Party, 1989

Judicial

First appointed to judiciary

Ester Lelapitu, 1999

Somalia

Women

Right to vote: 1956
To stand for election: 1956

Since Somalia began its descent into political chaos in 1991, all functions of what might be considered a normal government have gradually ceased to exist. At present, there are no organizations that might either supply or confirm information on the country.

International Notable: **Waris Dirie** was appointed special United Nations ambassador, with responsibility for female genital mutilation issues.

Executive

First appointed to cabinet

Nur Ilmi Uthman, Minister of Health, 1994. In the early 1980s, several women, including **Fadumo Ahmed Alin** at the Ministry of Education, were appointed as vice-ministers. During the regime of President Siad Barre (1969–1991), no women were appointed as full ministers.

First appointed ambassador

No woman yet appointed

Legislative

First elected to national legislature (Golaha Shachiga, People's Assembly)

Eighteen women, December 1979

Political Entities: Somaliland and Puntland

With the collapse of the Somali central government, two regional governments have been established and are making their way slowly toward becoming separate nations. The first, Somaliland, is in the northwest of Somalia. Established in 1991, it has all the trappings of a modern state—executive, legislative, and judicial branches—although these are still in a rudimentary form. It is obvious from checking the roster of the personnel in these branches of government that women, thus far, appear to have been excluded from participation. No other nation has yet recognized the independence of Somaliland, but the government appears determined to ensure that Somaliland will not be reunited with the rest of what was Somalia again.

The other entity, Puntland, in the northeast of Somalia, was established in 1997–1998 and has chosen a slightly different path. It proclaims that it remains a "state" of Somalia and will reincorporate itself once all the feuding clans have resolved their differences and reestablished Somalia as a loose federal republic of states. It, too, has established a government, with a Parliament (the House of Representatives). Information is unclear as to whether this body has been elected or appointed. There are five women members of Puntland's Parliament, including **Shugri Sallat** and **Asha Gelle.**

South Africa

Women

Right to vote: May 21, 1930; March 30, 1984; January 14, 1994
To stand for election: May 21, 1930; March 30, 1984; January 14, 1994[48]

Executive

Ex–partner in power

Graça Simbine Machel Mandela, 1993–1999. Widow of Mozambique's first president, Samora Machel, who died in a plane crash in 1986, Machel became intimately involved with South Africa's President Nelson Mandela shortly after his separation from his second wife, Winnie. When she and Mandela married in July 1998, Machel became the first woman since Eleanor of Aquitaine (in the twelfth century) to have been married to the heads of state from two different countries (*see* Mozambique). According to the Mandelas, Machel will continue to play a role in Mozambique, dividing her time between living there and in South Africa.

Ex–partner in power

Winnifred (Winnie) Madikizela-Mandela, 1958–1995. Divorced second wife of Nelson Mandela, Winnie led the fight to keep his memory alive during his years in prison. A controversial woman, Winnie was long a thorn in the side of the white supremacist government in Pretoria. After her husband was freed from prison, Winnie played an increasingly prominent role in the African National Congress (ANC). In 1990, she was convicted on charges of kidnapping and assault, which grew out of her involvement with certain dubious associates in the black townships while her husband was imprisoned. The Mandelas separated in 1992, but two years later Winnie was awarded a deputy ministerial position in his government. Although she was dismissed from her government post in 1995, Winnie still retains a potent allure for many South Africans, particularly the more radical blacks. She doesn't mind uttering the occasional racially demagogic statement to convince such radicals that she's more on their side than her husband's ANC. Because of her past service to the cause of

[48]Women's right to vote and to stand for election was granted to whites on May 21, 1930; to coloreds and Indians on March 30, 1984; and to blacks on January 14, 1994.

black liberation, and because of her ex-husband's stature, politicians of all stripes tread carefully around Winnie. Once Nelson Mandela passes from the scene, Winnie has the potential to become a political power again, perhaps by building on her militant links.

First appointed to cabinet

Elizabeth H. Venter, Minister of National Health and Population, 1989

Notable service in cabinet

Thoko Didiza, Minister of Agriculture and Lands
Nkosazana Dlamini-Zuma, Minister of Health
Geraldine Fraser-Moleketi, Minister of Welfare and Population Development
Ivy Matsepe-Casaburri, Minister of Posts, Telecommunications, and Broadcasting
Sankie D. Mthembi-Mahanyale, Minister of Housing
Stella Sigcau, Minister of Public Enterprise
Zola Skweyiya, Minister of Public Services and Administration

First appointed ambassador

Cécile Schmidt, Ambassador to Austria, 1988

First black woman appointed ambassador

Barbara Masakela, Ambassador to France, 1995

First elected provincial premier

Ivy Matsepe-Casaburri, African National Congress, Free State, 1996

Legislative

First to serve in national legislature (Parliament)

Mrs. Deneys Ritz

First elected to national legislature (Parliament)

Mabel Malherbe, April 21, 1933. The next woman was not elected until 1953, when **Helen Suzman** (see below) of the United Party won a seat.

Head of national legislature

Frene Noshir Ginwala, National Assembly, 1994–1999. On May 9, 1994, Ginwala became the first woman in Africa to be elected speaker of a national assembly.
Naledi Pandor, National Council of Provinces (upper house), 1999

Miscellaneous

Helen G. Suzman, 1953–1993. For more than twenty years, Helen's was the sole liberal voice raised in Parliament against the racist outrages of South Africa's apartheid system. It was an unlikely role for the daughter of an immigrant Lithuanian Jewish family, but one she fulfilled magnificently. A trained academic (with a degree in economics) married to a Johannesburg physician and mother of two, Helen came by her seat in Parliament almost by accident. In 1953, she upset the United Party member representing her upscale, all-white neighborhood and took her seat. By 1959, she had left the United Party, along with several other members, to form the liberal Progressive Party. At the next election, all Progressive Party members lost their seats except Helen, leaving her as the sole voice of liberal reason and outrage in Parliament. Overnight, she had become the de facto representative of millions of disfranchised black South Africans. Helen fought, by herself, against every piece of apartheid legislation introduced in Parliament, while her opponents showered her daily with abuse and undisguised contempt. Undeterred, she fought on for years, winning her seat by a stronger majority in each election. Had Helen ever lost that parliamentary seat, it's likely that the racist government would have pounced quickly on her, either subjecting her to imprisonment or "banning" orders, as was done with so many of the regime's opponents. When majority rule finally came to South Africa, Helen announced her retirement. She didn't remove herself entirely from politics, though, serving as one of the members of the Independent Electoral Commission, which oversaw the first all-race elections in April 1994. President Mandela awarded Helen South Africa's highest civilian award for meritorious service in February 1997.

Judicial

First appointed judge

Leonara Neethling, 1969

First black woman appointed to supreme court

Yvonne Mokgoro

Minority: Gay

Judicial

First appointed to supreme court

Edwin Cameron, 1995

Transkei

Executive

Power past

Stella Sigcau, Prime Minister, October 5–December 30, 1987. Sigcau, daughter of the Transkei's first president, Manzolwandlee Sigcau, was installed as prime minister of the Xhosa "homeland" (recognized as an independent entity only by the Pretoria government) in 1987 after a military coup. After less than three months in office, a second military coup tossed her out. Sigcau reappeared in 1994 in the new South African cabinet of Nelson Mandela as minister for public enterprises, after Mandela's African National Congress had assumed power. This appointment was surprising, as the ANC had distanced itself from most leaders of the former "homelands" that had been established under the apartheid regime.

Spain

Women

Right to vote: December 9, 1931
To stand for election: May 8, 1931

Royalty

Sofia, Queen, November 22, 1975–present. When the Spanish monarchy was restored in 1975, Sofia became the first Spanish queen in more than forty years. Greek-born and a trained nurse, she was determined that her husband, Juan Carlos I, would not suffer the same fate as her brother, Greece's King Constantine II, who had lost his throne. She has worked skillfully with her husband to make the institution of the monarchy a viable part of Spain's still young democracy. Some of her first acts as queen had great symbolic importance: highly visible visits to both a Jewish synagogue and a Protestant church. Those steps heralded the liberalism that has marked the reign of her husband, a welcome change after the country had endured almost forty years of right-wing dictatorship. The royal couple have tried exceptionally hard to portray themselves as open and caring, as a symbol of the state around which all Spaniards can rally, whatever their political beliefs. Sofia's careful efforts have succeeded. Her husband now firmly approaches his silver jubilee on what was once regarded as Europe's shakiest throne, and the royal family is held in almost universal high regard.

Executive

First appointed to cabinet

Frederica Montseny, Minister of Health and Social Services, 1936

Notable service in cabinet

Esperanza Aguirre Gil de Biedma, Minister of Education and Culture
Cristina Alberdi, Minister of Social Affairs
Matilde Fernandez Sanz, Minister of Social Welfare
Margarita Mariscal de Gante y Miron, Minister of Justice
Loyola de Palacio del Valle-Lersundi, Minister of Agriculture, Fisheries, and Food
Isobel Tocino Biscarolasaga, Minister of the Environment

First appointed ambassador

Mercedes Rico Carablas, Ambassador to Costa Rica, 1985

Legislative

First appointed to national legislature

Thirteen women, 1923. These women were appointed by Spanish dictator Primo de Rivera to the Consultative National Assembly, a body that he had established.

First elected to national legislature (Cortes Españoles, Spanish Cortes)

Clara Campoamor, Left Coalition
Victoria Kent, Left Coalition

Both elected July 1931. In November 1931, they were joined by **Margarita Melken,** also a member of the Left Coalition.

Head of national legislature

Esperanza Aguirre Gil de Biedma, Senate, 1999–present

Power past

Dolores Ibarurri, 1936–1938. A small-town woman transformed into one of the great figures of leftist lore, Ibarurri blazed passionately for a short time. Elected as a communist deputy to the Cortes of Republican Spain in 1936, she is remembered for her radio speeches in defense of the republic when the Spanish Civil War erupted that same year. Dubbed "La Pasionara," she told listeners around the world: "It is better to die on your feet than live on your knees." When the Republic fell in 1938, she fled to Moscow, where she spent years in exile as head of the Spanish Communist Party, still making radio broadcasts, listened to by fewer and fewer people each year. With dictator Francisco Franco's death in 1975 and the restoration of democracy in Spain, Ibarurri returned home. In a move that would presage the political adroitness he would show in the years to come, newly installed King Juan Carlos I warmly welcomed her return as a loyal daughter of Spain. Ibarurri was again elected to Parliament by her old constituency, but the passion of her earlier presence was gone. She, along with Spanish communism, was now a spent force. Ibarurri served quietly in Parliament, a marginal figure at best, until her death in 1989.

Sri Lanka

Women

Right to vote: March 20, 1931
To stand for election: March 20, 1931

Executive

Chandrika Kumaratunga, Prime Minister, August 19–November 14, 1994; President, November 14, 1994–present. Kumaratunga, daughter of Sri Lankan prime ministers Solomon West Ridgeway Dias Bandaranaike and Sirimavo Bandaranaike (see below), was herself elected prime minister of the island state in 1994. After only a few months in office, she ran for and won a presidency with newly expanded powers. On being sworn in as president, Kumaratunga made her mother prime minister again, the first instance in history where both the elected head of state and the head of government were women. For the past thirty-odd years, Sri Lanka has been an extremely violent country, circumstances that seem to belie the country's name, which translates as "Blessed Land." This violence has touched Kumaratunga personally; both her father and her husband were killed by political assassination. She has had to contend with an ongoing, extremely bloody revolt by the minority Tamils of the island's north, which has been marked by terrorist attacks in the country's capital, Colombo, as well as military operations in Tamil-populated areas. Kumaratunga reportedly lives in a high-security, heavily fortified house and dreads public appearances. Given Sri Lanka's penchant for bloody assassinations and terror, it would not be surprising if she ultimately met the same end as did her father and husband.

In December 1999, Kumaratunga narrowly won a second presidential term, after surviving an assassination attempt. There was immediate speculation that she would attempt to revise the constitution again, reverting power back to a strong prime minister. Then, she would assume that position (making her mother president in her stead?) and use its strengthened powers to pursue an end to the conflict with the Tamils.

Sirimavo Ratwatte Dias Bandaranaike, Prime Minister, July 22, 1960–March 25, 1965; May 28, 1970–January 23, 1977; November 14, 1994–present. Bandaranaike, the widow of prime minister Solomon West Ridgeway Dias Bandaranaike, was first sworn into office to complete her husband's term after his assassination. When she assumed office, Bandaranaike became the first female head of government in the world, excluding monarchs. Generally, her first two terms as prime minister were marked by economic mismanagement and tenacious guerrilla warfare, waged at different times by several different groups. She was defeated in reelection campaigns in 1965 and again in 1977. In 1994, her daughter, Chandrika Kumaratunga, was elected prime minister in her own capacity. After serving a few months in the office, Kumaratunga assumed the presidency, then named her mother to a third term as prime minister.

Notable presidential candidate, 1994

Srima Dissanayake. Widow of assassinated presidential candidate Gamini Dissanayake, Srima stepped into his place as the candidate of the United National Party and ran against another woman, Chandrika Kumaratunga (see above). She placed second with almost 36 percent of the vote.

Notable presidential candidate, 1988

Sirimavo Ratwatte Dias Bandaranaike. Three-time prime minister (see above), Sirimavo ran against Ranasinghe Premadasa and placed second with 45 percent of the vote.

First appointed to cabinet

Wimala Wijewardhna, Minister of Health, 1956

Notable service in cabinet

Srimani Athulathmudal, Minister of Transport, the Environment, and Women's Affairs
Ranuka Herath, Minister of Health and Women's Affairs
Chandrika Kumaratunga, Minister of Defense; Minister of Finance
Sunethra Ranasinghe, Minister of Education
R.M.A. Piyaseeli Ratnayake, Minister of Social Welfare
Hema Ratnayare, Minister of Women's Affairs

First appointed ambassador

Lorani Senarathna, Ambassador to Ghana, 1962

Legislative

First appointed to colonial legislature (Senate)

Adlin Molamure, November 14, 1931

First elected to national legislature (House of Representatives)

Flowrence Senanayaka, August 1947

Judicial

First appointed judge

Sudharma Dharmadasa, circa 1962

First appointed to supreme court

Shirani Bandaranayaka, 1996

Sudan

Women

Right to vote: November 1964
To stand for election: November 1964

Executive

First appointed to cabinet

Fatima Abd al-Mahoud, Minister of Social Affairs, 1976. In 1971, **Nafisah Ahmad al-Amin** had been appointed as deputy minister of youth and sport.

Notable service in cabinet

Marian Osman al-Khatim, Minister of Social Planning
Agnes Lukudo, Minister of Public Service

First appointed ambassador

Zeinab Muhammad Mahmoud Abd al-Karim, 1999. When her appointment was announced, no country of accreditation was included. Some skeptics have voiced the opinion that the appointment was made only as a "window display" because of Sudan's rather spotty record on women's rights.

First state governor

Agnes Lukudo, Bahr al-Jabal, 1994

Legislative

First elected to national legislature (Parliament)

Fatima Ahmed Ibrahim, November 1964

Judicial

First appointed judge

Ihsan Fakhri, 1965

First appointed to supreme court

Farida Ibrahim, 1994

Suriname

Women

Right to vote: December 9, 1948
To stand for election: December 9, 1948

Executive

First appointed to cabinet

Siegmien Staphorst, Minister of Social Affairs and Housing, August 1980. Staphorst had already been appointed as vice-minister of labor and housing in February 1980, along with **Nel Stadwijk-Kappel** as vice-minister of education.

Notable service in cabinet

Evelyn M. B. Alexander-Vanenberg, Minister of Home Affairs
Yvonne Raveles-Resida, Minister of Regional Development
Ellen Smit-Naarendorp, Minister of Health

First appointed ambassador

No woman yet appointed

Legislative

First to serve in colonial legislature (Staten)

Grace R. Schneiders-Howard, 1938

First elected to national legislature (Nationale Assemblee, National Assembly)

Albertine Liesdek-Clarke
Bella Richaard

Both elected October 1975

Head of national legislature

Indradevi M. Djwalapersad, National Assembly, 1996–present

Judicial

First appointed judge

Cynthia Valsteijn, 1998

Minority: Amerindian

Legislative

First elected to national legislature (Nationale Assemblee, National Assembly)

Ronald Karwafodi, National Party of Suriname
Frank Yong, National Democratic Party

Both elected 1996

SWAZILAND

Women

Right to vote: September 6, 1968
To stand for election: September 6, 1968

Royalty

Power past

Ntombi Thwala, Queen Regent, August 10, 1983–April 25, 1986. One of the wives of the deceased King Sobhuza II and mother of Prince Mokesetive, who was chosen to succeed him, Ntombi achieved power when the previous regent was deposed as a result of factional strife (see below). She managed to satisfy the demands of Swaziland's traditionalist faction, keeping the country calm until her nineteen-year-old son was crowned King Mswati III on April 25, 1986.

Dzeliwe Shongwe, Queen Regent, August 21, 1982–August 10, 1983. Dzeliwe was one of the senior wives of King Sobhuza II, who had reigned for sixty years, siring some 600 children by nearly a hundred wives; she was appointed regent for his underaged heir (and son) Prince Mokesetive, who was completing his studies in Great Britain. Dzeliwe required the patience of an elephant, for she was promptly caught between competing traditionalist and modernist factions within Swaziland's ruling Liqoqo (National Council). She appointed a fifteen-man group from the council, as well as an "Authorized Person," to help her navigate these turbulent waters, but it was all to no avail. After plots, threats of a coup, and fierce infighting, Dzeliwe was deposed when she refused to sign a document acknowledging the supreme authority of the Liqoqo.

Labotsibeni, Queen Regent, December 1899–December 22, 1921. Swaziland is a matriarchal society. A deceased king's elder wife, given the Swazi title Idlovukazi (Great She-Elephant), is typically appointed regent for the next king. To ensure a lengthy reign, a very young male child is always chosen, selected by a group of elders who base their choice on the reputation of the boy's mother! Labotsibeni, senior wife of deceased King Ngwane V, was also grandmother of the new six-month-old king, Sobhuza II. It was during her regency, in 1903, that Swaziland passed from the nominal control of the South African Republic (Transvaal, just defeated in the Boer War) to direct British rule. Labotsibeni relinquished her power on December 22, 1921, when Sobhuza II came of age.

Executive

First appointed to cabinet

Fanny Friedman, Minister of Health, 1988

Notable service in cabinet

Phetsile Dlamini, Minister of Health
Stella Lukhele, Minister of Housing and Urban Development

First appointed ambassador

Madzandza Khanya, Ambassador to Canada, 1990

Legislative

First elected to national legislature (House of Assembly)

Mary Mdziniso, April 1972

First appointed to national legislature (Senate)

Mary Mdziniso, April 1967

Minority: European

Legislative

First appointed to national legislature (House of Assembly)

Four persons, 1978

Sweden

Women

Right to vote: 1862; 1918; May 1919; 1921
To stand for election: 1907; 1918; May 1919; 1921[49]

Royalty

Power to be

Victoria, Crown Princess. If she succeeds her father, King Carl XVI Gustaf, Victoria will become Sweden's first reigning queen since the mysterious Queen Christina of the mid-1600s. Her power, however, will be almost negligible. The constitution of 1975 stripped the Swedish monarch of almost all power and prerogatives, leaving the position as little more than a figurehead. Although she was born in 1977, Victoria did not receive the right to inherit Sweden's throne until 1980, when the law was changed to permit female succession. At the time, she was the king's sole child; since then, a son has been born, but Victoria's first right to the throne is now secure.

Executive

Potential power

Gudrun Schyman, leader of the once communist Left Party. When she led her party to third place (garnering 12 percent of the vote) in 1998, Schyman put Prime Minister Goran Persson in a hard place. He was forced to accept her party into a coalition government, mostly on their terms. Following her party's traditional platform, she demanded additional spending on welfare, higher taxes on wealth, and a curb on privatization, as well as a four-year guarantee that the Left Party would remain in the government. Whether she and Persson can continue to coexist for that long remains to be seen.

---

[49]Women were granted the right to vote in local elections at different stages between 1862 and 1918, and were progressively granted the right to stand for election to local bodies between 1907 and 1918. For national elections, women were granted the right to vote and to stand for election in May 1919; however, these rights came into effect only in 1921.

Failed bid for power

Mona Sahlin, 1995. It looked like Mona, Sweden's vice-premier, was set to become the nation's first female prime minister when Ingvar Carlsson of the Social Democratic Party announced that he would resign the following spring, in 1996. Unfortunately, her rise to power was stymied by a financial mishap. After Sweden's tabloid press reported on her questionable use of a government credit card—supposedly to purchase diapers for her children among other things—Mona called it quits in October 1995. She resigned from her cabinet posts but kept her parliamentary seat, and Carlsson was succeeded by another man. In 1998, after a parliamentary election won by her Social Democratic Party, Mona made a reappearance in the government; she was appointed a junior minister by Prime Minister Persson, a move that could lead to her full rehabilitation and perhaps another try for power in the future.

First appointed to cabinet

Karen Kock-Lindberg, Minister Without Portfolio for the Economy, 1947

Notable service in cabinet

Margaretha af Ugglas, Minister of Foreign Affairs
Annika Ahnberg, Minister of Agriculture, Food, and Fisheries
Karen Ahrland, Minister of Public Health
Anitha Bondestam, Minister of Communications
Birgitta Dahl, Minister of Industry and Energy
Laila Freivalds, Minister of Justice
Birgit Friggebo, Minister of Housing
Anita Gradin, Minister of Foreign Trade
Lena Hjelm-Wallén, Minister of Foreign Affairs; Minister of International Development; Minister of Education
Ylva Johansson, Minister of Schools and Adult Education
Maj-Inger Klingvall, Minister of Social Affairs
Anna-Greta Leijon, Minister of Labor; Minister of Justice
Anna Lindh, Minister of Foreign Affairs; Minister of the Environment
Ulla Lindström
Ulrika Messing, Minister of Equality Affairs
Britt Mogard, Minister of Education and Cultural Affairs
Alva Reimer Myrdal, Minister of Disarmament[50]
Hildur Nygren
Camilla Odhnoff
Elvy Olsson, Minister of Housing and Physical Planning
Mona Sahlin, Minister of Labor

---

[50]Myrdahl's appointment to this portfolio in 1967 marked the establishment of the first such ministry in history.

Gertrud Sigurdsen, Minister of Health and Social Affairs; Minister of Sexual Equality
Karin Söder, Minister of Foreign Affairs
Ingela Thalen, Minister of Labor; Minister of Health and Social Affairs
Görel Thurdin, Minister of Physical Planning; Minister of the Environment
Ingegerd Troedsson, Minister of Health
Marita Ulvskog, Minister of Culture
Ines Uusmann, Minister of Transport and Communications
Margot Wallstom, Minister of Health and Social Affairs
Margareta Winberg, Minister of Labor

First appointed ambassador

Alva Reimer Myrdal, Ambassador to India, Burma, Nepal, and Ceylon, 1951. In 1632, **Katharina Stopia Möller** was accredited as the Swedish ambassador to Moscow, where she served for two years.

Legislative

First elected to national legislature (Riksdagen, Parliament)

Kerstin Hesselgren, Liberal–Social Democratic Party, First Chamber
Agda Östland, Social Democratic Party, Second Chamber
Elisabeth Tamm, Liberal Party, Second Chamber
Nelly Thüring, Social Democratic Party, Second Chamber
Bertha Wellin, Ruralist Party, Second Chamber

All elected September 1921

Head of national legislature

Birgitta Dahl, Parliament (Riksdagen), 1994–1998
Ingegerd Troedsson, Parliament (Riksdagen), 1991–1994

Judicial

First appointed to supreme court

Ingrid Gärde Widemar, 1968

Minority: Gay

Legislative

First elected to national legislature (Riksdagen, Parliament)

Kent Carlsson, Social Democratic Party, 1991

Notable service in national legislature (Riksdagen, Parliament)

Andreas Carlgren, Center Party, Deputy Chairman

Switzerland

Women

Right to vote: February 7, 1971
To stand for election: February 7, 1971

Executive

Power past

Ruth Dreifuss, President, January 1, 1999–January 1, 2000. Dreifuss was one of seven members of the Swiss Federal Assembly elected to become a Federal Councillor on March 10, 1993. Each of the seven assumes responsibility for one broad aspect of the Swiss government, and hers was the Department of Home Affairs. The councillors select a president and vice-president each year to serve a one-year term. Dreifuss was selected vice-president for the 1998–1999 term. Generally, the vice-president assumes the presidency the following year, becoming the de facto Swiss chief executive. When Dreifuss followed suit in 1999, she became not only Switzerland's first female president, but also its first Jewish one.

Dreifuss followed a very nontraditional route to power. She began her career as a journalist, then moved on to academia. Later, she joined the government's Department of Overseas Aid as a bureaucrat, and soon became affiliated with the trade union movement, in accordance with her socialist leanings. Since the president's job is largely ceremonial, Dreifuss did not have much immediate impact on Swiss policies. Her greatest achievement was that she served as president less than thirty years after the Swiss finally granted woman the right to vote. And, given all the bad press the Swiss banks received in the mid-1990s about their ties to Nazi Germany and looted Jewish assets, Dreifuss's being Jewish helped remove some of that tarnish, too.

First elevated to the Federal Council

Elisabeth Kopp, Federal Councillor of Justice and Police, 1984

First appointed ambassador

Francesca Pometta, head of the political division of the Department of Foreign Affairs with the title of Ambassador, 1977; appointed as head of the Swiss Observer Mission at the United Nations, 1982; Ambassador to Italy, 1987

First head (Landammann) of a canton

Margit Weber-Röllin, Schwyz, 1993

Legislative

First elected to national legislature (Federal Assembly)

Elisabeth Blunschy, Christian Democratic Party
Tilo Frey, Radical Democratic Party
Hedi Lang, Social Democratic Party
Josi Meier, Christian Democratic Party
Gabrielle Nanchen, Social Democratic Party
Martha Ribi, Radical Democratic Party
Liselotte Spreng, Radical Democratic Party
Hanny Thalmann, Christian Democratic Party
Lilian Uchtenhagen, Social Democratic Party
Nelly Wicky, Communist Party

All elected to the National Council October 31, 1971, and seated November 30, 1971

Lise Giradin, Radical Democratic Party, elected to the Council of States October 31, 1971, and seated November 30, 1971

Head of national legislature

Trix Heberlein, National Council, 1998
Judith Stamm, National Council, 1996
Gret Haller, National Council, 1994
Josi Meier, Council of States, 1992
Hedi Lang, National Council, 1982
Elisabeth Blunschy-Steiner, National Council, May 2–December 31, 1977

Syria

Women

Right to vote: September 10, 1949; 1953
To stand for election: 1953[51]

Executive

First appointed to cabinet

Najah al-Attar, Minister of Culture, 1976

Notable service in cabinet

Salihah Sanqar, Minister of Higher Education

First appointed ambassador

Siba Naser, Ambassador to the Netherlands, Belgium, and Luxembourg, and accredited to the European Union, 1988

Legislative

First elected to national legislature (Majlis al-Chaab, People's Council)

Hana Hamwi, Socialist Arab Ba'ath Party
Boshra Kanafani, Socialist Arab Ba'ath Party
Munuar Mackluta, Socialist Arab Ba'ath Party
Salma Najeeb, Socialist Arab Ba'ath Party
Hajar Sadek, Socialist Arab Ba'ath Party

All elected May 1973

---

[51]The right to vote was initially given to women who had reached a sixth-grade educational level; it was then extended to all literate women, and in 1953 all educational restrictions on voting were lifted for women.

Religious Minority: Alawite

Executive

Hafez al-Assad, President, February 22, 1971–present. In the Alawite religious faith, multiple theological and philosophical influences coexist. Regarded as heretics by some orthodox Muslims and as a branch of the Shi'ites by others, the Alawites, who account for some 10 percent of Syria's population, blend a sense of Phoenician paganism and Christian trinitarianism with various Islamic notions. Traditionally excluded from politics, many Alawites, beginning during the period of French rule in Syria, used the armed forces as a place to exert power. Assad continued that tradition. A former defense minister and head of the air force, he has run a repressive regime, one best described as "kinship-based." Relying on the assistance of four brothers, countless nephews, and other extended family members—as well as fellow Alawites—he has managed to secure his power base and provide Syria with a stable government for more than twenty-five years. One moment he's fostering international terrorism, the next he's cozying up to the Western nations, all the while maintaining close ties to the former Eastern bloc. Until his death in an auto accident, Assad's son Basil was being groomed as a successor. Now, based on the billboards of praise sprouting around the country, it appears that another, younger son, currently a doctor, is the heir apparent. When Assad passes from the scene, it may be hard for the minority Alawites, particularly Assad's family clique, to continue to keep Syria under their personal rule.

Tajikistan

Women

Right to vote: 1924
To stand for election: 1924

Executive

First appointed to cabinet

Tamara M. Abdushurova, Minister of Culture, 1990. Abdushurova was serving in the cabinet at the time independence was declared. **Zebo Aminzoda** was appointed deputy prime minister in 1992.

Notable service in cabinet

Munia Inoyatova Abdulloyevna, Deputy Prime Minister; Minister of Education
Bozgul Dodkhudoyeva, Deputy Prime Minister

First appointed ambassador

No woman yet appointed

Legislative

First elected to national legislature (Majlisi Oli, National Assembly)[52]

Husnoro Mirzoeva
Rafika Musoeva
Adolat Rakmonova

---

[52]Tajik women had previously been elected to both the Supreme Soviet of the Soviet Socialist Republic of Tajikistan and to the Parliament of the Soviet Women.

Kimmat Rustanova
Gulafzo Savriddinova

All elected 1991

Judicial

First appointed to supreme court

T. Azizova, 1958

Tanzania

Women

Right to vote: 1959
To stand for election: 1959

Executive

First appointed to cabinet

Julie C. Manning, Minister of Justice, 1975
Tabitha Siwale, Minister of Lands and Housing, 1975

Notable service in cabinet

Anna Abdullah, Minister of Agriculture, Livestock, Development, and Cooperatives; Minister of Works
Fatima S. Ali, Minister of State for Civil Service
Anna Makinda, Minister of Social Development and Women's Development
Zakhia Meghji, Minister of Natural Resources and Tourism; Minister of Health
Gertrude Ibengwe Mongella, Minister of Natural Resources and Tourism
Mary Nagu, Minister of Commercial Development, Women's Affairs, and Children

First appointed ambassador

Tatu Nuru, Ambassador to Ethiopia, 1961. **Dorah Bantu** was appointed as an ambassador in 1963.

Legislative

First elected to national legislature (Bunge, Parliament)

Lucy Lameck
Titi Mohamed

Both elected 1961

Judicial

First appointed to supreme court

Julie C. Manning, 1973

Minority: European

Executive

First appointed to cabinet

Derek Bryceson, Minister of Agriculture and Cooperatives, 1963

THAILAND

Women

Right to vote: December 10, 1932
To stand for election: December 10, 1932

Royalty

Sirikit, Queen, May 5, 1950–present. The Thais exhibit a deep reverence for their monarchy, more so than in most other countries that sustain a royal family. Sirikit has wisely built on that support. Internationally famed for her beauty and sense of style—she's been a regular on the "best dressed" lists for years—Sirikit is more familiar among Thais as a queen who will travel on horseback in casual clothes through rough terrain to the most remote regions of the country promoting the progress and well-being of her people. It was largely due to the efforts of her and her husband, King Bhumibol Adulyadej, that in the aftermath of the Vietnam War the much-discussed "Domino Theory," whereby Southeast Asian countries would tumble to the communists one by one, did not come to pass in Thailand. A minor guerrilla war did spark up, mainly in the impoverished Thai northeast, which could have ignited the country, but Sirikit worked tirelessly to increase income and raise the standard of living, particularly in that region. Her efforts paid off: As Thailand entered the 1990s, its economy was growing rapidly, and the rural standard of living was showing improvement every year. Even with the economic crisis that overtook Thailand in 1997, the king was secure on his throne, having celebrated his golden jubilee in 1996. So great is the esteem in which the royal couple is held that when the king retreats on occasion to a Buddhist monastery to serve penitence as a monk, Sirikit oversees Thailand as regent in his stead.

Potential power

Princess Maha Chakri Sirindhorn. Eldest daughter of Bhumibol Adulyadej and Sirikit, the princess is particularly well respected among Thais. There has always been some doubt about Crown Prince Vajiralongkorn's ability to be an effective monarch after his father passes from the scene. In his late forties, the crown prince is reputed to be temperamental and brash, decidedly un-Thai traits that are particularly unsuited to dealing with the nation's often tumultuous politics. Given a choice, the Thais would probably prefer that his sister follow her father onto the throne instead. Perhaps her father thinks so, too. In 1978, she was granted a special new title in recognition of her services to the throne and to the nation. Also, constitutional amendments were effected stipulating that if there is no suitable male heir, Parliament may approve the succession of a royal daughter. Many have speculated that both moves were meant to convey a subtle message to the crown prince: His succession might not be automatic.

Executive

First appointed to cabinet

Wimonsiri Jamnarnwej, Minister of University Affairs (Government)
Thanpuying Lusakdi Sampatisiri, Minister of Transport and Communications

Both appointed October 1976

Notable service in cabinet

Khunying Suprata Masdit, Minister attached to the Office of the Prime Minister

First appointed ambassador

Suchira Hiranprueck, Ambassador to Russia, 1993

First provincial governor

Khunying Charactsri Teepirach, Nakorn Nayok Province, 1993

First mayor

Jintana Nopakun, Muang Photharam municipality, Ratchaburi Province, 1969

Legislative

First appointed to national legislature (Vuthisapha, Senate)

Thanpuying La-iad Phibunsongkhram
Khunying Lekha Apaivongse

Both appointed November 18, 1947

First elected to national legislature
(Saphaphoothan Rajsandhorn, House of Representatives)

Orapin Chaiyakarn, June 5, 1949

Judicial

First appointed judge

Chalorjit Jittarutta, 1965

First appointed to supreme court

Churunee Tantayakom, 1995

Religious Minority: Muslim

Legislative

First head of national legislature
(Saphaphoothan Rajsandhorn, House of Representatives)

Wan Muhammad Nur, Speaker, 1999

Togo

Women

Right to vote: August 22, 1945
To stand for election: August 22, 1945

Executive

First appointed to cabinet

Biyémi Kekeh, Minister of Social Affairs, Health, and Women
Bibi Yao S. Toré, Minister of Justice

Both appointed 1978

Notable service in cabinet

Ayssa Agberta, Minister of Third and Fourth Cycle Education
Aissa Ahlokoba, Minister of Social and Women's Affairs
Massa Dagadzi, Minister of Parliamentary Affairs
Sheffi Meatchi, Minister of Social Affairs and Women's Promotion
Kissem Tchangi-Walla, Minister of Labor and Civil Services

First appointed ambassador

Biyémi Kekeh, Ambassador to Cuba, 1980

First appointed mayor

Marie Gbikpi, Lomé, 1967

Legislative

First elected to national legislature
(Assemblée nationale, National Assembly)

Joséphine Hundt, April 9, 1961

Tonga

Women

Right to vote: 1960
To stand for election: 1960

Royalty

Power past

Salote (Charlotte) Mafile o Pilolevu Veionga Tupou III, Queen, April 12, 1918–September 4, 1965. A strikingly regal and exceptionally statuesque woman, Salote, the only regnant queen in the South Pacific, was best known for her appearance at Queen Elizabeth II's coronation in 1952. When a sudden downpour caused the other dignitaries to scamper for cover and raise their umbrellas, Salote rode serenely uncovered in her open landau carriage, waving to the massed crowds, which elicited their cheers. When asked for the identity of the small man riding with Salote in her carriage (actually her prime minister), famed wit Noel Coward replied, "Her lunch." A piously devout Christian who was deeply loved by her subjects, Salote promoted the strength of Polynesian culture and advanced the cause of women in her small island-nation throughout her nearly fifty-year reign. She died four years before Tonga, a British protectorate, gained its independence. As commented in a recent biography about Salote, were it not for the fact that the Wesleyan Church (Tonga's state religion) objects to saints, Tongans would have long ago deified their beloved queen.

Executive

First appointed to cabinet

No woman yet appointed

First appointed ambassador

'Akosita Fineanganofo, High Commissioner (Ambassador) to the United Kingdom, accredited as ambassador to various other European nations, 1996

Legislative

First elected to national legislature (Fale Alea, Legislative Assembly)

Papiloa Bloomfield Foliaki, 1978
Princess Mele Siuilikutapu Kalaniuvalu-Fotofili, 1975

Trinidad and Tobago

Women

Right to vote: 1946
To stand for election: 1946

Executive

First appointed to cabinet

Isabel Ursula Tesha, Minister of Health and Housing, 1963

Notable service in cabinet

Linda Baboolal, Minister of Health
Elmira Clark-Allen, Minister of Housing and Resettlement
Muriel Donawa-McDavidson, Minister of Commercial Development and Local Government
Marilyn Gordon, Minister of Sports, Culture, and Youth Affairs
Muriel Green, Minister of Information
Margaret Hector, Minister of Education
Gloria Henry, Minister of Education; Minister of Social Development
Jennifer Johnson, Minister of Youth, Sport, Culture, and Creative Arts
Pamela Nicholson, Minister of Settlement and Public Utilities; Minister of Youth and Youth Affairs
Kamala Persad-Bissessar, Minister of Legal Affairs
Daphne Phillips, Minister of Commercial Development, Culture, and Women's Affairs
Eugenia Pierce, Minister of Youth and Sport
Camille Robinson-Regis, Minister of Consumer Affairs
Joan Yuille-Williams, Minister of Commercial Development, Culture, and Women's Affairs

First appointed ambassador

Isabel Ursula Tesha, Ambassador to Ethiopia, 1970

Legislative

First appointed to colonial legislature (Legislative Council)

Audrey Jeffers, 1946

First elected to national legislature (House of Representatives)

Isabel Ursula Tesha, People's National Movement, December 4, 1961

First appointed to national legislature (Senate)

Verna Crichlow, People's National Movement, December 29, 1961
Beatrice Olive Walke, Independent, December 29, 1961

Head of national legislature

Occah Seapaul, House of Representatives, 1991–1996

Tunisia

Women

Right to vote: 1957[53]; June 1, 1959
To stand for election: June 1, 1959

Executive

First appointed to cabinet

Fathia M'zali Mali, Minister of Family and Women's Affairs, 1985. In 1984, she had been appointed secretary of state (deputy minister) for the same portfolio.

Notable service in cabinet

Nozia Herzefor
Faiza Kedi, Minister of the Environment and Land Management
Neziha Zarrouk, Minister of Women and Children's Affairs

First appointed ambassador

Zeinouba Khomsi Maaref, Ambassador to Malta, 1993

Legislative

First elected to national legislature (National Assembly)

One woman, November 8, 1959

[53]Women were allowed to take part in municipal elections beginning in 1957.

Turkey

Women

Right to vote: April 3, 1930
To stand for election: December 5, 1934

Executive

Power past

Tansu Çiller, Prime Minister, June 13, 1992–March 12, 1996. Çiller, an American-trained economist and academic, was leader of the right-leaning True Path Party (and economics minister in the cabinet) when she was chosen as the head of a coalition government in June 1992. A strong-willed woman, she made her husband take her maiden name after their marriage. Most observers felt that she spent more time fighting to retain power rather than wielding it. After her party failed to win a majority in new elections, she became deputy prime minister in a coalition government, agreeing to a "power swap" after a few years. Before she was able to take her turn for a second stint as prime minister, however, the government fell and was replaced by another coalition in which she had no part. Çiller was the third woman to head a Muslim nation.

First appointed to cabinet

Türkân Akyol, Minister of Health, 1971

Notable service in cabinet

Imren Aykut, Minister of the Environment; Minister of Labor and Social Security
Tansu Çiller, Deputy Prime Minister
Isilay Saygin, Minister of State for Women and the Family

First appointed ambassador

Filiz Dincmen, Ambassador to the Netherlands, 1982

First provincial governor

Lale Aytaman, 1991

First elected mayor

Müfide Ilhan, 1950

Legislative

First to serve in national legislature (Kamutay, National Assembly)[54]

Benal Ariman
Türkân Baştuĝ
Sati Çirpan
Nakiye Elgün
Sabina Gökçül
Mebrure Gönenç
Sabina Görkey
Ferrun Güpgüp
Senina Hizal
Ekibe Insel
Fatma Memik
Bediz Morova
Esma Nayman
Huriye Öniz
Fakihe Öymen
Hatice Özgener
Mihri Pektaş
Meliha Ulaş

All Republican People's Party, seated February 1935

First elected to national legislature (Kamutay, National Assembly)

Salise Abanozoĝlu
Mebrure Aksoley
Benal Ariman
Belkis Baykan
Muammer Develi
Nakiye Elgün
Sabina Gökçül
Mebrure Gönenç
Hasene Ilgas
Şemsa Işçcan
Saadet Kâĝitçilar

---

[54]These women were technically elected, although there was no competition for the seats, as Turkey was a one-party state at the time.

Fatma Memik
Fakihe Öymen
Mihri Pektaş
Tezer Taşkiran
Şehime Yunus

All Republican People's Party, seated March 1943

Head of national legislature

Neftçi Neftei, Deputy Speaker

Judicial

First appointed to supreme court

Samia Akbulut, 1990. Some reports claim that Turkey was the first country to appoint a woman to its supreme court, in the mid-1930s at the instigation of the modernizing dictator Kemal Atatürk. The Turkish Ministry of Foreign Affairs, however, notes Akbulut as the court's first female member.

Minority: Kurd

Executive

First to serve as president

Ismet Inönü, 1938

Legislative

First woman elected to national legislature
(Türkiye Büyük Millet Meclisi, Turkish Grand National Assembly)

Leyla Zana, Social Democratic Party, 1991

Religious Minority: Jewish

Executive

First appointed to cabinet

Nasim Mazliah, Minister of Finance, 1913

Legislative

First elected to Parliament

Four men, 1877

Turkmenistan

Women

Right to vote: 1927
To stand for election: 1927

Executive

First appointed to cabinet (Turkmenistan SSR)

Khally Nazarova, Minister of Social Affairs, 1959

First appointed to cabinet (since independence)

Tuvakbibi Amagl'Dyeva, Minister of Foreign Affairs, 1990

Notable service in cabinet

Ataeva Aksoltan Torayevna, Minister of Health
Djamal Geklenova, Minister of Consumer Goods
Bibi Palvanova, Minister of Education
Abad Sehedovna Risaeva, Deputy Prime Minister

First appointed ambassador

Ataeva Aksoltan Torayevna, Ambassador to the United Nations, 1995

Legislative

First elected to national legislature (Mejlis, Parliament)[55]

Eight women, January 1990

Head of national legislature (Turkmenistan Soviet Socialist Republic)

Roza Atamuradovna Bazarova, Chairwoman, Presidium, 1988

---

[55]Turkmen women had previously been elected to the Supreme Soviet of the Soviet Socialist Republic of Turkmenistan and to the Parliament of the Soviet Union.

Tuvalu

Women

Right to vote: January 1, 1967
To stand for election: January 1, 1967

Executive

First appointed to cabinet

Naama Maheu Laatasi, Minister of Health, Education, and Human Resources Development, 1989

First appointed ambassador

No woman yet appointed

Legislative

First elected to national legislature

Naama Maheu Laatasi, September 1989

Uganda

Women

Right to vote: 1962
To stand for election: 1962

Executive

Specioza Wandira-Kazibwe, Vice-President, 1994–present. Appointed by president Yoweri Museveni, Specioza is a surgeon and former cabinet minister. It was rumored that her appointment—she is from the north of the country—was an effort by the president to shore up his support in that area, many inhabitants of which continue to support former dictators Milton Obote and Idi Amin Dada. Specioza found herself caught up in a damaging political scandal in April 1999. The imbroglio resulted from funds allegedly misappropriated from the construction of a dam. She was hauled before Parliament and forced to defend her actions in overseeing the project. Museveni, perhaps showing some distrust, took away her portfolio as minister of agriculture, animal industries, and fisheries. At the same time, he reaffirmed his continuing commitment to involve women in Ugandan politics by giving two other women increased responsibilities in his cabinet.

Notable presidential candidate, 1996

Adonia Tiberondwa

First appointed to cabinet

Princess Elizabeth Bagaya of Toro, Minister of Foreign Affairs, 1973

Notable service in cabinet

Syda Bbumba, Minister of Energy and Mineral Development; Minister of Economic Monitoring
Namirembe Bitamazire, Minister of Education
Rebecca Kadaga, Minister of Parliamentary Affairs; Minister of Communications
Jane Frances Kuka, Minister of Gender and Community Development
Miriam Matembe, Minister of Ethics and Integrity
Joyce Mpanga, Minister of Women's Development

Janat Mukwaya, Minister of Gender and Community Development
Amanya Mushega, Minister of Public Services
Elizabeth Okwir, Minister attached to the Office of the Vice-President
Mary Senkatuka-Astles, Minister of Culture and Commercial Development
Victoria Ssekitoleko, Minister of Agriculture and Forestry

First appointed ambassador

Princess Elizabeth Bagaya of Toro, Ambassador at Large, 1971; accredited to Egypt and Ethiopia, 1973. An interesting ambassadorial appointment to note is that of **Bernadette Olowa,** accredited to the Holy See (Vatican City) in 1975. She was the first woman ever appointed as ambassador to the Vatican, breaking a 900-year-old tradition of male dominance in the papal state's diplomatic community.

First mayor

Janet Wesonga, Mbale, 1967

Legislative

First Europeans appointed to colonial legislature (Legislative Council)

Alice Boase
Barbara Saben

Both appointed 1954

First African appointed to colonial legislature (Legislative Council)

Pumla Kisosonkole, 1957

First to serve in national legislature (National Assembly)

Florence Lubenga, The King Alone Party
Sugra Visram, The King Alone Party

Both appointed April 1962

First elected to national legislature (National Consultative Council)

Rhoda Kalema, 1979

Minority: Asian

Legislative

First appointed to colonial legislature (Legislative Council)

Chrunabai Jekabhai Amin, 1926

Ukraine

Women

Right to vote: March 10, 1919
To stand for election: March 10, 1919

Executive

Notable presidential candidate, 1999

Natalia Mykhaylivna Vitrenko, candidate (and leader) of the Progressive Socialist Party. A Soviet-educated economist and self-styled "true Marxist," this mother of three campaigned on a program of populism, nostalgia for the Soviet Union, anti-Western sentiment, and pledges of government support to help the needy. Vitrenko began the election campaign leading in the polls, then slipped to a consistent second place behind incumbent Leonid Kuchma. Violence rocked the campaign in early October 1999, when assailants hurled two grenades into a crowd at one of Vitrenko's election rallies. She suffered shrapnel wounds to her stomach and legs; more than thirty other people were wounded as well, some quite seriously. Police quickly caught the assailants, who were linked to the campaign of one of the other candidates. Despite her early poll numbers, Vitrenko ultimately placed fourth, with slightly more than 11 percent of the votes. She tried another tactic in the runoff between Kuchma and his communist opponent: an endorsement for the communist if he would appoint her prime minister should he win.

First appointed to cabinet (preindependence)

Eugenia Bogdanova Bosh, People's Commissar (Minister) for Internal Affairs, 1918

First appointed to cabinet (after independence)

Suzanna Stanik, Minister of Family and Youth Affairs, 1997. **Ivanivna Khorolets,** appointed minister of culture in 1990, was still serving when Ukraine declared its independence; she continued in office until 1992.

Notable service in cabinet

Raisa Bohatyryova, Minister of Health

Valentyna Dovzhenko, Minister of Family and Youth Affairs
Suzanna Stanik, Minister of Justice

First appointed ambassador

Nina Kovalska, Ambassador to Switzerland, 1998

Legislative

First elected to national legislature (Verkhovna Rada, Parliament)[56]

Hanna Arkhipova
Raisa Bohatyryova
Kateryna Boyko
Valentyna Eschenko
Maria Gumeniuk
Iryna Kalynets
Svitlana Ostroushenko
Lidiya Sivkova
Larysa Skoryk
Halyna Vasylieva
Tetyana Yakheeva
Stanislava Yanushevych
Kateryna Zavadska

All elected March 1990. They were elected to the last Parliament of the Soviet Socialist Republic of Ukraine and continued in office after independence on December 25, 1991. The first parliamentary elections after independence were held in April 1994, with seventeen women winning seats.

Head of national legislature (Ukrainian Soviet Socialist Republic)

Valentina Semyonovna Shevchenko, Chairwoman, Presidium, 1984–1990

[56]Ukrainian women had previously been elected to the Supreme Soviet of the Soviet Socialist Republic of Ukraine and to the Parliament of the Soviet Union.

United Arab Emirates

The right to vote does not exist in the United Arab Emirates. There is no parliament, and political parties are forbidden. There is a federal national council, the Majlis Watani Ittihad, which has forty appointed members. The council performs only advisory tasks and no woman has ever been appointed as a member, nor has any woman been appointed to the cabinet.

The UAE passed a notable landmark in 1999, however. The ruler, Sheikh Zaid, named his wife, **Sheikha Fatima,** as de facto ambassador to represent the country at the funeral of Jordan's King Hussein.

United Kingdom

Women

Right to vote: February 2, 1918; July 2, 1928
To stand for election: February 2, 1918; July 2, 1928[57]

As early as 1869, single women who were taxpayers were granted the right to vote in municipal elections in some jurisdictions.

International Notable: **Rosemary Higgins** was the first woman to be elected to the International Court of Justice, in 1997.

Royalty

Elizabeth II Alexandra Mary, Queen, February 6, 1952–present. Elizabeth's reign has been marked by great changes in the power and prestige of the British nation. She has seen her empire shrink considerably; more than forty former British colonies have won their independence since she ascended the throne. Before Elizabeth's rule, the English royal family was held in high respect; that now seems to have changed. Although Elizabeth is personally well liked, republican sentiment has never been higher, much of it brought on by the indiscretions of her family—three of her four children have divorced, along with her only sister. She has also been hurt by the common accusation that the royals cost too much, deliver too little, and don't pay enough taxes. Elizabeth, although her position is ceremonial, has a keen political mind and knows how to subtly sway her ministerial government. She should; the incumbent prime minister, Tony Blair, is the tenth of her nearly fifty-year rule. Only time will tell if Elizabeth will be able to salvage the monarchy and ensure its continuation.

Power past

Elizabeth, 1936–1952. Dubbed by Hitler as "the most dangerous woman in Europe," the wife of King George VI was a mainstay to her husband and his subjects throughout World War II. The first commoner to wed a prince of the realm since 1660, she was thrust unexpectedly into the role of queen when her husband succeeded his brother (see below). Elizabeth's upper-class but decidedly nonroyal upbringing allowed her to move easily among the

[57] Women over thirty years of age were granted voting rights in 1918; full voting equality with men was achieved in 1928.

Britons during the darkest days of the war, rallying their courage against the enemy. When others suggested that the royal family flee abroad, she shrugged them off, saying: "The children won't leave without me, I shan't leave without the King, and the King will never leave." When Buckingham Palace was bombed, she commented: "Now I can look the East End in the face," referring to the lower-class section of London, which suffered heavy damage almost nightly from German aerial poundings. After her husband's death, Elizabeth assumed the role of Queen Mother. Affectionately dubbed the Queen Mum, she still makes her share of royal public appearances despite the fact that she is a near centenarian and often plagued with physical ailments. Opinion polls rank Elizabeth as one of the best-loved and most respected royals.

Bessie Wallis Warfield Spencer Simpson, Duchess of Windsor, 1936. A twice-divorced American, Wallis changed the course of the British Empire during three months in 1936, prompting *Time* magazine to select her as its first Woman of the Year. Edward VIII, who had ascended the throne on the death on his father, George V, gave up his crown because he couldn't remain king and marry Wallis at the same time. The couple married shortly after his abdication and were styled the Duke and Duchess of Windsor. Accused of pro-German sympathies—there are rumors that Edward would have been returned to the throne if the Germans had won the war—the couple roamed about the haut monde spots of Europe, frequently making intemperate remarks and doing unseemly things like visiting Nazi Germany. Afraid of the mischief they might cause, Prime Minister Winston Churchill dispatched them to the Bahamas, where the duke was made governor-general, mainly to neutralize them in an out-of-the-way spot. Once Britain was victorious in the war, the couple returned to their society life, far removed from any semblance of power. Until Wallis's death, the British royal family refused to acknowledge her as a "royal" highness, even though her husband was once king and uncle of the reigning queen.

Executive

Power past

Margaret Hilda Roberts Thatcher, Prime Minister, May 4, 1979–November 22, 1991. One of the most controversial prime ministers in British history, Thatcher led her Conservative Party to a smashing victory in 1979. In office, she pursued a militant sell-off of Britain's government-owned industries and a dismantling of the welfare state, and in doing so introduced the term "Thatcherism" to laissez-faire economics. After winning two reelection bids (in 1983 and 1987), Thatcher's popularity waned, causing her to resign under pressure from members of her own government. After her resignation, she was elevated to the House of Lords as Baroness Thatcher of Kesteven, where she has been uncharacteristically quiet. Thatcher always evoked interesting political comments. French president François Mitterrand once said of her, "She has eyes like Caligula and the mouth of Marilyn Monroe."

First appointed to cabinet

Margaret Bondfield, Minister of Labour, 1929

Notable service in cabinet

Margaret Beckett, Minister of Trade and Industry
Barbara Castle, Minister of Overseas Development; Minister of Transport
Lydia Chalker, Minister of Overseas Development Assistance
Edwina Currie, Minister of Health
Harriet Harman, Minister of Social Security
Judith Hart, Minister of Social Security
Margaret Herbison, Minister of Pensions and National Insurance
Florence Hosbrugh, Minister of Education
Tessa Jowell, Minister for Public Health
Jennie Lee, Minister of Arts
Marjorie Mowlam, Minister of State for Northern Ireland
Joan Ruddock, Minister for Women
Clare Short, Minister of Overseas Development Assistance
Edith Summerskill, Minister of National Insurance
Margaret Thatcher, Minister of Education and Science
Ellen Wilkinson, Minister of Education
Shirley Williams, Minister of Education and Science

First appointed ambassador

Barbara Salt, Ambassador to Israel, 1962

First mayor

Elizabeth Garrett Anderson, Aldeburgh, 1908. It is an interesting side note that Anderson was also the first female British physician by virtue of passing the Society of Apothecaries examination in 1865 and being granted a certificate that permitted her to practice medicine.

Legislative

First elected to national legislature (House of Commons)

Countess Constance Markiewicz, St. Patrick's, Dublin, Sinn Fein, December 14, 1918. Due to her strong feelings about Irish independence, Markiewicz, along with the other Sinn Fein members elected, refused to take her seat in the House of Commons. The first woman to sit in the House was **Nancy Astor** of the Conservative Party, who was elected on November 28, 1919, and seated three days later.

Youngest elected to national legislature (House of Commons)

Bernadette Devlin, Independent Unity Party, age twenty-one, 1969

First female twins elected to national legislature (House of Commons)

Angela and Maria Eagle, both Labour Party, May 1997

Longest service in national legislature (House of Commons)

Irene Ward, Conservative Party, thirty-eight years, 1931–1945; 1950–1974

Longest continuous service in national legislature (House of Commons)

Barbara Castle, Labour Party, thirty-four years, 1945–1979

First appointed to national legislature (House of Lords)

Dame Katherine Elliot
Barbara Wooten

Both appointed October 21, 1958, joining the Dowager Marchioness of Reading and the Baroness Ravensdale, who had become members because of hereditary rights.

Head of national legislature

Elizabeth (Betty) Boothroyd, Labour Party, House of Commons, 1992–present

First woman to preside over House of Commons

Betty Harvie Anderson, Conservative Party, July 2, 1970

First parliamentary election in which all major party candidates were female

Hampstead and Heath, May 1997. The winner was the Labour Party candidate, **Glenda Jackson,** a two-time winner of the Academy Award for Best Actress.

Judicial

First appointed to supreme court

Elizabeth Lane, 1965

Minority: African-British

Executive

First elected mayor

John Archer, Labour Party, Battersea, 1913

Legislative

First elected to national legislature (House of Commons)

Diane Julie Abbott, Labour Party
Paul Boateng, Labour Party
Bernie Grant, Labour Party

All elected 1987. Boateng, on June 18, 1987, became the first of the three to formally take his seat.

First appointed to national legislature (House of Lords)

Lord Taylor of Warwick, 1996

First woman appointed to national legislature (House of Lords)

Baroness Valerie Amos and **Baroness Scotland of Asthal,** 1997. Both life peerages were announced on August 2, 1997; Baroness Amos was made a life peer on September 24, 1997, and Baroness Scotland of Asthal on October 30, 1997.

Minority: African-Caribbean

Legislative

First appointed to national legislature (House of Lords)

Baron Learie Nicholas Constantine of Maraval and Nelson, 1969

First elected mayor

Lloyd Leon, Lambeth, Labour Party

Minority: Chinese-British

Legislative

First woman appointed to national legislature (House of Lords)

Baroness Lydia Dunn, 1990

Minority: Gay/Lesbian

Executive

First appointed to cabinet

Christopher Smith, Labour Party, Secretary of State for National Heritage (renamed Culture, Media, and Sport), 1997. Undoubtedly others have served, but Smith is the first "open" gay to do so.

Notable service in the cabinet

Nicholas Brown, Minister of Agriculture
Peter Mandelson, Minister of Trade

Legislative

First appointed to national legislature (House of Lords)

Waheed Alli, 1998

First elected to national legislature (House of Commons)

Christopher Smith, Labour Party, Islington South and Finsbury, 1983. Smith, elected in 1983, did not openly declare his homosexuality until 1984.

First woman elected to national legislature (House of Commons)

Angela Eagle, Labour Party, Wallasey, 1992. First elected in 1992, Eagle did not openly declare her homosexuality until 1997.

Notable service in national legislature (House of Commons)

David Borrow, Labour Party, South Ribble
Ben Bradshaw, Labour Party, Exeter
Michael Brown, Conservative Party, Brigg and Cleethorpes
Nicholas Brown, Labour Party, Newcastle-upon-Tyne East
Maureen Colquhoun, Labour Party, Northampton North
Tom Driberg, Labour Party, Maldon; Barking
Peter Mandelson, Labour Party, Hartlepool
Gordon Marsden, Labour Party, Blackpool South
Matthew Parris, Conservative Party, Derbyshire West
Stephen Twigg, Labour Party, Enfield Southgate

Minority: Indo-British

Executive

First elected mayor

Mohammed Ajeeb, Labour Party, Bedford, 1985

First woman elected mayor

Shreela Flather, Conservative Party, Royal Borough of Windsor and Maidenhead, 1986. Flather had previously been the first Asian-British woman elected as a local councillor.

Legislative

First elected to national legislature (House of Commons)

Dadabhai Naoroji, Liberal Party, Finsbury Central, Parsee, 1892

Notable service in national legislature (House of Commons)

Mancherjie Bhownagree, Conservative Party, Bethel Green North East
Nirj Deva, Conservative Party, Brentford and Isleworth
Piara Singh Khabra, Labour Party, Ealing Southall
Ashok Kumar, Labour Party, Middlesbrough South and Cleveland East; Langbaurgh
Shapurji Saklatvala, Labour Party, Battersea North
Mohammed Sarwar, Labour Party, Glasgow Govan
Jonathan Sayeed, Conservative Party, Bristol South East
Marsha Singh, Labour Party, Bedford West
Keith Vaz, Labour Party, Leicester East

First appointed to national legislature (House of Lords)

Lord Sinha of Raipur, 1919

First woman appointed to national legislature (House of Lords)

Baroness Shreela Flather, 1990

Religious Minority: Jewish

Legislative

First elected to national legislature (House of Commons)

Baron Lionel de Rothschild, 1858

Religious Minority: Mormon

Legislative

First elected to national legislature (House of Commons)

Terry Rooney, Labour Party, Bradford North, 1990

Religious Minority: Muslim

Legislative

First elected to national legislature (House of Commons)

Mohammed Sarwar, Labour Party, Glasgow Govan, 1997

First woman appointed to national legislature (House of Lords)

Polla Manzia Uddin, 1998

Religious Minority: Sikh

Legislative

First elected to national legislature (House of Commons)

Piara Singh Khabra, Labour Party, Ealing Southall, 1992

Scotland

Executive

First appointed to cabinet

Wendy Alexander, Minister of Social Inclusion, Local Government, and Housing
Sarah Boyack, Minister of Transport and Environment
Susan Deacon, Minister of Health and Community Services

All appointed 1999

Legislative

First elected to legislature (Scottish Parliament)

Wendy Alexander, Labour Party
Jackie Bailie, Labour Party
Sarah Boyack, Labour Party
Rhona Brankin, Labour Party
Cathy Craigie, Labour Party
Christine Creech, Scottish National Party
Roseanna Cunningham, Scottish National Party
Margaret Curran, Labour Party
Susan Deacon, Labour Party
Helen Eadie, Labour Party
Dorothy Grace Elder, Scottish National Party

Margaret Ewing, Scottish National Party
Winnie Ewing, Scottish National Party
Linda Fabiani, Scottish National Party
Patricia Ferguson, Labour Party
Trish Godman, Labour Party
Annabel Goldie, Conservative Party
Rhoda Grant, Labour Party
Janis Hughes, Labour Party
Fiona Hyslop, Scottish National Party
Sylvia Jackson, Labour Party
Cathy Jamieson, Labour Party
Margaret Jamieson, Labour Party
Johann Lamont, Labour Party
Marilyn Livingston, Labour Party
Tricia Marwick, Scottish National Party
Marge McDonald, Scottish National Party
Irene McGugan, Scottish National Party
Lyndsay McIntosh, Conservative Party
Kate McLean, Labour Party
Fiona McLeod, Scottish National Party
Maureen McMillan, Labour Party
Pauline McNeill, Labour Party
Mary Mulligan, Labour Party
Elaine Murray, Labour Party
Irene Oldfather, Labour Party
Cathy Peattie, Labour Party
Nona Radcliffe, Liberal Democrat Party
Shona Robison, Scottish National Party
Mary Scanlon, Conservative Party
Elaine Smith, Labour Party
Margaret Smith, Liberal Democrat Party
Nicola Sturgeon, Scottish National Party
Elaine Thomson, Labour Party
Karen Turnbull, Labour Party
Kay Ullrich, Scottish National Party
Sandra White, Scottish National Party
Karen Whitefield, Labour Party

All elected May 1999

Wales

Executive

First appointed to cabinet

Rosemary Butler, Minister of Education

Christine Gwyther, Minister of Agriculture and Rural Economy
Edwina Hart, Minister of Finance
Jane Hutt, Minister of Health and Social Services

All appointed 1999

Legislative

First elected to legislature (Welsh Assembly)

Lorraine Barrett, Labour Party
Rosemary Butler, Labour Party
Christine Chapman, Labour Party
Jane Davidson, Labour Party
Jocelyn Davies, Plaid Cymru
Janet Davis, Plaid Cymru
Sue Essex, Labour Party
Val Field, Labour Party
Janice Gregory, Labour Party
Christine Gwyther, Labour Party
Alison Halford, Labour Party
Edwina Hart, Labour Party
Christine Humphreys, Liberal Democrat Party
Jane Hutt, Labour Party
Pauline Jarnan, Plaid Cymru
Ann Jones, Labour Party
Bin Jones, Plaid Cymru
Helen Mary Jones, Plaid Cymru
Lynn Neagle, Labour Party
Jenny Randerson, Liberal Democrat Party
Janet Ryder, Plaid Cymru
Karen Sinclair, Labour Party
Gwenda Thomas, Labour Party
Kirsty Williams, Liberal Democrat Party

All elected May 1999

United Kingdom Dependency: Anguilla

Executive

First appointed to cabinet

Albena Lake Hodge, Minister of Social Services, 1976

Legislative

First elected to colonial legislature (House of Assembly)

Adalia Gumbs, People's Progressive Party
Albena Lake Hodge, People's Progressive Party

Both elected 1976

United Kingdom Dependency: Bermuda

Executive

Jennifer Smith, Prime Minister, November 11, 1998–present. Smith, a former "dancercise" instructor who collects matchboxes and first-day covers as hobbies, led her Progressive Labour Party, which she had headed for two years, to its first victory since it was founded in the mid-1960s. The formerly left-wing party—regarded as the more "black" of Bermuda's two main parties—has moved toward a center position in recent years, promising to work with the business establishment to preserve Bermuda as a tax and insurance haven.

Power past

Pamela Felicity Gordon, Prime Minister, March 27, 1997–November 11, 1998. Gordon, head of the United Bermuda Party, was serving as minister of the environment, planning, and natural resources when the previous prime minister resigned. At the age of forty-one, she became the youngest person ever to become Bermuda's prime minister. Gordon's rise to prominence came as a result of a most unusual scandal: Her predecessor was forced from office because of local outrage over the opening of Bermuda's first McDonald's restaurant. Her party, even though it polled a majority of black voters, had always been regarded as the more "white" of Bermuda's two main parties, a factor that led to her defeat in the 1998 general elections.

First appointed to cabinet

Gloria McPhee, Minister of Youth and Sport, 1972

Legislative

First elected to colonial legislature (House of Assembly)

Hilda Aitken, Independent
Edna Watson, Independent

Both elected 1948

United Kingdom Dependency: British Virgin Islands

Executive

First appointed to cabinet

Eileene Parsons, Minister of Health, Education, and Welfare, 1997

Legislative

First to serve in colonial legislature (Legislative Council)

Emmogene Creque, 1965

First elected to colonial legislature (House of Assembly)

Eileene Parsons
Ethlyn Smith

Both elected 1995

United Kingdom Dependency: Cayman Islands

Executive

First appointed to cabinet

Juliana O'Connor-Connally, Minister of Youth, Sports, Culture, and Community Affairs, 1997

United Kingdom Dependency: Falkland Islands

Executive

First appointed to cabinet

Mary Jennings, Executive Council, 1980

United Kingdom Dependency: Gibraltar

Executive

First appointed to cabinet

Conchita Anes, Minister of Public Works and Housing, 1969

Legislative

First elected to colonial legislature (House of Assembly)

Conchita Anes, Integration with Britain Party, 1969

United Kingdom Dependency: Guernsey

Legislative

First elected to colonial legislature

Marie Randall, 1924

United Kingdom Dependency: Isle of Man

Some women on the Isle of Man were among the first in the world eligible to vote. In 1881, women who were property owners were granted that right, and in 1913 the franchise was extended to women who met the same electoral qualifications that applied to men. Universal suffrage was introduced in 1918.

Executive

First appointed to cabinet

Hazel Hannan, Minister of Education, 1990

Legislative

First elected to legislature (Tynwald, House of Keys)

Marion Shimmin, Independent, 1933

First elected to legislature (Legislative Council)

Betty Quirk Hanson, Independent, 1982

United Kingdom Dependency: Jersey

Legislative

First elected to legislature (States of Jersey, lower house)

Ivy May Forster, Jersey Progressive Party, 1948

First elected to legislature (States of Jersey, upper house)

Gwyneth Clore Huelin, 1966

United Kingdom Dependency: Montserrat

Executive

First appointed to cabinet

Mary R. Truitt, Minister of Education, Health, and Welfare, 1973

United Kingdom Dependency: Turks and Caicos Islands

Executive

First appointed to cabinet

Arabella R. Smith, Minister for Natural Resources, 1991

Legislative

First elected to colonial legislature (TCI Legislative Council)

Rosita Butterfield, 1984

United States of America

American women and minorities were comprehensively referenced in *The Almanac of Women and Minorities in American Politics* (Westview Press, 1999) by the same author.

URUGUAY

Women

Right to vote: December 16, 1932
To stand for election: December 16, 1932

Executive

First appointed to cabinet

Alba Roballo, Minister of Education and Social Welfare, 1968

Notable service in cabinet

Raquel Lombardo de De Betolaya, Minister of Education and Culture
Ana Lia Piñeyrua, Minister of Labor and Social Welfare
Adela Dias Rosa Reta, Minister of Education and Culture

First appointed ambassador

Pura Sasca de Sundblad, Ambassador to Costa Rica, 1984

Legislative

First elected to national legislature (Asamblea General, General Assembly)

Sofia Alvarez Vignali de Demichelli, Colorado Party, Senate
Magdalena Antonelli Moreno, Colorado Party, Chamber of Representatives
Julia Arevalo de Roche, Communist Party, Chamber of Representatives
Isabel Pinto de Vidal, Colorado Party, Senate

All elected November 1942

Head of national legislature

Alba Roballo, Senate, 1963; 1965; 1967

Judicial

First appointed to supreme court

One woman, 1985

Uzbekistan

Women

Right to vote: 1938
To stand for election: 1938

Executive

First appointed to cabinet (Uzbek Soviet Socialist Republic)

Yadgar S. Nasriddinova, Minister of Construction Industry, 1952

First appointed to cabinet (after independence)

Shaklo Makhmudova, Minister of Foreign Affairs, 1991

Notable service in cabinet

Dilbar Ghulomova, Deputy Prime Minister
Sanobar A. Khodzhayeva, Minister of Social Affairs

Legislative

First elected to national legislature (Oliy Majlis, Supreme Council)[58]

Buritosh Shodieva, 1995

Head of legislature (preindependence)

Yadgar S. Nasriddinova, Supreme Council of the Soviet Socialist Republic of Uzbekistan, 1959–1970 (*see also* Russia)

---

[58]Uzbek women were previously elected to the Supreme Soviet of the Soviet Socialist Republic of Uzbekistan and to the Parliament of the Soviet Union.

Judicial

First appointed to supreme court

Tatiana Anisei
Farrukha Mukhitdinova
Mashkura Safaeva
Alfia Shurova

All appointed May 5, 1995

VANUATU

Women

Right to vote: November 1975
To stand for election: November 1975

Executive

Power past

Marie-Noelle Ferrieux-Patterson, Ex-ombudsman, 1994–1999. Although Vanuatu's 1980 constitution established the office of the ombudsman, it wasn't until 1994 that the office was actually filled. One wonders what the men who chose Ferrieux-Patterson were thinking. Would a woman be deferential, or easy to push around? Would a Frenchwoman be at a loss trying to operate amid Vanuatu's clan-driven politics? Whatever they may have thought, Ferrieux-Patterson proved more than a match for any of Vanuatu's politicians, who are overwhelmingly male. She was an assertive advocate of open and good government, regardless of which self-serving politicians' feet got trampled in the process. Ferrieux-Patterson investigated in an assertive manner, then issued strongly written reports—in what some considered to be an acerbic style—that usually recommended the maximum punishment for any irregularities she documented. In one report, she stated that the then–deputy prime minister was "not fit to hold any ministerial post." Parliament threatened to remove her from office, or at least curtail her activities, which led to a public outcry. Perhaps the people of Vanuatu liked to hear what she had to say. She was undoubtedly the most powerful woman in Vanuatu, having established the ombudsman's office as a virtual fourth branch of government.

Then, her contract ended. Ferrieux-Patterson reapplied for another five-year term, but the government declined to reappoint her. Ferrieux-Patterson's male replacement had close links with the ruling party, which led to one final official blast from her, a threat to investigate how the new ombudsman had been appointed. Having made her point, Ferrieux-Patterson left office, then announced in October 1999 that she would head the Vanuatu branch of Transparency International, a worldwide anticorruption organization. Ferrieux-Patterson obviously intends to continue to have her own say in Vanuatu's politics.

Ex–power behind the scene

Grace Molisa, 1979–1990, Special adviser to longtime prime minister Walter Lini. Molisa vetted all civil service appointments and was the second most influential women in the government, after the ombudsman (see above). She is also a poetess, whose work reflects her strong feelings about colonial powers, expatriate workers in Vanuatu, and the Western world in general. She lost her position when her husband, a finance minister, disagreed with Lini and was ousted from the cabinet.

First appointed to cabinet

Hilda Lini, Minister of Health, 1991

First appointed ambassador

No woman yet appointed

Legislative

First elected to national legislature (Parliament)

Maria Crowby
Hilda Lini

Both elected November 1987

Judicial

First appointed to supreme court

Dawn Bachinski, 1989

Vatican City

The right to vote does not exist. There is no parliament, and political parties do not exist. The only elected office (that of pope) is filled by a vote from an extremely limited franchise (members of the College of Cardinals). It is unlikely that a woman will receive an official appointed position in the Vatican hierarchy that would correspond to those of other nations in the foreseeable future. The most likely future appointment might be that of ambassador (or Papal Nuncio) from the Vatican City.

VENEZUELA

Women

Right to vote: March 28, 1946
To stand for election: March 28, 1946

Executive

Notable presidential candidate, 1998

Irene Saez. A former Miss Universe (1981) with a degree in political science, Saez was elected mayor of Chacao, the wealthiest district of Caracas, in 1992. Running for reelection in 1996, she won again with 96 percent of the vote. Still in her mid-thirties, Saez was regarded by many as just the cure for Venezuela's many political ills. In May 1998, the Christian Social Party (COPEI), one of the nation's two largest political parties, endorsed her as its official presidential candidate. Then her campaign began to fall apart. Long the front-runner in the contest, Saez saw onetime coup leader and independent candidate Colonel Hugo Chavez surge ahead of her in the opinion polls. As the major political parties struggled to contain the upstart Chavez, Saez ended up being dumped by COPEI and running as the candidate of her own IRENE Party. By the time the actual voting took place in November 1998, Saez managed only a miserly 3 percent of the vote, far behind the winner Chavez. She did not let her defeat dampen her political ambitions, however. In 1999, she was elected governor of Nueva Esparta state, with the assistance of her former rival Chavez, a surprising turn of political events.

Notable presidential candidate, 1988

Ismenia Villaba. Villaba was leader and candidate of the Democratic Republican Union.

First appointed to cabinet

Daria Parra, Minister of Education, 1953

Notable service in cabinet

Maria Bello de Guzman, Minister of State for Women's Affairs
Maria Bernardoni de Govea, Minister of Labor and Social Security

Aura Celina Casanova, Minister for Development, 1969
Imelda Cisneros de Perez, Minister of Development
Aura Loret DeRange, Minister of Women's Affairs
Evangelina Garcia Prince, Minister for the Promotion of Women
Maritza Izaguirre, Minister of Finance; Minister of Development
Marisela Padrón Quero, Minister of Family Affairs
Maria del Pilar Iribarren de Romero, Minister of Youth
Mercedes Pulido de Bricero, Minister for the Integration of Women in Development
Milena Sardi de Selles, Minister of Youth

First appointed ambassador

Ida Gramcko, Ambassador to the Soviet Union, 1948

First elected governor

Dora Maldonaldo de Falcón, Trujillo state, 1976

Legislative

First elected to national legislature (Constituent Assembly)

Nine women, October 1946

First elected to national legislature (Cámara de Diputados, Chamber of Deputies)

Two women, February 1948

First elected to national legislature (Senado, Senate)

Two women, February 1948. **Mercedes Fermán** and **Dorra Parra,** 1968, are noted in some sources as the first elected senators.

Head of national legislature

Ixora Rojas, Chamber of Deputies, 1998–1999
Carmen Lavria, Chamber of Deputies, 1994–1995

Judicial

Notable service on supreme court

Cecilia Sosa Gómez, Chief Justice, 1996

Vietnam

Women

Right to vote: January 6, 1946
To stand for election: January 6, 1946

Executive

Nguyen Thi Binh, Vice-President, September 23, 1992–present. Nguyen became well known during the Vietnam War when she was foreign minister of the National Liberation Front of South Vietnam, at the time a supposedly "patriotic," noncommunist group devoted to the liberation of that country. At the Paris peace talks, she headed their delegation; by then, the front had become a communist puppet entity called the Provisional Revolutionary Government. With the communist takeover of the south, Nguyen's true colors emerged, and she was soon education minister in the government of reunited Vietnam. She was elevated to the vice-presidency of the country in 1992, obviously a reward for her long years of service to the cause.

Power past

Madame Ngo Dinh Nhu (Tran Le Xuan), 1956–1963, sister-in-law of South Vietnamese president Ngo Dinh Diem. Madame Nhu was derided by the American press as the embodiment of a notorious "Dragon Lady." Tiny in stature (five feet, two inches tall in high heels), she wielded formidable power in South Vietnam until the overthrow and death of both president Diem and her husband, Ngo Dinh Nhu, éminance grise and commander of the national police in his brother's regime. From a seat in the national assembly and her position as de facto "first lady" to the bachelor president, Madame Nhu preached a fierce combination of militant feminism and fervent anticommunism. Largely forgotten now are her campaigns to upgrade the status of Vietnamese women by outlawing polygamy and concubinage. Today, she is best remembered for her comments about "Buddhist barbecues," in response to fanatically religious Vietnamese monks who doused themselves with gasoline and immolated themselves in protest against Diem's authoritarian Catholic regime. Fortunately for her, Madame Nhu was out of the country when Diem's regime was overthrown in a military coup. Otherwise, she would have undoubtedly met the same fate as her brother-in-law and her husband: captured and quickly executed. She reportedly lives quietly in a

Rome convent or monastery, still blaming the United States for the loss of both her family and her country to the communists.

First appointed to cabinet (Democratic Republic of Vietnam)

From 1954 onward, the position of minister of state of social affairs (deputy minister) was reserved for women.

First appointed to cabinet
(National Liberation Front of South Vietnam)

Nguyen Thi Binh, Minister of Foreign Affairs, 1969

First appointed to cabinet
(Provisional Revolutionary Government of South Vietnam)

Duong Quynh Hoa, Minister of Health, Social Affairs, and the Disabled, April 1975

First appointed to cabinet (Socialist Republic of Vietnam)

Duong Quynh Hoa, Minister of Health, Social Affairs, and the Disabled
Nguyen Thi Binh, Minister of Education

Both appointed July 1975

Notable service in cabinet

Mai Ky, Minister of Population and Family Planning
Tran Thi Thanh Thanh, Minister of Child Care and Protection
Tran Thi Trung Chien, Minister of Population and Family Planning

First mayor

Nguyen Thi Hau, Dalat, 1966

Legislative

First elected to national legislature (Democratic Republic of Vietnam)

Ten women, January 6, 1946

First elected to national legislature (Republic of Vietnam)

Madame Ngo Dinh Nhu (Tran Le Xuan) was elected to either the Constituent Assembly on March 4, 1956, or to the National Assembly on August 30, 1959. It is also possible that several other women were elected at the same time.

First elected to national legislature of reunified Vietnam (Quoc-Hoc, National Assembly)[59]

One hundred and thirty-two women, April 1976

Minority: Tay

Legislative

Head of national legislature (Quoc-Hoc, National Assembly)

Nong Duc Manh, 1992

[59]This statistic refers to the 1976 election, held after the reunification of Vietnam. Vietnamese women had previously been elected to legislatures in both the Socialist Republic of Vietnam (North Vietnam) and the Republic of Vietnam (South Vietnam).

YEMEN

The Arab Republic of Yemen (North Yemen) and the People's Democratic Republic of Yemen (South Yemen) merged in May 1990 to form the Republic of Yemen.

Women

Right to vote: 1967; 1970
To stand for election: 1967; 1970[60]

Executive

First appointed to cabinet

Before the merger, in 1986, a woman was appointed as deputy minister of information and culture in South Yemen. This was the highest cabinet position attained by a woman in that nation. North Yemen has also been reported as possibly having had female deputy ministers before the merger.

Amat al-Aleem al-Sosowah, Deputy Minister of Information, 1997. She had previously been an undersecretary in the same ministry since 1994.

First appointed ambassador

Amat al-Aleem al-Sosowah, Ambassador to the Netherlands, 1999. The first female ambassador accredited to Yemen was **Helga von Strachwitz,** ambassador from Germany, 1994.

---

[60]Women were granted voting rights in 1967 in the People's Democratic Republic of Yemen (South Yemen) and in 1970 in the Arab Republic of Yemen; the two countries have since merged.

Legislative

First to serve in national legislature
(South Yemen, Supreme People's Temporary Council)

Aiedah Ahmed Alwai
Fawzyah Mohammed Ja'afer
Aiedah Ali Saeed
Raja'a Ahmed Saeed
Khawlah Ahmed Sharaf

All appointed 1971

First to serve in merged national legislature
(Majlis Annowab, House of Representatives)

Shafiqa Morshed Ahhmed
Hasseinah Salem Ali
Hasseinah Mohessen Aubied
Fatema Mohammed Balahmer
Mona Basharahiel
Melki Abdullah Hassan
Mozna Saleh Mohessen
Gamilah Ali Mohessen
Aiedah Ali Saeed
Nadia Mohammed Salem

All appointed May 1990

Yugoslavia

Women

Right to vote: January 31, 1946
To stand for election: January 31, 1946

Executive

Power past

Milka Malada Planinc, Prime Minister, May 16, 1982–May 15, 1986. Planinc, an economist, served in communist Yugoslavia, before the country broke apart. She was a Croat who had fought as one of Tito's partisans in World War II, joining the Communist Party after the war and serving in the federal Parliament. Her appointment resulted when a new policy was introduced into the country in which the prime minister position was rotated among nationals of the states making up the federal republic.

Partner in power

Mirjana Markovic, 1989–present, wife of Serbian strongman Slobodan Milosevic. Markovic, who often comes across as an unreconstructed communist, is rumored to be an even tougher customer than her husband. She is a frequent contributor to the pro-Serb Yugoslav press, and her columns are often touted as her saying aloud what her husband is thinking but cannot air publicly himself. Markovic has been known to occasionally criticize some Serbian hard-liners—like Bosnian Serb radical Radovan Karadzic—so people do lend credence to what comes out of her mouth and pen.

Ex–Red Queen, partner in power

Jovanka Budisavljevic Broz, 1952–1980. Second (third? fourth?) wife of longtime (1945–1980) quasi-communist dictator Marshal Tito (Josip Broz). Thirtyish and reportedly secretary to Tito's security guards when they met, Jovanka was also rumored to have been a protégé of the sinister head of national security and intelligence, Aleksandar Rankovic. A Serb from the Lika region of Croatia, she was a youthful Partisan soldier during World War II. Tito had Jovanka schooled in diplomatic protocol, and given a sense of fashion, at the Yugoslav embassy in Rome before their marriage. She became an elegant, well-dressed woman, sporting a fashionable 1960s beehive hairdo, and was at Tito's side as he traveled about the world promoting his Third World unitarianism.

Jovanka placed herself in charge of all of Tito's personal affairs: the forty palaces, his yacht, his "missions of peace" to Third World countries. The Yugoslavs found Jovanka fun: She provided some homegrown glamour, gaiety, and fashion in the midst of their otherwise mostly dreary existence. To them, Jovanka was a Cinderella come true: rising from being a poor soldier to becoming the wife of one of the most powerful men in the world. Occasionally she'd slip with a faux pas, like dispatching a plane to Cairo to fetch home some watermelons, but usually Jovanka seemed content to parade around as Mrs. Marshal Tito. Beginning in 1966, Jovanka's power over her husband began to wane. Powerful people around Tito began to plot against her. Tito was gradually relinquishing his power, and they wanted to make certain that Jovanka didn't try to interfere by insisting that he retain full control. Ever more gradually, Jovanka was removed from his orbit, until the husband and wife were virtually separated, even living apart from each other. One of Jovanka's last formal public appearances was at Tito's funeral in 1980. Tito had wanted her to be cared for after his death with all the rights and benefits of a president's wife. That did not happen. Her rights and privileges disappeared almost overnight; she became a nonperson politically and socially in Yugoslavia. Jovanka still lives in Belgrade, but almost under house arrest. There's been an occasional rare sighting, usually on the anniversary of Tito's death, when she brings flowers to his grave.

First appointed to cabinet

Mitra Mitrovic-Djilas, Minister of Education, 1945

Notable service in cabinet

Sinisa Korica, Minister of Market and Economic Affairs
Milka Kufrin, Minister of Tourism
Radmila Milentijevic, Minister of Information
Bratislava Morina, Minister of Refugees
Nevenka Neralic-Mlivojevic, Minister Without Portfolio
Margit Savovic, Minister Without Portfolio
Nada Sljapic, Minister of Science, Development, and the Environment

First appointed ambassador

Stana Tomasevic, Ambassador to Norway, 1963

Legislative

First elected/appointed to national legislature (Constituent Assembly)

Spasenija Babovic
Anka Berus

Ljiljana Ahilova Calovska
Bosa Cvetic
Bozidarka Damnjanovic
Aceva Vera Donceva
Malinska Veselinka Gjorgjeva
Pepca Kardelj
Radmila Manojlovic
Naceva Mara Milanova
Ljubinka Milosavijevic
Mira Milosevic
Milka Minic
Mitra Mitrovic
Stanka Muncan
Zora Nikolic
Kata Pejnovic
Lidija Sentjuro
Vida Tomsic

All People's Front of Yugoslavia, elected/appointed November 11, 1945

Head of national legislature

Bogdana Glumac-Levakov, Federal Chamber, May 15, 1989–June 11, 1992
Milka Gligorijevic-Takeva, Federal Chamber, May 15, 1986–May 15, 1987
Stana Tomasevic-Arnesen, Federal Chamber, October 31, 1979–May 15, 1982
Vida Tomsic, Federal Chamber, May 16, 1967–May 16, 1969
Olga Vrabic, Federal Assembly, June 29, 1963–May 16, 1967

Political Entity: Kosovo

Executive

First female head of regional executive council
(Provincial Executive Council of the Autonomous Province of Kosovo)

Kaqusha Jashari, 1987

ZAMBIA

Women

Right to vote: October 30, 1962
To stand for election: October 30, 1962

Executive

Ex–potential power

Alice Mulenga Lenshina, 1963–1975. Educated in a Church of Scotland mission, Lenshina, an ethnic Bembe, had a vision shortly before her thirty-ninth birthday instructing her to wage war on the witches of Zambia. She claimed that she had died and been reborn four times and that Jesus had appeared to her, presenting her with the "one true Bible." Expelled by the Church of Scotland for her heresy, Lenshina set about forming her own group, the Lumpa Church, to do her bidding. When Zambia became independent in 1963, Lenshina turned her followers—she claimed 100,000—against the new government in a rural and ostensibly religious peasant rebellion, refusing to pay taxes or acknowledge the authority of the central government. The conflict soon turned bloody when President Kenneth Kaunda's government forces killed some 700 of Lenshina's adherents, mainly in the northern part of the country, while burning many of her churches. In August 1964, Lenshina surrendered to the government, which immediately banned her church. When she was imprisoned, many of her followers fled across the Congolese border, where they still reside today. Kaunda had proclaimed Lenshina one of the gravest threats to Zambian democracy (he later actually turned out to be almost as dangerous to democracy himself) and kept her locked up until 1975. After she was released, the government kept her under close watch by confining her to the capital, Lusaka, where she died in 1978.

First appointed to cabinet

Mutumba Mainga Bull, Minister of Health, 1973

Notable service in cabinet

Kabunda Kayongo, Minister of Service, Technology, and Vocational Training
Nkandu Luo, Minister of Health
Mavis Muyunda, Minister of Water, Lands, and Natural Resources

Edith Nawakwi, Minister of Finance; Minister of Agriculture; Minister of Energy and Water Development
Princess Nakatindi Wini, Minister of Community Development and Social Welfare

First appointed ambassador

Gwendoline Konie, Ambassador to Sweden, Norway, Denmark, and Finland, 1974. **Lombe Phyllis Chibesakunda** was appointed ambassador to Japan, Italy, and the Netherlands in 1975.

First elected mayor

Patricia Nawa, Lusaka, 1999

Legislative

First appointed to national legislature (National Assembly)

Princess Nakatindi Wini, January 1964

First elected to national legislature (National Assembly)

Ester Banda, United National Independence Party
Margaret Mbeda, United National Independence Party
Princess Mukwae Nganga Nakatindi, United National Independence Party

All elected January 1964

ZIMBABWE

Women

Right to vote: 1957[61]
To stand for election: March 1978

Executive

Woman to watch

Margaret Mtetwa Dongo, former guerrilla freedom fighter (her nom de guerre was Tichaona Muhondo, "we will sort it out on the battlefield") turned parliamentarian. Married and the mother of three, Dongo is the most outspoken voice in Zimbabwe against the corrupt rule of President Robert Mugabe and his Zimbabwe African National Union–Patriotic Front Party. First elected to Parliament on that party's ticket, she was assigned to a committee overseeing how state funds were spent. Her outspokenness against government injustices, including corrupt officials and ministers, led to attempts to remove her from Parliament. Dongo fought back when ZANU-PF attempted to seize her seat (via a dubious election), taking her case to Zimbabwe's high court. She won that fight and reentered Parliament as the only truly "independent" member of the chamber, where she has continued to lash out even more vocally against corruption and misrule. Dongo is a fearless fighter with a high level of credibility among Zimbabweans. She obviously feels, as do many Zimbabweans, that her nation's struggle for true freedom and independence has resulted in merely swapping one set of dictators (white) for another (African). In April 1999, she mustered biracial support to launch a new multiracial party (the Zimbabwe Union of Democrats) with a strong anticorruption platform. Given her high standing among Zimbabweans and her feisty, combative nature, it's not difficult to imagine the diminutive Dongo as the country's first female president sometime in the future.

First appointed to cabinet

Joyce Teurai-Ropa Nhongo Mujuru, Minister of Sports, Youth, and Recreation, 1980

---

[61]Prior to 1957, only men and European women could vote. Beginning in 1957, a qualified right to vote was gradually extended over the years to black women.

Notable service in cabinet

Florence Chitauro, Minister of National Affairs, Employment, and Cooperatives
Victoria Chitepo, Minister of Information and Telecommunications
Fay Chung, Minister of Education and Culture
Thenjiwe Virginia Lesabe, Minister of National Affairs, Employment, and Cooperatives

First appointed ambassador

Angelina Makwavarara, Ambassador to Kenya, 1993

Legislative

Notable first, 1920: **Ethel M. Tawse-Jollie** became the first woman in Africa to sit in a parliamentary body when she was elected to the Legislative Council of Southern Rhodesia. In 1923, after a new constitution was adopted, she was elected from Umtali to the Legislative Assembly of Southern Rhodesia, where she continued to serve until 1927.

First appointed/elected to national legislature (Senate)

M. Clark, Zimbabwe African National Union
T. Munyati, Zimbabwe African National Union
S. Takawira, Zimbabwe African National Union

All appointed/elected May 1980

First elected to national legislature (House of Assembly)

R. L. Chinamano, Zimbabwe African People's Union
Victoria Chitepo, Zimbabwe African National Union
M. Chivaura, Zimbabwe African National Union
Thenjiwe Virginia Lesabe, Zimbabwe African People's Union
J. L. Ngwenya, Zimbabwe African People's Union
N. P. Nhiwatiwa, Zimbabwe African National Union
T. R. Nhongo, Zimbabwe African National Union
S. Tavarwisa, Zimbabwe African National Union
J. T. Zvobgo, Zimbabwe African National Union

All elected May 1980

Minority: European

Executive

First appointed to cabinet

Dennis Norman, Minister of Agriculture

David Smith, Minister of Finance

Both appointed 1980, shortly after independence

Minority: Gay

Executive

First elected president

Canaan Banana, 1980. Banana was convicted in 1998 of sexual offenses against several members of his presidential staff. Married to a woman, he continued to proclaim his innocence, despite much evidence to the contrary. The whole affair erupted when a police officer shot one of his seniors (who happened to be one of Banana's aides-de-camp). The killer claimed that his victim had taunted him as being "Banana's wife." Several other men came forward before and during Banana's trial to state that they, too, had been subjected to sexual assaults from him during his presidential term. To complicate the whole matter, homosexuality is illegal in Zimbabwe, with practicing homosexuals subject to severe discrimination. Banana infuriated what exists of the country's gay and lesbian community, who labeled him a hypocrite, when he continued to disparage them throughout his trial.

Special Research Contacts

Dona Abdurazakova, UN Gender in Development Bureau, Kyrgyzstan
Pauline Abela, Department of Equal Status of Women, Office of the Prime Minister, Malta
Jesus Antonio Lopez Aguilar, Minister of Youth, Women, Children, and the Family, Panama
Ashraf Q. Ahmad, Library, Sultan Qaboos University, Oman
Junga Stella Ahn, Inter-Library Cooperation Division, National Assembly of Korea Library
Durbek Amanov, Second Secretary, Embassy of Uzbekistan, Washington, D.C.
Karl Erik Andersen, Sound and Image Archive, National Library of Norway
Brian Armstrong, Coordinator, Training and Information, Northwest Territories, Canada
Aruina, FeminetAsia, Mongolia
Arxiu Historic Nacional (National Historic Archive), Andorra
Daria M. Bartulin, Communications Office of the Croatian Government
Mabel Batto, Subdirector, National Library of Uruguay
Rita Bertenstam, Information Secretary, Parliament of Sweden
Biblioteca Nacional do Brazil, Divisão de Informacão Documental
Biblioteca Nazionale Centrale, Italy
E. Blakelock, Parliament of Fiji
Nada Bratina, Government of Slovenia
Jesper Brinkman, Ministry of Justice, Denmark
Charles M. Brown, Librarian, Parliament of Ghana
Ann Cacacellos, University of Athens, Greece
Claude Cahn, Belgium
Angela Callus, Office of the Prime Minister, Malta
Ana Isabel Calvo, Ministry of Labor and Social Services, Spain
Andreas Carlgren, Parliament of Sweden
Karina Castro, Centro de Estudios e Investigaciones de la Mujer Ecuatoriana, Ecuador
B. M. Cederboom, Coordinator, National Gender Bureau, Suriname
Yasmine Chatila, Federal Department of Foreign Affairs, Switzerland
Mrs. Cheah, Librarian, Parliament of Singapore
Mwango Chisala, National Assembly of Zambia
Martin Iversen Christensen, Denmark
Chris Christophorou, Press and Information Office, Cyprus
Khayrou Cissé, Parliament of Senegal
Stan Combs, Canada
Claire Cooper, Chief Minister's Office, Government of the Isle of Man
Rob Cover, Centre for Comparative Literature and Cultural Studies, Monash University, Australia
Helen de Del Cid, Directora de Biblioteca Nacional, El Salvador
Noelle Deville, Parliament of Switzerland
Mehrangiz Dolatshahi, Iran
Helena Doleckova, Library, Parliament of the Czech Republic

Richard Dorman, British Friends of Vanuatu
Eppie Edwards, Deputy Director, User Services Division, National Library of Jamaica
Simon J. Engitu, Senior Assistance Librarian, Parliament of Uganda
Thomas Hylland Eriksen, University of Oslo
L. Ernesta, Assistant Director, National Library of the Seychelles
Wheeba Faree, Rector, Arwa University, Yemen
Florencine Fernandez, International Affairs Committee, Legislative Branch, Costa Rica
Michael J. Field, Agence France-Presse
Emma Fookes, Office of the Clerk of the House of Representatives, Parliament of New Zealand
Marianne Fosland, Ministry of Foreign Affairs, Norway
Karen Furness, National Collection Librarian, Belize National Library Service
Heather Garven, Ministry of Foreign Affairs, New Zealand
Robert Gasperoni, San Marino
Martha Giefing, Austrian Parliamentary Administration
Helgi Gislason, Foreign Ministry, Iceland
Maksim Gjinaj, Head, Department of Bibliography, Albanian National Library
Michael Goldsmith, University of Waikato, New Zealand
Government Information Service, Saint Lucia
Sir Douglas Graham, Attorney General, New Zealand
B. K. Grandsaull, National Library of Trinidad and Tobago
Nigel Gravesande, Director of Tourism, Grenada
Lisete Gravito, Jurist, Parliament of Portugal
Margarida Guadalpi, Head of Division, Parliament of Portugal
Tapas Das Gupta, Parliament of India
Iván Guzmán de Rojas, Vicepresidente Corte Nacional Electoral, Bolivia
Ahmed Zaki Hafiz, Director, Ministry of Information, Arts, and Culture, Republic of Maldives
Yves Hanotiou, Parliament of Belgium
Joy Harris, Director of Women's Affairs, Nauru
G. Hartman, Peoples National Party, Guyana
Fauziah Abu Hassan, Parliament of Malaysia
Rainer Hiltunen, Secretary General, SETA, Finland
Anke Hintjens, Flemish Federation of Gay and Lesbian Organizations
Annemiek Hoeksma, National Library of the Netherlands
J. M. Hogan, Jersey Library, Jersey
Marika Holmblad, National Library of Sweden
Shahar Banun Jaafar, Deputy Director General, National Library of Malaysia
Francisco Huenchumilla Jaramillo, Parliament of Chile
Hanne Brehm Johansen, National Library of Greenland
Giff Johnson, Marshall Islands
Solveig K. Jónsdóttir, Information Officer, Parliament of Iceland
Akira Kado, International Cooperation Division, National Diet Library, Japan
Haver Kambaizadeh, Azerbaijan
Caroline Kangalee, Parliament of Trinidad and Tobago
Kenya Library Service, Nairobi Kenya
Mon Khalaf, Director, Institute for Women's Studies in the Arab World, Lebanon
Sharief Khan, Peoples National Party, Guyana
Kristine Kikiza, Information Department, Government of Latvia

Deyan Kiuranov, Director, Research and Publications Department, European Roma Rights Committee
Nelli Kopola, University of Stockholm
Ilona Korgema, National Library of Estonia
Said Kreidieh, Reference Librarian, LAU Library, Lebanon
Marie-France Kremer, National Center of Literature, Luxembourg
D. Ghassan Lahham, National Library of Syria
Pirjo Laiho, Ministry of Justice, Finland
Dora Lamberty, Parliament of Belgium
Emily Lau, Hong Kong Special Administrative Region Legislature
Tyrone Laurenson, National University of Samoa, Samoa
R. A. Lee, Director CBS, Aruba
M. Lenyatso, National Assembly, Botswana
Gary B. Little, United States of America
Chris Lodge, Public Affairs Officer, Government of Bermuda
René A. Long, National Library, Faeroe Islands
Roberta Louch, Director, Bureau of Women's Interests, Palau
Valentin Lytvynchuk, Parliament of the Ukraine
Marie Gloria Macedo, Gibraltar Tourist Board, Gibraltar
Keboitse Machangana-Lekuntwane, Botswana
Jihad Makdissi, Syria
Ghazwa Malhas, Press and Information Office, Jordan
Ismail Mamedov, Azerbaijan
Irene Manda, National Assembly of Zambia
Gustavo Marenco, Library, University of El Salvador
Dragan Markovic, Yugoslavia
Khunying Supatra Masdit, Thailand
Susan Maskey, Asmita Women's Publishing House, Nepal
Elma MaUa, Cook Islands Media Information, Cook Islands
Marika Meskhishvili, Parliamentary Research Department, Parliament of Georgia
Chris Meti, National Library of Papua New Guinea
Katherine Metres, U.S. Department of State, Mauritania
Demetrius S. Mgalami, Protocol and International Relations, Parliament of Tanzania
Yumiko Mikanagi, Division of Social Sciences, International Christian University, Tokyo, Japan
T. N. Minchena, Secretary of Politics, National Library of Belarus
Ala Mindicanu, Member of Parliament, Moldova
Ministry for the Promotion of Women, Luxembourg
Ministry of Foreign Affairs, Turkey
Bridgette Misick, Government Information Service, Turks and Caicos Islands
Nomsa Mkhwanazi, Parliament of Swaziland
Monaco Tourist Office
Derek P. Montague, McCrae University, Australia
Maria Victoria Mora, Special Commission of International Relations, Parliament of Costa Rica
Angus Morrison, Australia
Helen Morton, La Trobe University, Australia
David Naita, National Library of Papua New Guinea
National Assembly of Togo
National Information Center of Yemen

National Library of Namibia, Reference Desk
National Library of Poland
National Library of Russia
National Library of Serbia
National Library of Slovenia, Reference Desk
National Library of South Africa
Aminata Mbengue Ndiaye, Minister, Senegal
Jaime Ela Ndong, Parliament of Equatorial Guinea
Wim Neeleman, Eduardo Mondlane University, Mozambique
Niue Information Center
Luseane T. 'Ofa, Women and Development Centre, Tonga
Anna Okruhlicova, National Council of the Slovak Republic
Jeanie Ollivierre, Director, Women's Bureau, United Labor Party, St. Vincent and the Grenadines
Eugenia O'Neal, Women's Desk, Government of the British Virgin Islands
Rudolf Ortner, Foreign Ministry, Austria
Laszlo Ottovay, National Library of Hungary
Jose Herrera Ovalle, Secretariat of the Presidency, Guatemala
Richard Overy, Kiribati
Oyuntulga, Parliamentary Library, Parliament of Mongolia
Ms. A. Palaniappan, Parliament of Singapore
Kyung-ae Park, University of British Columbia
Karen Peacock, University of Hawaii
(Mrs.) Alex F. Phillip, clerk of the House of Assembly, Parliament of Dominica
Sandra S. Pierantozzi, Palau
Leslie Pierce, Managing Editor, *Grenadian Voice,* Grenada
Tatiana Placinta, Head, Department of Parliament and Government Assistance, National Library of Moldova
Carina Popovici, International Exchange Division, National Library of Romania
Martine Provence, Conseil National, Monaco
Inta Pujāte, Librarian, Parliament of Latvia
Annelise Quistorff, Parliament of Denmark
Louis Ralaisaholimanana, National Library, Malagasy Republic
E. N. Ramokotjo, Senior Librarian, Lesotho National Library Services
Russel Reid, Director, Anguilla Library Service, Anguilla
S. Reynolds, National Library Service, Barbados
David Robillard, Guernsey
Victor Joy-Way Rojas, Parliament of Peru
Miriam Ruiz, Comunicacion e Informacion de la Mujer, Mexico
Tekarei Russell, Kiribati
Tseten Samdup, Office of Tibet in the United Kingdom
Carlos Sampei, Brazil
Carles Santacreu, Secretari General, Parliament of Andorra
Makedonka Sardzovska, Parliament of Macedonia
T. Sarkar, National Library of India
Noman Sattar, Pakistan
Tere Schwarz-Blokhuis, Reference Department, National Library of the Netherlands
Orla Scott, Public Relations Office, Parliament of Ireland
Mrs. M.B.J. Senevirathne, Head, Reader Services, National Library of Sri Lanka

Riita Sihvonen, Archivist, Parliament of Finland
Jorge Sosa, Library, Universidad San Francisco de Quito, Ecuador
Sousada, Chief Librarian, Parliament of the Lao People's Democratic Republic
Lynn Stoner, University of Arizona
Christopher P. Storcks, Universitaet zu Koeln
Sherriley Strachan, Department of Archives, Commonwealth of the Bahamas
Maryan Street, Director, Centre for Labour Studies, University of Auckland, New Zealand
Iris Strovuen, Parliament of Belgium
Elin Suleymanov, Second Secretary/Press Officer, Embassy of Azerbaijan, Washington, D.C.
Francis Tan, Ministry of Foreign Affairs, Singapore
Martinho Tavares, Parliament of São Tomé and Príncipe
Gevorg Ter-Vardanian, Director, National Library of Armenia
Manju Thapa, Asmita Women's Publishing House, Nepal
Aslaug Thorlacius, Samtökum um kvennalista (Women's Alliance), Iceland
Patricio Aranda Torres, Chief, Library of Congress, Peru
Togi Tunupopo, Library, National University of Samoa, Samoa
University of Mauritius, Library Reference Desk, Mauritius
Vilimaina Vakaciwa, Librarian; University of the South Pacific Centre, Solomon Islands
Mereani Vakasisikakala, Pacific Collections Librarian, University of the South Pacific, Fiji
S. Velaviciene, National Library of Lithuania
Marieke Visser, Suriname
Barbara Vogt, Liechtensteinische Landesbibliotek, Liechtenstein
Lenka Vytlacilova-Petrova, Czech Republic
Michael Wilhelmer, Parliament of Germany
Women in Development Bureau, Tajikistan
E. Yanakieva, Reference Department, National Library of Bulgaria
Seyit Yolak, Director of International Relations, Turkish Republic of Northern Cyprus
Sevdou K. Zagre, Parliament of Burkina Faso
Rachid Zegrane, Alakhawayn University Library, Morocco
Zagorka Gligora Zeman, Public Relations Department, National and University Library, Zagreb, Croatia

Reader Submissions for the Next Edition

Submissions for inclusion in the next edition of *The Almanac of Women and Minorities in World Politics* are welcomed. Please complete as much of the following information as possible, then submit it to:

Mail: *The Almanac of Women and Minorities in World Politics*
c/o Westview Press
5500 Central Avenue
Boulder, Colorado 80301-2877 USA

Or e-mail: jhm@sirius.com

Name of person, minority, event, or year for inclusion:

Notable achievement of event that happened:

Pertinent facts (be as specific as possible):

References available (please any list books, articles, or other materials that will provide additional information):

Submitted by:

Address:

Phone: E-mail address:

May we contact you for further information on the submission?

Yes No

Index